DATE DUE

JAN 3 0 2017		
APR 1 5 2017		
		PRINTED IN U.S.A.

IRON MAC

ANDREW M. HOMAN

IRON MAC

THE LEGEND OF ROUGHHOUSE CYCLIST REGGIE McNAMARA

University of Nebraska Press • Lincoln & London

Library of Congress Cataloging-in-Publication Data
Names: Homan, Andrew M., 1964– author.
Title: Iron Mac: the legend of roughhouse cyclist
Reggie McNamara / Andrew M. Homan.
Description: Lincoln: University of Nebraska Press, [2016]
Includes bibliographical references and index.
Identifiers: LCCN 2015036859
ISBN 9780803254800 (cloth: alk. paper)
ISBN 9780803290556 (epub)
ISBN 9780803290563 (mobi)
ISBN 9780803290570 (pdf)
Subjects: LCSH: McNamara, Reggie, 1887–1971. | Cyclists—
United States—Biography. Bicycle racing—History.
Classification: LCC GV1051.M25 H66 2016 | DDC 796.6092—
dc23 LC record available at http://lccn.loc.gov/2015036859

Set in Ehrhardt MT Pro by Rachel Gould.

For my mother, Anne Marshall Homan

Contents

Acknowledgments

The commitment to produce this book demanded the work of a great many people, to each of them I owe a great debt.

In Australia there exists a great passion for cycling history, and I am grateful to so many, including Ann Wymark, Ian Pitt, Bruce Robinson, Leon Sims, and Ron Grenda.

Several people have shared family stories and firsthand accounts in interviews, emails, letters, social media, and scrapbooks, including, Alan Noel, Ted Ernst, Bob Walthour III, Harry Hopkins, and Christopher Seufert.

I am thankful for the *Newark Evening News*, which once printed many stories on professional cycling, just as today's American newspapers write about football, baseball, and basketball. Two *Newark Evening News* sportswriters, Willie Ratner and Howard B. Freeman, deserve much credit for capturing the era's historical cycling record in an entertaining and witty fashion. I was able to access the *Newark Evening News* microfilm only by the coordinated efforts of Doris Murphy, a supervising librarian at the New Jersey State Library, and Nancy Leonti, a circulation supervisor at the El Dorado County Library. Thank you to those at the El Dorado County Library in Placerville, who put up with my constant need for more paper and more quarters, especially Bonnie Battaglia.

I am also thankful to the online capabilities of the Library of Congress, the National Library of Australia (Trove), the Bibliothèque Nationale de France (Gallica), and Old Fulton

County New York Post Cards (fultonhistory.com) as well as EllisIsland.org.

Cheers to my fellow cycling researchers, collectors, and historical cycling enthusiasts, including Jeff Groman, Peter Stephens, Peter Nye, George Mount, Andrew Ritchie, Owen Mulholland, Michael Gabriele, Charlie Kelly, Buck Peacock, Feargal McKay, Bill McCann, Renate Franz, and David Herlihy.

This book would not have been complete without help and support from Reggie McNamara's extended family: his surviving grandchildren, Kenneth Zink, Joseph K. Horter, and Theresa Passione; and his great-grandchildren, Lori McGowan and Joseph D. Horter.

Thanks to Robert Taylor, Courtney Ochsner, the folks at University of Nebraska Press, and Elizabeth Gratch for her expert copyediting. Thanks to Elizabeth Demers and those at Potomac Books.

I cannot thank my family enough for their love and support. My mother, Anne, diligently read through each chapter, offering many critiques and correcting grammatical mistakes. She and my father, Don, have always been a great source of inspiration. My uncle, James Marshall, spent time in New Jersey, where I believed the record of the McNamara's marriage certificate was held. After days of effort he ran into a dead end. But when he decided to look elsewhere, in New York, the certificate was found in ten minutes. Thanks to my cousin Alison Stone, who helped with indexing. My sister, Becky, her husband, Jeff, and their children, Arly and Vinzent, and my brother, Ted, and his wife, Julia, have all lent helping hands. And of course, thanks to Shelli, the love of my life, and her family.

Introduction

Extinction is not a term often linked with sport. For more than five decades a sport once robust generated millions of dollars in revenue. Hundreds of highly tuned professional athletes earned a good living. Enthusiasts paid good money for the privilege of watching the excitement unfold. Today this sport has disappeared into an abyss. To purchase tickets, thousands once waited outside in the cold, shivering for hours in long lines that wrapped around Madison Square Garden. The wealthiest and most famous people of the day, such as Babe Ruth, Knute Rockne, Will Rogers, Mary Pickford, Charlie Chaplin, William Randolph Hearst, and Bing Crosby paid top dollar to sit in the best box seats. Today the sport, and nearly any knowledge of its great athletes, rests in oblivion.

That sport is six-day bicycle racing. Although six-day racing still exists in Europe, it has been wiped out in the United States for a long time—virtually killed off by the 1950s. Several unsuccessful attempts were made to revive the sport to its former glory in America, but it could not adapt to its new climate.

Reggie McNamara rose to fame in the 1920s, at the zenith of the sport's prominence. He was the son of an Australian farmer. His career earnings of approximately $500,000 (about $7 million in today's dollars) rivaled those of the best baseball players of his generation. He was the so-called Iron Man of cycling, and for almost thirty years—until he was nearly fifty years old—McNamara battled against younger, older, and more talented riders. For fans, sportswriters, and fellow professionals of his era, no six-day race was complete without him.

In 1913, very early in his career, McNamara received the Iron Man label. As the years went by, the suitability of his nickname was confirmed over and over again. McNamara possessed an inhumanly high tolerance for pain. What biker would go right back into a race after a doctor was compelled to use a pair of pliers to pull a spoke out of his arm? McNamara would—and McNamara did. From innumerable crashes he suffered many broken bones, had lacerations that required umpteen stitches, and had countless contusions, concussions, and internal bleeding. He finished more than one six-day race with broken ribs.

McNamara was one of the very few to ever win six-day races on three different continents—Australia, Europe, and North America. Throughout his professional career, which spanned nearly thirty years, he won a total of seventeen six-day races, along with an inestimable number of shorter-distance races.

As a self-described "little punk kid" living in New Jersey, Bob Walthour III once remarked that there were two people who used to scare him. Walthour did a lot of his growing up in and around cycling tracks in the 1930s, when his father competed with and against McNamara. The first person to scare young Walthour was Frank Turano. Turano used to purposely scare him just for laughs. Going slowly and quietly on his fixed-gear bike with highly pressurized tires, Turano would sneak up on kids like Walthour from behind. When the opportunity presented itself, Turano would touch Walthour on the shoulder and at the same time yell, "Hey kid!" Turano would take off and look back at the startled boy and chuckle.

The second person who scared Walthour was Reggie McNamara. But the difference between being scared by Turano and McNamara was that McNamara didn't have to do anything. His mere presence made young Walthour uneasy because of the pervasive wounds on McNamara's hands, arms, legs, and especially his face.

But these "battle scars" didn't bother McNamara's grandson, Kenneth Zink Jr. To him McNamara was Grandpa, and Ken loved him just the way he was. In the 1950s, decades after he retired from professional racing, Reggie's hands worked well; they fixed Ken's bike when something broke or if he got a flat tire. His legs worked fine; the pair took long walks and bike rides and even went swimming. To Ken, McNamara was a hero.

Ted Harper, a six-day rider from the mid-1930s, said of McNamara: "This remarkable man was a very kind person, who was very good with the younger riders and always willing to give them advice. I learned a lot from Reggie's instructions, and I owed a lot to him for any success that I had as a professional bicycle racer. He was always my idol."[1]

But he was neither indestructible nor far from perfect. McNamara became estranged from his wife and family. Later in his life he lost a fortune built up through the sport he so dearly loved and developed a serious drinking problem that nearly ruined his life.

Comparing professional six-day racing with today's professional road cycling would be like comparing NASCAR with Formula 1 or baseball with cricket or rugby with American football—a lot of similarities but also enough differences to make understanding them both equally and thoroughly quite a task. Any fan dedicated to both sports may be considered offbeat—or worse, a traitor.

In cycling "roadies" make fun of "trackies," and vice versa. Most of it is all in good fun. Several years ago, after submitting an article to a cycling magazine, I was duly informed by the editor that if I had first read his magazine's byline, I would forever know that it reported exclusively on road cycling and positively no track cycling articles, under any circumstances, were welcome or considered. Okay, maybe I exaggerate a little—shortly thereafter the story was published in a competing magazine.[2]

Although road cycling in the United States is currently at the top in professional popularity, in McNamara's day American road cycling was strictly for amateurs.

Willie Ratner, a sportswriter and radio commentator of McNamara's era, said of six-day racing: "One visit to a six-day bike race and the picture is with you forever. There's nothing else like it in the world. Hard to talk about, perhaps—over the air—but nothing else but easy to look at. Panoramic motion constantly. Excitement of a character that leaves one wet with perspiration. A whirl of color accompanied by the throaty thunder of a great indoor bowl filled with fans who are as rabid as yourself. Endurance and grit and stamina, which can only be marveled at. Hidden wells of energy which mere spectators cannot even understand. Marvelous!"[3]

Although this is a biography of Reggie McNamara, it also encapsulates the cycling career of many other great cyclists and six-day races forgotten by time. With the publication of this book, I don't expect a six-day revival in the United States, but if the sport were somehow resuscitated from extinction, McNamara would be its most worthy inspiration.

1

Rabbits and Slingshots

Inheriting toughness and longevity from a father and mother is not a requirement to become a great athlete, but for Reginald James McNamara it didn't hurt. Between 1876 and 1895 Reggie's mother, Honora, gave birth to fourteen children; she lived to ninety years old. His father, Timothy McNamara, spent his entire life in New South Wales following grazing and farming pursuits. He and Honora were married at Sydney's St. Francis Church on January 1, 1875. They remained married until Timothy died of his first and only sickness in 1934, at the age of eighty-six.

Timothy and Honora's first farm was in the Grenfell district, roughly 250 miles directly east of Sydney. All the McNamara children were born on or near the farm. Reggie was the ninth child, born on November 7, 1887.[1] The McNamaras tilled the red soil and raised sheep on the flat dry landscape. Local newspapers kept close track of rainfall, which never seemed to be enough. But when rain did fall, it came in torrents. The entire family worked hard and played hard; everyone pulled their weight.

With the assistance of a professional tutor, Reggie and his brothers and sisters were homeschooled. Perhaps there was no public school nearby the farm. Reggie's penmanship, as witnessed in examples made decades later, gives evidence of an attention to detail. His writing was very neat, with distinctive loops done in a calligraphic style. When they weren't working, being schooled, or sitting down to eat, the McNamara children enjoyed boundless freedom on the fringe of the Australian Outback.

That freedom to roam was sometimes costly, and for the McNamara family it certainly was. Their first son, Ernest James, died at the age of nine in a drowning accident. Not only had his body been discovered days after the tragedy, but Timothy and Honora, who had been away gathering provisions for the farm, knew nothing of their dreadful loss until their arrival home, when they came across the coroner just back from the inquest.[2] Thereafter, the McNamaras probably made it a household rule not to stray far from home all alone.

In what may be the oldest existing photo of Reggie, surrounded by some of his blond-haired and brown-haired brothers and sisters and his mother, there is no doubt which one he was. He was about ten years old and neatly attired in a coat, white collar, and cap. His ears stuck out distinctively—exact replicas of his father's.

There are few people who in childhood encounter a single event that alters the course of their lives, for better or worse. If such an event did alter the course of Reggie's life, it would be impossible to know. One event from his youth, however, was recounted over and over in newspapers and magazines after he became famous; it happened one day in the heat of the Australian Outback. "I had a lot of adventures when I was a youngster in Australia," McNamara once related. "That finger is a little memento of one of them."[3]

Rabbits were first introduced to Australia in 1788, brought over from Europe aboard the ship *First Fleet*. For decades they were kept isolated in rabbit-farming warrens. But in 1859 Thomas Austin released twenty-four wild rabbits on his property for hunting purposes. Instead of getting shot at and killed, the rabbits did what rabbits do best in a warm climate—they bred. Ten years later rabbits became so prolific in the Australian bush that two million could be trapped or shot each year without any appreciable difference in their population. Vast amounts of

Australian taxpayer money were spent on thousands of miles of "rabbit-proof" fences that did little to contain the spread of the vermin. Besides ruining farmers' crops, rabbits caused the loss of many species of plants and animals unique to Australia.

Like so many farmers, the McNamaras did what they could to control the pests on their own property. On one of many occasions the McNamara boys equipped themselves with handmade slingshots, much like the ones Reggie fashioned for his grandchildren some fifty years later, and set out to hunt rabbits. The event most likely took place on their enormous piece of property in either Grenfell or Dubbo, where they moved when Reggie was about ten. The Dubbo farm was roughly 130 miles due north of Grenfell.

The boys scared a rabbit into a fallen hollow tree. Reggie volunteered to go in to fetch the rabbit or at least scare it out so they could get a shot off with slingshots at the ready. He felt around with his left hand for the frightened creature. "It was black in there," he recalled later, "and I was feeling my way forward when my hand closed—not on the fur of a rabbit but on the cold, scaly body of a snake. The next instant I felt the fangs close into the end of my finger. You can bet I crawled out of there quicker than I crawled in. I remember I was mighty frightened. So were my brothers."[4]

The eldest brother, John, announced that the end of the finger had to come off—they were not going to wait to identify the snake as poisonous or not—and the others agreed. Most accounts claim it was done with an ax. But because the boys were probably far away from home, it is more likely they used whatever they had handy—such as a hunting knife.

"'Go ahead and cut it off!' I said as stoutly as I could," McNamara recounted, "and tried hard not to wince when the steel bit through the flesh, bone and fingernail. It was a successful operation in more than one way. I learned what it was to be brave; what it was to take punishment like a man without whimpering."[5] Small and bloody as it was, the brothers wrapped up the remaining piece of Reggie's finger in a portion of a shirttail.

From that day on, McNamara knew what to expect from pain, knowing that he could manage it.

Reggie's older brothers acquired bikes at an early age— probably before Reggie was born. Given the time frame, one of the bikes could have been an old-fashioned "high-wheel." With the introductions of both the diamond-framed "safety" bicycle, with two equal-size wheels, and the pneumatic tire at the same time in the late 1880s, it was more likely the boys owned the kind we are all familiar with today.

Whatever the case, young Reggie longed for the day he could have his own bicycle. By the time he got one, he was already proficient from riding his brothers' bikes. It was purported that he first straddled and rode a bike at the age of two.[6] No doubt, it was a fixed-gear bike without brakes, like the ones he'd race on for his entire career.

The boys built their own dirt racetrack on the McNamara property by having a team of horses pull a weighted drag around. They worked on the track whenever there was a break from chores, and it was built up with banked turns. The brothers raced each other, kicking up the red dirt as they rode around that track until each knew the slightest bump and impression. Like most brothers, they were competitive against one another and constantly pushed each other. They fought, wrestled, and had plenty of laughs together too. Reggie's two oldest brothers, John Cecil (J.C.) and Denis, were eight and seven years older, respectively. Joe was only a year older than Reggie, and there were two younger brothers, Leo Vincent and Ignatius Patrick, who were five and six years younger, respectively. Then there were his sisters, who no doubt joined in the merriment on the track and rode bicycles on and off the farm as much as they were able. Margaret was two years older than J.C.; Alice, Bertha, and Sybil were between Denis's and Joe's age. Reggie's younger sisters were Eileen, Kathleen, and Mary Anne, the baby of the entire flock.

In New South Wales, where Reggie grew up, and in most other sections of Australia, there was no such thing as amateur racing. When they could, youngsters Joe and Reggie went along with J.C. and Denis when they competed in local races. The young lads got inspiration seeing their brothers amid the dust, noise, and rough-and-tumble high-speed excitement.

When Joe and Reggie went up on their home track against their older brothers, they had a real fight on their hands. No big brother was going to let a younger brother beat him on purpose. As Joe and Reggie honed their cycling skills, J.C. and Denis moved on with other things. But for Joe and especially Reggie racing bikes started to become more than just a pleasant diversion.

On May 30, 1906, in what may have been his first entrance into professional racing, eighteen-year-old Reggie did well in a series of races to support the local hospital. He won the one-mile Empire Wheel Race as well as the one-mile District Handicap (starting from scratch) and took second in the half-mile Pulican's Purse. For his efforts he earned a good amount of money. Months later he had a race fifty miles from home. He strapped a few spare wheels on his back and rode out to the race and won enough money to take a train home. Earning money doing what he loved motivated him to train harder. By the time he turned twenty, he had made up his mind to pursue a racing career and left the farm for good.

Whether it was long road races or short track races, on grass, on dirt, or on pavement, Reggie did all he could do to earn a living. He began to earn a reputation as a rider, not gifted with a great sprint at the end of races but, rather, with a remarkable ability to sustain high intervals of speed over a long period of time. His modus operandi was to zap the sting out of sprinters' legs and lungs before they had a chance to go against him at the end. Reggie's stamina and strength were phenomenal.

He found another way to make money—or at least free bicycles and bike parts—by advertising an "Austral" bike, which he rode. The ad was in the *Sydney Morning Herald* and encouraged patrons to come to the "Austral Cycle Dept" at 73 Market Street in Sydney. Reggie's youthful exuberance was unmistakable: "I have won races everywhere. I won a wheel race at Cobar on 7th October, from scratch, also the wheel races at Willington; seven days later I defeated A. J. Davies and A. P. Quinlan at Dubbo on the 28th October, giving me only 14 yards. Won scratch race the same day, in which Quinlan and Davies also started. In the 50 Speedwell Mile Road Race I won, and made the fastest time on 3rd July. . . . I might mention that I have five gold medals, fifteen first, five from scratch, seven second, four third, and only been riding eighteen months and am nineteen years old."[7]

By late 1909 Reggie was known as the "Western Champion" and the "Country Champion" and had changed his allegiance from an Austral to a Massey-Harris bicycle. He was riding against the best riders in Australia, including Alf Goullet, Gordon Walker, George Horder, A. J. Davies, Frank Corry, and Alf Grenda. On September 15, 1909, he won the forty-mile Forbes to Parkes and back road race sponsored by the Forbes Federal Bicycle Club. McNamara started fifteen minutes after many of the riders and took first place in a time of one hour, fifty minutes, and forty-nine seconds. Months later, on a day when it was 110 degrees Fahrenheit, he won the Coolamon Wheel Race in front of four thousand people and took home twenty-five pounds (US$2,100 today).[8]

In case he needed more money, Reggie always had the family farm to fall back on. But with his passion in pursuit of a sustainable and successful professional bike racing career, along with his great physical and mental abilities, he continued to improve year after year. He never went back to the farm. To McNamara professional cycling was so much more exhilarating; he wanted it to be part of his life forever.

Rabbits and Slingshots

2

Bushes to the Big Leagues

Tempted by fame and fortune, most of today's professional elite cyclists, primarily road racers, spend much of the year training and racing in Europe. They adapt to its traditions, food, weather, and culture. They learn new languages and develop lifelong relationships. Many would otherwise go to college or establish "normal" careers, but instead, they sacrifice time and untold amounts of energy (not to mention risk of terrible injury) dedicating themselves to compete at the sport's highest level.

More than one hundred years ago dozens of young Aussies like McNamara, with determination and talent that would have equaled that of today's top cyclists, were similarly seduced by success. Although lacking modern communications, they, too, traveled thousands of miles from their homes and families. But rather than Europe, they dreamed of racing in America. Alfred Goullet said that coming to the United States from his native Australia "was like entering the Big League from the bushes."[1] A generation of young Aussie riders, including McNamara, attained inspiration from two Americans who had come to Australia—Arthur Augustus Zimmerman and Marshall Walter "Major" Taylor. Before crossing into the Southern Hemisphere, both Zimmerman and Taylor had gone up against the best competition in the United States and in Europe, and both had come out on top. They won American championships and world championships, achieved worldwide notoriety, and gained fabulous wealth.

In September 1895, just before Reggie's eighth birthday, the tall and lanky "Zimmy" made his first stop in Australia. At a time when the average Australian worker earned one hundred pounds (US$8,400 today) per year, Zimmerman received a two thousand–pound (US$167,000 today) appearance fee. Months earlier, "the papers had been full of Zimmerman, his performances, his movements, and in fact, everything about him."[2]

Zimmerman came directly from London aboard the steamer RMS *Oruba*. His plan was to train in Adelaide for a month prior to any racing. By his own admission Zimmerman was not highly motivated to race. "I did not come out altogether with a view to showing what I can do in racing, for although I am going to ride," Zimmerman said, "I regard my visit more as a friendly call."[3] It is unlikely that McNamara or his brothers traveled to go see Zimmerman in person, but certainly the brothers read about him in the newspaper.

Zimmerman raced in Sydney, Melbourne, Brisbane, and Newcastle. But largely due to influenza, he didn't race as much as he hoped, nor was he as dominating as he had been earlier in his career. More noteworthy than his racing were the phenomenal crowds. On November 17 the Sydney Cricket Ground "was massed from the barrier to the outskirts in such a solid body that their swaying carried away a strong fence separating them from the oval. . . . The attendance in round numbers was fully 27,500, which is a record."[4] Although Zimmerman's racing did not live up to competitive expectations, never did Australia draw larger and more voracious crowds of spectators who took pleasure in the colorful high-speed excitement of cycling. Zimmerman's visit caused a big stir Down Under, and many new cycling fanatics were born.

Seven years later, in December 1902, when Reggie had just turned fifteen, Major Taylor, who had the same short and stocky build as McNamara did in his prime, was cycling's biggest superstar sensation, and he arrived in Australia for the first time to a

Bushes to the Big Leagues

huge assemblage of fans. "I could not restrain my tears," Taylor said, "as I looked over the side of the liner and saw hundreds of boats . . . decked out with American flags."[5] Like Zimmerman before him, Taylor received a hefty appearance bonus—fifteen hundred pounds (US$2,500 today). He also needed time to train and adjust. Thousands came out to the Sydney Cricket Ground just for the opportunity to watch Taylor's workouts. Newspapers reported at the time that "record attendances during Zimmerman's visit are expected to be eclipsed."[6]

Like Zimmerman, huge crowds flocked to see Major Taylor. Many came to see him for the sheer novelty—a non-Aboriginal black man in Australia was a rare sight. But to witness Taylor on cycling's highest professional stage was extraordinary. Unlike the United States, "white Australia" accepted Taylor and treated him very kindly. In the press, however, there were racist remarks and cartoons, but much more was made about his religious convictions, particularly his steadfast refusal to race on Sundays. Given that the McNamara brothers were older now than when Zimmerman had raced Down Under, it's possible that at least one McNamara went to see Taylor. But in all likelihood the brothers eagerly read about Taylor from newspaper accounts, just as they had done when Zimmerman arrived in Australia.

Taylor's racing Down Under was more impressive than Zimmerman's. He went up against and beat the best sprinters, including Don Walker, George Morgan, R. W. Lewis, Ernest A. Pye, and, from New Zealand, J. Chalmers.

Even with a threat of rain, more than fifteen thousand fans and a Naval Brigade Band packed the Sydney Cricket Ground on Monday, January 19, 1903, under brilliant electric lights. Taylor won the fifth heat and subsequent final of the coveted Centennial Mile. He also won his heat of the "Taylor Plate" quarter-mile race. Two days later twenty-five thousand spectators braved the rain again to see him win the semifinal and the final of the Taylor Plate; he also won the International Mile race.[7]

Taylor said, "Australia has the best public, the best prizes, and the worst tracks in the world."[8] This comment may have been due to the fact that much racing was done on grass, which up to that point was completely unknown to him. During his stay Taylor racked up "almost £4,000 [US$335,000 today]— equivalent to what an average Australian worker would have earned during his entire 40-year working lifetime."[9]

The success of Taylor's visit was staggering, and almost as soon as he left, in mid-April 1903, negotiations had begun with the dark-haired and mustachioed Australian promoter Hugh D. McIntosh to bring him back. Taylor and his pretty wife, Daisy, had only one child, who was born on their second visit to Australia on May 11, 1904. They named her Rita Sydney after the city where she was born.

But another American may have had more influence than anyone else fetching young talent to the United States. His name was Floyd MacFarland. In late 1903 he arrived in Australia from his hometown of San Jose, California, along with sprinting ace Iver Lawson. At six foot four MacFarland cut an imposing figure on the bike. Not only was he one of the best professional sprinters of his day; he was also skilled at motor-paced racing, and he had ridden successfully in several long-distance six-day races.

MacFarland was a savvy businessman, and he was an excellent promoter of himself and others. Although he was a very likable man, MacFarland had a bit of Jekyll and Hyde in him. It seemed that if he wasn't making friends, he was making enemies. If he were crossed, whether by friend or foe, he reacted with the fury of a mother grizzly bear protecting her cubs. His traveling partner, Lawson, knew firsthand about MacFarland's temper. In 1901 MacFarland, claiming Lawson had fouled him and caused him to fall, pulled him off his bike and punched Lawson in the face.[10] Four months later, at a Boston six-day race, MacFarland nearly started a riot by attacking the six-foot, two hundred–pound Chicago racer George Leander at the finish. According to the *Boston Globe*, "Guns were left at the office, but fists were good, as were handlebars, clubs and sections of the training stands."[11]

In the 1970s, when Alf Goullet, perhaps the most talented bike rider ever to draw oxygen (yes, I include Eddy Merckx), was in his eighties, his recollection of MacFarland was strong: "When I was a boy in knee pants, cycling was the rage in Australia. Everybody rode a wheel. I used to read about Major Taylor, Iver Lawson and Floyd MacFarland. When I finally got a peek at MacFarland in Australia, he struck my fancy. I followed him wherever he went on the streets. It was then I took to racing and trained between my working hours on the ranch."[12] If the news of these Americans inspired Goullet to train harder, others, like Reggie McNamara, were sure to follow suit.

Major Taylor had many battles with MacFarland in the United States. According to Taylor's biographer Andrew Ritchie, MacFarland threatened him physically and verbally after Taylor had won a race through "skillful tactical maneuvering." MacFarland and his cronies came after him. Taylor wrote: "As they came into my room, I was waiting for them with a length of two-by-four which I had picked up from a lumber pile near the grandstand. Before they had a chance to lay a hand on me I made one vicious, healthy swing at MacFarland, but he dodged the blow. Then the entire outfit tried to close in on me, and I was too fast for them even on foot. . . . Fortunately, there was no bloodshed."[13]

In January 1904 Major Taylor and his pregnant wife, Daisy, arrived in Australia for the second time. Rather than taking time for a week or two of workouts and becoming acclimated with the weather and tracks, Taylor went straight to racing. MacFarland and Lawson were well aware that Taylor was due to arrive again in Australia, and they worked together to create a hostile atmosphere in which some Aussies, once friendly with Taylor, turned against him.

Taylor was again treated poorly in the press—much like in the United States. He was regularly referred to as "darkie" or the "Flying Darkie." One publication wrote: "Major Taylor, the coon champion cyclist, is not scooping all the fat prizes this time. Two other Yanks—Iver Lawson and Floyd MacFarland—have both beaten him several times at the big cycle meetings held recently in Melbourne and Sydney."[14]

On one such occasion MacFarland was penalized and suspended for a month. He had forced Taylor off the track and onto the grass inside. MacFarland tried to appeal the ruling, saying that Taylor had come off his line after looking under his arm to see where his competition was. But his appeal did not impress anyone, and his suspension stood.

On February 8, at Melbourne's Exhibition Ground, in front of twenty-four thousand excited fans, a match race was run between Taylor and Lawson. This time Lawson didn't have MacFarland there to help. In the half-mile event the two riders "crawled round the track at a pace sufficient to keep the machines upright." Then Taylor suddenly shot out, propelled rapidly by every fiber of muscle in his body. Lawson went a half-second later, but it was too little too late; Taylor won by three lengths.

A week later the two met again in Melbourne. In the first of three heats Taylor was in the lead with a quarter-mile (one lap) to go. Around the first turn Lawson was right on Taylor's wheel. By the second turn Lawson made a move to pass. With one hundred yards to go, both were on even terms flying down the home stretch. As they went by the grandstands, the crowd could see Taylor inching ahead. It was too much speed for Lawson to handle, and he lost by a length and a half.

In the second heat both riders were on even terms at the sound of the bell lap, "when Taylor's machine skidded. He lost ground momentarily, but soon regained it, and at the Exhibition Building, he was slightly in the lead, riding on the inside. The machines came into collision and Taylor was thrown violently to the track."[15]

Taylor was taken to the hospital for one of the most serious accidents of his career. He was badly bruised and lacerated. Lawson was suspended by the Victorian League of Wheelmen for a year, which was later reduced to three months. Unable to compete, Lawson took a steamship to London, where in September he claimed victory to one of the most coveted titles of the day, the 1904 World's Sprint Champion.

Once Taylor got out of the hospital, he began preparing for what would potentially be his biggest payout in Australia and maybe the world: the Sydney Thousand. The Sydney Thousand was a multi-program event that culminated in the race Taylor was ultimately competing for, the One-Mile International Handicap, for which the winner would receive 750 Australian dollars, second place would get 100, third place 50, and the remainder would go to the individual heat winners. Eleven riders qualified: three Americans, Taylor, MacFarland, and Hardy Downing; three from Victoria, Don Walker, F. H. Scheps, B. P. Kett; and five from New South Wales, Larry Corbett, D. J. Plunkett, H. Gordon, A. E. O'Brien, and C. Bathe.

An American, Norman C. Hopper, had won the previous year's Sydney Thousand in front of nearly thirty thousand spectators at the Cricket Ground. Many fans pinned their hopes and bets on another American victory. But there was much work to be done because Taylor and MacFarland were starting at scratch and Downing was starting at 10 yards, whereas all the New South Wales riders were starting at least 120 yards ahead.

On the evening of March 23, 1904, a record-breaking crowd of more than thirty thousand people came out. The spacious grandstand was overflowing and included hundreds of women attired in colorful dresses. In contrast, the "shilling pavilion" was a sea of mostly young men in dark overcoats and hats. Dozens of races were run before the grand finale, and the crowd buzzed with excitement and anticipation as they waited for the last race.

Taylor was the first rider on the track for a warm-up under the track lights. He was met with a thunderous ovation, which he acknowledged with a big smile and a wave of his hand. As the riders lined up in their starting positions and rider announcements were made, all of the lights, with the exception of the track lights, were turned off. The spectacle they had all been waiting for was soon to begin. The big crowd was on its feet and quiet.

The pistol fired, and off the riders went. The crowd came

alive and roared with excitement. Downing and Walker, both at ten yards off the starting mark, were quickly caught by Taylor, with MacFarland bringing up the rear. Of the four only Taylor and Walker put in any effort at the front of their group to catch the leading team, with its seven riders. Because MacFarland and Downing sat on wheels and didn't help with the chase, it was all quickly over. With a quarter-mile to go, however, Taylor took off to catch the leading division. Although it was a lost cause for first place, he did catch and pass the tailenders and finished in fourth overall.

Larry Corbett, with a 120-yard start advantage, took home the £750 (US$63,800 today), edging out O'Brien, who had started at 180 yards, by half a bike length. The disgusted crowd had not expected a race like this. When MacFarland and Downing came across the finish, they were met with a resounding cacophony of dissatisfaction for spoiling what could have been an exciting race from the scratch men. Taylor was asked what had happened. "What am I to think?" he shrugged, "Walker did his share of the pacing and I did mine. MacFarland did not do his. That was all."[16]

Second-place finisher O'Brien quickly made an appeal to the council of the New South Wales League of Wheelmen about whether there had been collusion among the riders. On March 30 a meeting was held at the Gosford Hotel to consider O'Brien's case.

Behind closed doors they carefully examined all evidence and came up with a sensational announcement. Floyd MacFarland was to be suspended for three years and Corbett for two. Bathe, Downing, Kett, and Plunckett were each served with one-year suspensions and Gordon a half-year. O'Brien was awarded the £750 (US$63,800 today), and Taylor won £100 for second place. Walker and Scheps did not receive prize money but were not handed suspensions.[17] Several members of the council claimed that even if O'Brien had not protested, there would have been an inquiry anyway. Seven riders were on the take, and based on the punishment, MacFarland was the ringleader.

Incredibly, less than two months after MacFarland returned to the United States, rumors began to circulate that he would soon be back to Australia. The *Sydney Morning Herald* reported that because MacFarland "cannot take part in any race meeting until his three years' suspension is up, there is probably some mistake in the announcement."[18]

MacFarland sent a letter to the council to appeal his suspension. In the letter he offered no apology, nor did he take any responsibility in the matter other than to say that in the future he would comply with the rules. He stated that the punishment was too severe. "Inasmuch as I was not given a hearing upon the charge upon which I was suspended," he wrote, "I would like to have your council reconsider my case."[19] Despite a report in August that MacFarland's appeal "did not meet with any sympathy" and that "every member of the council was opposed to the American's appeal," by November 1905 the united front had reversed its decision, and MacFarland was free to race in Australia again.

But racing wasn't the only thing MacFarland had on his docket. He was given a task by John M. Chapman, the manager of the Salt Lake City Velodrome, to recruit young Australian riders to the United States. And so began MacFarland's career as a promoter.

McNamara was too young and inexperienced at this time and may not have met MacFarland until many years later. But the two riders MacFarland had his eye on were Ernest Pye and A. J. "Jackie" Clark.[20] Australians had raced in America before, including Don Walker, F. H. Scheps, and Peddler Palmer, but none were to have a more lasting impact up to this point than Pye and Clark. With help from MacFarland, their introduction to the United States paved the way for others such as Alf Goullet, Reggie McNamara, and dozens of other young Aussies who came out over the next twenty-plus years.

Both Pye and Clark lived permanently in the United States and became U.S. citizens. Pye was dark-haired and looked a little older than his years. He was an all-around rider and could sprint with the best, could race behind the motors, and was also well suited to endurance races. Short in stature and sometimes referred to as the "chubby" kid from Melbourne, Clark was more of a pure sprinter, the caliber of the chisel-chinned American Frank Kramer. Clark was immediately embraced by fans in the Northern Hemisphere, who gave him the moniker "the Australian Rocket."

Pye and Clark, both from Victoria, signed contracts to race in Salt Lake City during the summer of 1906.[21] They also signed an engagement letter to compete in the December 1906 six-day race at Madison Square Garden in New York City. As Mac-Farland, Pye, and Clark prepared to leave Australia bound for San Francisco, Australian promoter and secretary of the New South Wales League of Wheelmen, Hugh McIntosh, could not resist sending a parting shot at MacFarland in the form of a letter to the editor of the *Sydney Morning Herald*. "Dear Sir," he wrote, "I read in your issue of this morning an interview with the American cyclist Floyd MacFarland, in which he says the sport here requires a lift, and to accomplish that requires a governing body more in sympathy with the men who race for a living. This is certainly amusing to those of the general public who remember Mr. MacFarland's 1904 Thousand, when the officials displayed their sympathy to the extent of three years' disqualification of Mr. MacFarland."[22]

The trio arrived in San Francisco sometimes around May 20, 1906—just about a month after the great earthquake. The devastation they observed was horrific. Approximately 3,000 people had perished, and as many as 300,000 of the 410,000 people who lived in San Francisco were homeless, and 80 percent of the city had been destroyed.

They visited MacFarland's hometown, San Jose, which had suffered far less than San Francisco. San Jose, about fifty miles south of San Francisco, had no shortage of water and thus was able to put out fires, which had been contained to small areas and single buildings, whereas the fires in San Francisco had consumed whole city blocks. The three men visited with members of MacFarland's former club, the Garden City Wheelmen, before they boarded an early-morning train on May 23 that took them to Salt Lake City.

According to newspaper accounts, Pye and Clark both had difficulty mastering the steep curves of the wooden velodrome track. Clark would not try it for days. In Pye's first attempt around, he crashed twice. Pye rode the embankments "as if he were dodging boulders in a creek bottom." [23] Both got the hang of it, however, and each had successful summer seasons in Utah.

For Pye it was not just success on the bike path that he enjoyed that summer, but he also found the love of his life. Grayce M. Newborn and Pye wasted little time and were married in July 1906. Grayce reportedly said, "I want to become Mrs. Pye just as soon as I can." [24]

In 1908 Pye became manager of the Salt Lake City Velodrome. Years later he started a business manufacturing bicycle tires. Many of the best cyclists in the world rode on Pye-Musselman tires, including Reggie McNamara, whose image and quotes were used for advertising. Pye died an early death, in 1923, and Grayce continued on with the business, becoming one of the few women in the United States at that time to lead such an organization.

On August 31, 1910, Clark married Rena Bray at her parents' home in Salt Lake City. Floyd MacFarland was the best man. [25] But by 1913 Clark and MacFarland's relationship had soured to the point that Clark refused to race on any track associated with MacFarland. Clark never won an American sprint title, a prize that was monopolized by Frank Kramer year after year, but he did come close on a number of occasions.

Another Aussie with lasting impact on the American scene was the aforementioned blond-haired and blue-eyed Alfred Timothy Goullet. He had not yet built up his 160-pound muscular frame when he first turned professional at the age of seventeen; that was in 1908, when he first met Floyd Mac-Farland. He mustered up the courage to ask a trainer if he could talk to MacFarland, and the trainer showed Goullet into the promoter's training quarters. MacFarland was getting a rubdown.

"Hello kid," MacFarland greeted him. "So you're going to ride against us, eh? Bob, you put some weight into that rub from now on. I'm not taking any chances." Goullet guffawed and stammered something to the effect that he couldn't win. "Why not?" MacFarland answered. "You're just a boy and we aren't getting any younger. You just go ahead and live clean and play hard and you will get there, and make up your mind that this is the only way you will get there. The game is as hard as any other, and it's the boys who take care of themselves that reach the top in the end."[26]

Goullet would never forget the wise advice MacFarland gave him that day in Melbourne. He got serious about self-discipline and practice over the next two years and developed physically and mentally into a more seasoned professional. In the early months of 1910 he received what every novice bicycle rider in Australia craved—a contract from John M. Chapman, a former professional rider turned promoter, to ride for him in America.

According to Goullet, he first arrived at the New York Harbor in early May "in a snowstorm, wearing a sleeveless shirt and a straw hat because it was summer at home."[27] His first race at Vailsburg in Newark indicated that here, too, he was ill prepared. In fact, he only collected a single victory at Vailsburg in his rookie season. But he did have success at seaside tracks—like those at home in Victoria—in Boston and Providence.

Chapman thought Goullet would do well in pursuit racing, in which riders start at opposite sides of the track until one rider overtakes the other. His first opponent in this style of racing was Percy Lawrence, from San Francisco, who was one of the best pursuit racers in the United States. It took Goullet eighteen miles to catch Lawrence for the win. In his second pursuit race he knocked down a bigger adversary, the king of sprinters, Frank Kramer, in fourteen miles.

What Goullet did not realize at the time was that pursuit racing provided excellent training for six-day racing. In December 1910 he rode his first six-day race in America on the world's grandest stage, Madison Square Garden in New York City. His partner was fellow Aussie Paddy Hehir.

Hehir predicted the pair would have great success. But the nineteen-year-old Goullet, by his own admission, had "no more idea of the rudimentary laws of taking care of myself during a grind than a jack rabbit has of arithmetic" and failed to feed himself properly. They did extraordinarily well and were in a great position for the win at the very end; they were on even terms with three other teams. The final victory came down to a one-mile sprint in which they decided Hehir would compete. Hehir took last in the sprint, so they split $600 in fourth-place prize money, plus expenses.

By the time he permanently retired from cycling, in 1926, Goullet had amassed the greatest winning percentage in six-day racing history. Sammy Gastman, who rode twenty-two six-day races in the 1920s, said in an interview that Goullet was the "greatest rider to ever sit on a bicycle. He could sprint, and he could do the long ones. You can't do both. But Goullet did. He was a hell of a bike rider." Other Aussies would follow Goullet's lead in six-day racing, including Alfred Grenda, Robert Spears, Gordon Walker, Cecil Walker, Frank Corry, Alex McBeath, Harris Horder, Fred Keefe, and of course Reggie McNamara.

3

A Promoter Goes to Hollywood

With the best young cycling talent leaving home for greener pastures, it was time for Australia to stand up and fight to keep professional cycling healthy and alive at a high level before it became just a breeding ground for John Chapman to pick from. What was needed was a man with creativity, a sharp mind, and deep pockets. A man who had all this and more was James Dixon Williams.

Better known as "J.D." Williams, he was born in 1877 in Ceredo, West Virginia. At age sixteen Williams entered the theatrical business, when he became treasurer of his home-town theater. In 1910 he came to Australia, where he organized the Greater J. D. Williams Amusement Company, headquartered in Sydney. In a just a few short years he was responsible for introducing motion pictures on a large scale to Australia.

In 1913 Williams sold his Australian interests and toured the world as a representative of several American film producers. Upon his arrival back in the United States, Williams helped build a national distribution company, which later became Paramount Pictures. In 1918 Williams signed Charlie Chaplin to the first ever million-dollar contract for a motion picture actor. The comedian was to produce eight movies for this amount. Chaplin later called attention to his expenses, which far exceeded his income, whereby Williams agreed to pay an additional $100,000 for each picture. Williams also signed a deal with Mary Pickford for three movies, at $250,000 each. Like Chaplin, Pickford later pointed out her financial struggles, and she, too, received an additional $100,000 per picture. Williams also signed Norma Talmadge, Rudolph Valentino, and many others.[1]

But in May 1911 Williams was put under great pressure to quickly build the Melba Theatre in Melbourne. In order to obtain the maximum effort from the bricklayers, Williams offered a large bonus to the man who could lay the most bricks. Although the trade union attempted to step in, work shifts were continuous, and competition was fierce among the workers. Williams achieved his objective in record time, and the building opened on June 8, 1911.[2]

Two weeks after the theater's opening night, Williams made an announcement that in agreement with the New South Wales League of Wheelmen, he had initiated plans for Australia's first ever six-day race in Sydney and quite possibly the first outdoor six-day race in the world.[3] The next day he also announced his intention to establish an additional six-day race in Melbourne.

Although he desired the best riders from Australia, Europe, and the United States, Williams hit a bit of a snag right away in his choice of dates for Sydney. His idea to start on New Year's Day was a good one, but there was a problem: the most famous and historic of all six-day races, the New York race inside Madison Square Garden, was always held in the first or second week of December.

Every year the cream of the crop from around the globe were handpicked for the New York race—the best track riders and the best road riders, including Tour de France and Paris-Roubaix champions. In 1911, the inaugural year of the Sydney event, the race at Madison Square Garden was to start on December 11, which meant that any rider competing in the New York six-day would not be able to make the Sydney six-day.

By the end of the 1910 outdoor season, Frank Kramer had been crowned the coveted title of the American national sprint champion for the tenth year in a row. Kramer won his first title in 1901, when he wrestled it away from the defending champion,

Major Taylor. Kramer was a model of consistency and varied his schedule as little as possible. He liked regular routine in sleeping, training, eating, and nearly everything else. Unlike so many young riders, who enjoyed traveling to different faraway places, Kramer chose to stay home if he could. Although he occasionally went north to Boston, out west to Salt Lake City, or sometimes to Europe, everyone knew Kramer was a homebody. One writer labeled him "the Hermit of East Orange."[4]

Points for the sprint title were typically arranged and agreed upon in May, at the beginning of the outdoor season, which lasted into October. Riders with this knowledge could plan their schedules to qualify for those open events that could earn them points. Points were obtainable at tracks in Boston, New Haven, Philadelphia, Providence, and Salt Lake City, but most were awarded in Newark. For many decades Newark was the epicenter of professional cycling in the United States, very much like Boulder is today.

During the 1911 outdoor season Kramer's main opponent was Jackie Clark; the two riders were in a seesaw battle for sprinting supremacy. By early September, Clark and Kramer were nearly tied, with about fifty points apiece. On September 3 five points were up for grabs in the five-mile national championship at the Newark Velodrome. Clark had defeated Kramer earlier in the day in a one-mile match race. But there were no points—only bragging rights and a lot of money.

At the bell lap of the five-mile race for sprint championship points, Clark suddenly pulled off and quit. Clark ran his bike across the grass inside the track and over to the referee's stand. He protested that Kramer had teamed with Alf Goullet to hinder Clark's performance. The argument became more assertive, and tempers began to run high; soon Floyd MacFarland had joined in the mix. By then some of the seven thousand fans had gotten into private disagreements of their own, and pandemonium broke loose all over the stadium. The referee stuck to his guns, however, and refused to change his decision. Calm was restored, and Kramer got his points.[5]

With only a few weeks remaining in the season, Clark had more bad luck. He got a flat tire in a race and crashed to the boards, taking down about a half-dozen riders with him, including Goullet and Iver Lawson. Due to injuries sustained from the crash, Clark was unable to compete in the next round of title points, leaving Kramer to win his eleventh championship in succession, earning seventy-two points to Clark's sixty.[6]

With the New York and Sydney six-day races fast approaching, riders and promoters had to make quick decisions. Three Aussies living in America—Alf Goullet, Paddy Hehir, and Gordon Walker—went back home to compete. Americans Iver Lawson and Worthington Mitten, who specialized in motor-paced racing, also went to Sydney.

Although Australian newspapers indicated that Clark was coming out for the Sydney six-day, he remained in the United States to race at Madison Square Garden. Clark's teammate was Joe Fogler, from Brooklyn, who was a talented all-around man and a seasoned professional who had won six-day races at the Garden on two previous occasions. Clark had a great chance to dig up some revenge on Kramer. In many tries Kramer had never won a six-day race, and he was teamed with Jimmy Moran, from Boston. Like Fogler, Moran was a very good and experienced rider and had won the previous six-day at the Garden with his partner, Eddie Root.

Sixteen two-man teams gathered at the starting line inside Madison Square Garden on the freshly built ten-lap-to-the mile yellow pine board track, in front of some ten thousand cycling-mad fans. Included was the 1910 Tour de France champion, Frenchman Octave Lapize. Lapize had also won three straight Paris-Roubaix races. He was teamed with Cyrille Van Hauwaert, who in 1908 had become the first of many Belgians to win Paris-Roubaix.

At one minute past midnight, on Monday, December 11, the starting line was lit up by the pop of many flashlight photographs as the official starter, Sheriff Tom Foley, provided comic relief in his struggle to operate the starting pistol. Finally, it discharged, and the riders were off.[7]

Five days, or 122 hours, later, after so many laps had been ridden, so many rider exchanges, so many crashes, so many attempts to break up the field, so many tickets purchased, so many cigarettes and cigars smoked, so many beers drunk, and so little sleep, seven teams remained tied for first place, including Clark-Fogler and Kramer-Moran.

At two o'clock Saturday morning Clark began a sprint at a very opportune time, when many teammates off the bike were half-asleep. Clark put distance between himself and the field, and the crowd came to life. Fogler was ready for it and straddled his bike to come out for a rider exchange. A trainer gave Fogler a good shove, and he was off on the inside of the track, waiting for Clark to come around. The two performed a perfect pickup. The lap was earned, and they were on top, with twenty hours to go.

Clark and Fogler were on high alert so that none of the other six teams tied for second could steal a lap back from them. In the end they accomplished the feat and won the overall victory. Clark got his revenge on Kramer, but it was close, especially because in a sprint off for second place overall, Kramer won. Kramer would have surely beaten Clark if they were racing for first overall. It was to be one of the most successful six-day races of Kramer's career—though he would never win a six-day. Fogler, however, won his third and Clark his second New York six-day at Madison Square Garden.

Back in Australia, competitors for the inaugural six-day event were getting ready. Alf Grenda, the lanky powerful Tasmanian, was considered the fastest sprinter left in Australia. He rode with a 108 gear, while others were typically geared at 90. In 1907, when Grenda first started racing, he claimed it was "much easier than chopping wood."[8] At that time Reggie McNamara was considered the "king of the dirt tracks."[9] Each had won victories that August and September both in road racing and on the track.

McNamara was turning twenty-four that November. Up to that point in his career he had never raced on a well-engineered track. The newspaper *Referee*, which reported extensively on professional cycling in America, Australia, and Europe, claimed that the three-lap-per-mile asphalt track that surrounded the Sydney Cricket Ground's field of grass would be McNamara's initial appearance on a first-class track.[10]

McNamara, Grenda, and several other riders set up shop and trained nearly every day on the track, starting at ten o'clock in the morning. Grenda, who chopped wood and played football to keep in shape during the off-season, was seemingly the fastest of the bunch. But McNamara was a glutton for punishment and worked harder than anyone.

In the beginning of November, Goullet, Hehir, and Gordon Walker left New York and winter and arrived in Sydney, where it was summertime. Immediately, they set out to train and race in preparation for the upcoming six-day. On November 20, in one of the races that led up to the big six-day race, Goullet was in a half-mile heat with Grenda. They bumped into each other, and Goullet raised his hand, in what appeared to be a protest against Grenda.

Goullet was fined by the referee for taking his hand off the handlebar. He was allowed to appeal to the league to oppose the fine. "I would not protest against Grenda for what I'm sure was an accidental bump," he wrote to the league, perhaps sarcastically. "It is not the first time I have met the big Tasmania flyer, and I'm sure that he is too good a sportsman to deliberately foul anyone in a race. But he is a heavy man, and when he bumps anybody, the usual thing is that the other fellow has to move."[11]

A week later McNamara and Goullet split a pair of victories against each other in front of eighteen thousand fans at the Sydney Hospital Centenary Carnival. In the first race Goullet won in a furious battle to the finish line. For the moment the crowd forgot that Goullet had abandoned his home country and reservedly accepted him as one of their own. But in their second race McNamara turned the tables on Goullet and won by a mere tire length.

To make certain that the public knew about the six-day race, J. D. Williams took out full-page advertisements in several Sydney newspapers. He claimed, "no idle boast," that it would be "the world's biggest six-days' bicycle race and sports carnival."[12]

One of the greatest challenges Williams faced was lighting the track, for which he spared no expense. He had an electric light plant and traction engine installed in the grounds. To be safe, a special set of wires was run from the training power station. Four hundred and forty metal filament lamps were suspended over the track, each four feet apart. The lamps, shaded so that light was reflected toward the inside and away from the spectator stands, set off an incredibly brilliant sight in the middle of the night, drawing attention to the asphalt track and clean-cut grass.

In case the crowd grew weary during any significant lull in the six-day competition, Williams brought in extraneous entertainment such as the "Globe of Death," whereby a husband-and-wife team of motorcyclists would speed along within a contraption thirty feet in diameter; according to the *Sydney Morning Herald*, they looked "like birds in a huge cage, dashing wildly against the bars in an effort to escape." There was also a one-legged trick cyclist named "Daredevil Kilpatrick," who would delight the crowd by riding down the hundred-plus stadium steps with amazing agility in his scarlet coat.

The field was composed of thirteen two-man teams outside on an asphalt three-lap-to-the-mile track. Compared with the six-day race in New York City, which traditionally had seventeen teams inside on a wooden-surfaced ten-lap-to-the-mile track, there was much more elbow room, not to mention fresh air. The four favored teams were Americans Iver Lawson and Worth Mitten, Goullet and Hehir in blue uniforms, Grenda with Gordon Walker, and McNamara and Frank Corry in yellow.

Before the start of the race, a band played a concert outside the gates of the Sydney Cricket Ground, where thousands

A Promoter Goes to Hollywood

assembled to enjoy the music and bring in the new year. At midnight the lights were turned on with a spectacular effect, and the masses were dumfounded to see the grounds bathed in an electric glow that rendered the field and track as bright as day.

Fifteen thousand fans streamed their way into the stands as a scrum of athletes, trainers, referees, and photographers invaded the starting area below. At one o'clock in the morning of January 1, 1912, the minister of education, Fred Flowers, fired the pistol that sent the riders on their exhausting journey.[13]

To keep the long race more competitive in the short term, Williams arranged to have races within the main race. When a bell sounded three times, the six-day riders knew they had to get ready to ride onto the grass track inside the asphalt track proper. At two bells they'd roll off the track and resume their riding on grass. At one bell they would go back to the track. The reason for all this was to incorporate series of amateur and professional sprint races.

Two issues arose from the switching. First, the mileage that the six-day men rode became an inexact figure once they started on the grass. Second, although the plot was relatively free of rocks and lumps, the riders slowed down considerably while on the grass. They did not seem to mind, however, taking a bit of a rest on the grass.

By four o'clock in the afternoon on day 2, they had ridden seven hundred miles, averaging about eighteen miles per hour. The colorfully clad riders rode at a moderate pace most of the time, but there was a lot of jockeying for position, riders relieved each other, and many attempts to gain a lap livened up the pace.

By day 3 record summer temperatures hovered at more than one hundred degrees Fahrenheit, causing two teams to drop out. The oppressive heat that radiated from the asphalt track slowed the riders' rate of progression even further. The riders' favorite spot around the track was where a hose was set up to spray them as they went by.

According to the *Sydney Morning Herald*: "Trainers resorted to all sort of expedients to make matters cool for their charges.

Cabbage leaves, carried under the cap, were a favorite device, the cool packing of succulent vegetables being rather embarrassing to the wearers, and it did not make for artistic affect to see the stray ends of cabbage stalks poking forth beneath the headgear."[14]

If anyone wished for a change in the weather, that wish was granted. On day 5 dark clouds gave way to booming thunder and a dazzling display of lightning. Driving rain came down ruthlessly on the riders. The band left for cover, and many fans did too, but the riders, soaked to the bone, kept going through it all, including some hail and a steady wind. Murphy's Law would have suggested that Williams got what he deserved, weather wise, when he scheduled the first outdoor six-day race. Up to the end of day 5 the weather played a huge factor in the race.

The weather for day 6 was gorgeous, and unlike on the previous days of oppressive heat and driving rain, people began appearing in large waves. The trams became overtaxed and unable to cope with the great rush to the Cricket Ground. According to the *Sunday Times*: "Not a square inch was unoccupied, and the faces of the crowd pressed against the wire enclosure. Dimly lit by the fairytale lamps, it made a weird and thrilling sight. Nothing like it has ever been seen before on the ground."[15]

Fully fifty-five thousand people were present. It was perhaps the biggest crowd to have witnessed the end of a bicycle race anytime before or anytime since. J. D. Williams gushed: "I've never seen anything like it anywhere; it's certainly the biggest one I've had the pleasure of providing entertainment for in any part of the world. Why, at Madison Square Garden, where the New York race is held, the crowds of any three days would not equal tonight's."[16]

In the afternoon sunshine Goullet made a determined effort to put a lap on the field. Off he went, and the massive crowd came to its feet. Hehir came out to relieve Goullet, and together they put a half-lap on the field amid much excitement. But the other teams worked together, and the breakaway was slowly and steadily reeled in. Some teams did get lapped during the

A Promoter Goes to Hollywood

endeavor, however, and five of the ten teams remained tied on laps. The leading teams were Goullet-Hehir, Grenda-Walker, Lawson-Mitten, Kirkham-Colvin, and McNamara-Corry. In the event the teams were tied on laps at the end of the race, a three-lap sprint was scheduled to determine the overall winners.

At ten o'clock Saturday evening the five teams were still tied on laps and had ridden approximately 2,085 miles. The other five teams went to the grass—their race was done. Hanging in the balance were five hundred Australian dollars for first place, two hundred for second, one hundred for third, seventy five for fourth, and fifty for fifth. At the time one Australian dollar was worth about five American dollars, so the prize money was at least as lucrative as that of the New York six-day race.

There was one American team along with four Australian individuals, represented by New South Wales, Victoria, and Tasmania, in the final three-lap sprint. The first half-mile was a crawl. The order of the riders was Kirkham, McNamara, Grenda, Lawson, and Goullet. They watched each other closely; riders up front incessantly looking back, and Goullet in the rear took an angle to look at everyone in front of him.

"Lawson's away!" The crowd came to life. Lawson jumped at the half-mile spot, and Goullet went right with him, followed by Grenda, McNamara, and Kirkham. Lawson went into the bell lap at a terrific rate of speed, with Goullet still clinging to his wheel. Grenda had a little work to do to bridge the small gap that had formed. Just as Grenda got back on Goullet's wheel, Goullet made his jump and went around Lawson. Grenda could not hold Goullet's wheel in the final straight, but he did hold off a hard-charging McNamara, who came in third. Lawson finished fourth and Kirkham fifth.[17]

The *Sydney Morning Herald* reported: "And the finish, as Enobarbus said of Cleopatra, beggared all description. The vast concourse, nearly sixty thousand strong, rose at the winner and cheered him to the echo. They yelled and whistled and shrieked and threw up their hats and kerchiefs, laughing and shouting wildly. Men clasped hands with utter strangers and clapped each other on the back like old comrades, just (to put it vernac-ularly) because two wiry young Australians had triumphed in a surprise test of speed, strength, stamina, skill and strategy. There were continuous cheers for Goullet and Hehir, the vic-torious pair. The band in the pavilion struck up 'Conquering Hero,' and Goullet was hoisted shoulder high, and borne in tri-umph through the seething multitude to a well-earned rest."[18]

While Goullet was smothered by the crowd, Hehir spoke with the media: "When Lawson jumped with a half mile to go, he played right into Goullet's hands, for the latter had his wheel, and only had to sit there until it was time to go. Then he showed really how he could sprint. We came from America determined, if possible, to win Australia's first six days' race, and we have accomplished our ambition. Now we hope to repeat our victory in the Melbourne race."

Jackie Clark, free of any previous obligations, came back to his homeland accompanied by his wife and trainer, Maury Gordon, for the Melbourne six-day. He arrived the last week of January and had a brief stay at his parents' home in Shapparton before returning to training. Although he had success in the United States and made good money, he complained to the Australian press of his treatment there. "Well, I get too bad a deal over there. The officials are against me," he began, "and Kramer is allowed to get the majority of the best riders 'teamed' with him. I can't get these combinations. Do you know that in one race I was in front for the last four laps, and Fogler was five men behind me? When I made my sprint Fogler, from the rear, yelled out, 'Go on, Clarkie.' I won and Kramer was second, but they disquali-fied me for 'teaming' with Fogler, because the latter called out to me in the race. . . . I don't expect to win the world's champi-onship, nor the American championship, with officials against me and Kramer allowed to 'corner' all the best riders to work for him, but I will make them pay. My friends declare I'm the most popular rider in America, and whenever I ride there are big crowds. Yes, I certainly make the promoters pay; Kramer can have the championships. I'm making the money."[19]

A Promoter Goes to Hollywood

Initially, Clark was to team up with a good sprinter named A. J. Davies. But Clark needed someone who could do the grunt work and sprint—someone like Reggie McNamara. McNamara gave the bad news to his Sydney partner, Frank Corry, who didn't hold any grudge—there would be other six-day races to team up with McNamara. When the McNamara-Clark combination was officially announced, it became the team to beat and the favorite on everyone's lips.

Between being called out in the Australian press by Clark for teaming with Kramer (though, presumably, Clark didn't mention him by name) and becoming the second favorite team in the public's eye, Goullet may have been rubbed the wrong way. Perhaps it became the motivation that Goullet and Hehir needed—being the underdogs after winning such a brilliant race in Sydney.

Melbourne's Exhibition Oval track was also asphalt, but it was five laps to the mile, making it much easier to gain a lap in the race than it was at Sydney. Williams took out more newspaper advertising for his second campaign. He included all the pieces he had before: the Globe of Death, Daredevil Kilpatrick, and the races within the race. There would be twelve teams in the race—again, mostly Australian.

The Melbourne race began at one o'clock, the morning of Monday, February 19, 1912. This time the summer weather maintained mild temperatures with no rain; consequently, the size of the crowd was more consistent, typically around twelve thousand people for the first five days.

With thirty hours remaining in the race, six teams were tied on laps: McNamara-Clark, Goullet-Hehir, Grenda-Walker, Lloyd-Gascoyne, Lawson-Mitten, and Crook-Yeend. Goullet started a big jam, one of the many attempts to "steal" a lap from the other teams. A few minutes later Hehir came out to relieve Goullet, and there was an ugly rattle of metal scraping against asphalt. McNamara had gone down hard and was sprawled across the track. From behind Grenda could not avoid going straight into McNamara, and Grenda went down hard too.

Both riders got up right away, cut and bruised. But McNamara had the worst of it, and he needed immediate medical attention. McNamara actually had to undergo an operation for an abscess in his stomach, so for five hours Clark had to defend their position all alone.[20]

Given McNamara's condition, many riders would have quit the race. But in addition to realizing that Clark had come all the way from America for the race, there was no quit in McNamara. Swathed in bandages, McNamara came out to the track to relieve Clark. The crowd recognized his great pluck and gave him a standing ovation.

Nearly thirty thousand people assembled to see the end of the race. Time had run out, and the same six teams were tied at 2,026 miles. Just like Sydney, the race would come down to a final sprint. Each team decided who the best sprinter was. McNamara was still feeling the effects from his fall, and Clark had ridden more miles than most of the others. They pinned their hopes on Clark. For the other teams it was Crook, Goullet, Grenda, Lawson, and Lloyd.

The sprint was composed of a one-lap rolling start and then three laps to the end. Grenda took the lead position for the first two laps, as the speed wound up to a fevered pitch. With one lap to go, Goullet was hot on Grenda's wheel and passed him. Lawson jumped, and so did Clark, both riders passing Grenda at the finish line. Goullet-Hehir won again, with the Americans Lawson-Mitten second, Clark-McNamara third, Grenda-Walker fourth, Lloyd-Gascoyne fifth, and Crook-Yeend sixth.

After the incredible crowds, especially at the end of both the Sydney and Melbourne races, Australia, it seemed, had found a sport that generated an awesome buzz of excitement; perhaps six-day racing would be around for years and years to come. But just months after the Melbourne six-day, there were foul goings-on at the Greater J. D. Williams Amusement Company.

Troubles for Williams began to unravel; charges of forgery involving company stock came forth. An arrest warrant was issued for Frank Lloyd, the alleged forger. A manhunt followed as Lloyd made a getaway to New Zealand. One sensation followed another as the board of directors made a motion to dismiss Williams as managing director.[21]

"For a long time I have refrained from speaking," Williams said, "even when my best interests demanded that I should speak. I have been reluctant to admit publicly the disunion in control and management that has unfortunately existed for some months in the affairs of what ought to be one of the best money-making concerns on this continent. But I can keep silent no longer." He went on to defend his circumstances, largely the result of having borrowed a large amount of money to get the company out of debt. "As to dismissing me, the directors have no such power," Williams declared. "A thing [such] as that requires a two-thirds vote at a general meeting of the shareholders, and they ought to know that."[22]

Two days after Williams's public appeal, he was arrested on charges of receiving, harboring, maintaining, and assisting Frank Lloyd. Williams posted bail the same day, while Lloyd, accompanied by a Sydney senior detective, made his way back to Sydney.

On February 5, 1913, Williams was reinstated to his position of managing director, and all charges against him were dropped. "I do not suppose that any man," Williams stated outside the courthouse, "a comparative stranger in even a democratic country like this, has ever experienced such a warmth of demonstrative sympathy as has come to me in this sudden, and to me, entirely unexpected trouble. For myself, I can at present say nothing, but when the facts are all made public, it is my very strong conviction that I shall feel a great deal better than I have during the last few days."[23]

Williams had perhaps had enough of Australia. Shortly after his legal ordeal, he quickly and quietly sold his interest in his company and moved on to the next chapter in his life, which took the one-time cycling promoter to American film fame and fortune. For six-day racing in Australia it was practically the beginning of the end.

4

Accidental Romance

On April 8, 1912, or about a week before the *Titanic* sank in the Atlantic Ocean, the RMS *Marama* left Sydney and headed course for San Francisco. On board was a large gathering of professional cyclists and company, including Clark, Goullet, Grenda, Hehir, Lawson, and Mitten.[1]

It was Grenda's first trip to America. If John Chapman had sent a contract to McNamara to race in the United States, he, too, would have been on that ship. Perhaps he was a little miffed to be left behind, especially because he was roughly equal in talent with Grenda. Perhaps he was happy to stay and promote Australian cycling in his home country. Given McNamara's character, it was more likely that he was content to earn a good living by riding a bike, wherever he was.

Someone had to take up the torch that J. D. Williams had lit. A. E. O'Brien, the very man who had protested the outcome of the Sydney Thousand in 1904, in which he was awarded first place and Major Taylor second, had since replaced Hugh McIntosh as the president of the New South Wales League of Wheelmen.

In June 1912 a meeting of the council of the league was held. Whereas J. D. Williams, a man with boundless energy, had promoted six-day racing the previous year, duties would now be carried out by O'Brien. A proposal was put forth to award the riders one-third of the gross gate receipts as prize money, and the league would take 5 percent.[2]

With the growth of international six-day events in the United States and in Europe, the issue of conflicts was becoming a concern. Sydney was to start on December 29, 1912, and Melbourne on February 24, 1913. In the United States the first race on the six-day calendar was Boston, which was to begin on November 4, 1912. The Super Bowl of six-day races, in New York at Madison Square Garden, perhaps more successful than the Tour de France at the time, was set for December 9. In Europe, Berlin's start was January 9, which was in direct conflict with the first ever Paris six-day inside the Vélodrome d'Hiver, starting on January 13.

No rider wishing to race at the Garden would be able to join the contestants at Sydney. The vast majority of the talent—or the "cracks," as the best were called back then—did two or three six-day races on the calendar. Not surprisingly, few Americans, few Europeans, and few imported Australians were tempted to cross into the Southern Hemisphere for six-day races in Sydney and Melbourne.

At least seven riders—two Australians and five Americans— competed in three total six-day races in that period, from November to February: Jackie Clark, Joe Fogler, Freddie Hill, Jimmy Moran, Ernie Pye, Eddie Root, and Bobby Walthour. Fogler pulled off an incredible feat of winning three. He won in Boston, teamed with Moran; then in New York, with German Walter Rutt; and then in Paris, teamed with a well-rested Alf Goullet. Clark and Hill were victorious in Berlin. Leading up to the Sydney six-day, McNamara was riding well. On November 6, 1912, he scored two brilliant victories in front of twenty thousand cycling fans at the Sydney Cricket Ground.[3]

On December 29, 1912, eighteen teams were set for the start an hour after midnight. McNamara was reunited with his Sydney teammate Frank Corry. The team of A. Rosseau (French) and Willie Appelhans (German) was the only one from Europe to race, and the two men nearly didn't make the start because of a ship delay. There was also a rider from Great Britain,

Sydney Jenkins, but the remaining teams were from Australia, New Zealand, or Tasmania.

Some had suggested that by not having Americans there, the pace would be livelier because Lawson and Mitten apparently acted as lieutenants to ensure a slow pace. But the Aussies must have learned a thing or two from the Americans because this time they rode even fewer miles—less than two thousand at the end. Some of the low mileage was because of rainstorms during which they had to take shelter. But even before the rains, the pace was not especially fast, particularly measured against the annual six-day in New York City, which was generally twenty-five hundred miles.

Just as the year before, the people of Sydney began arriving in droves on the final day. Despite a weather forecast of rain and strong southerly winds, as many as forty thousand people were there, and McNamara was the clear favorite. As the final hour approached, one newspaper reported: "Whir! Round they go again! Now looking like a bright splash of motley color as they shoot under the brilliant lights of the grandstands . . . they are silhouetted thinly against the half-light of the thousands of upturned faces."[4]

A pistol was fired at ten o'clock at night, indicating that the riders' 141-hour journey was nearly complete. The seven teams, even on laps, each had one rider line up for the final mile to determine overall victory. McNamara was there, along with A. L. Crook, C. E. Glencross, P. O'Shea, E. Priestly, Bert Scott, and Robert Spears. McNamara was most concerned with Spears, a big youngster from his Dubbo hometown who packed the same kind of sprint as Alf Grenda.

The first two laps were reeled off slowly. On the final lap, with all the riders bunched up together and the crowd excitedly waiting, McNamara went all in. Spears was first to react but didn't quite make it to McNamara's wheel. The crowd went berserk, shouting and throwing hats and pieces of paper. Down the homestretch Spears crept closer and closer. But McNamara held him off and came across the line a clear winner.

Accidental Romance

The great assemblage began to chant, "Mac! Mac! Mac! Mac!" McNamara was gaunt, tired, and sunburned as people came out of the stands and carried him around on their shoulders, waving hats, sticks, and umbrellas.[5]

"Well, it was a very easy race to ride all the way through," McNamara said to reporters after calm was restored. "As you know, it is my third six days' race, and in both previous events— those in Sydney and Melbourne—I was a member of the team that placed third. Frank Corry, my teammate this year, was also partnered with me in Sydney, but in Melbourne, I had A. J. Clark. Last year, the Sydney race was a far severer one; we did considerably more mileage, we had a lot more work on the grass, and we struck so much cool weather. And then, in last year's awful hail-storm, we were required to keep riding instead of being allowed to take shelter as we did in Friday's thunderstorms.

"About myself? Well, I've been racing about five years and have won about 130 races, mostly in the country districts of New South Wales, where I did very well on rough tracks before coming to Sydney. I've also been riding successfully in Queensland and Victoria. I am twenty-four years of age, stand about five-foot ten-inches [he was actually closer to five foot eight] and weigh twelve stone [168 pounds] in condition. I rode a Sydney-built racer with a ninety-four gear and six-and-a-half inch cranks mostly in this race, but on the grass, like others, changed to a lower geared road machine.

"I will ride with Corry in the Melbourne six days' race, and after finishing the season in Sydney will probably visit America for a season or two in March or April. In fact, Spears and myself are now in communication with J. M. Chapman concerning a visit to Newark."[6]

With a dream contract to race in America and another six-day to race in Melbourne, McNamara was in seventh heaven. "I just love these six days' races," he confessed. "I enjoy riding them so much that I'd like to ride one every month."[7] Little did he know his wish would come true in twenty years.

Melbourne was hot. Temperatures closed in on one hundred degrees Fahrenheit. In the first few days McNamara and Corry made a number of desperate efforts to gain a lap on the field. Their plans were foiled mostly by determined chases of the Spears-Kirkham team. Close to the thousand-mile mark, Corry touched pedals with another rider and went down hard. McNamara came out immediately in relief. Corry was lucky enough to escape with just a little road rash on his arms and legs.[8]

Utilizing trickery, one team was successful in gaining a lap and being the first team ever, in the Australian six-day races, to acquire sole possession of the lead before the final sprint off. Hours after the Corry crash, around eight in the morning, the riders were lazily spinning along, singing comic songs to break up the monotony. S. J. Edwards, who was teamed with J. D. Kerr, joined in the merriment by faking an attempt to break away from the pack by going out front a few bike lengths ahead. Edwards amused the group by doing it again and again, and pretty soon all the guys were laughing.

Edwards and Kerr had noticed that at the trackside along the turn there was a marquee positioned in such a way that if any rider was far enough ahead, he could not be seen by the group. Without creating suspicion, Edwards went ahead for the fifth time. Just after rounding the marquee, he went for broke. Kerr was waiting and ready for the attack and was astounded at how much ground Edwards had put on the rest of the field. When Kerr relieved Edwards, he hitched to the back of the group with relative ease, succeeding in gaining a lap.

The other riders quickly switched from a mood of frivolity to one of retribution. For hours the pace shot up to well over twenty miles per hour. Not only did they gain back their lost lap, but they put an additional lap on the Edwards-Kerr team, which shortly thereafter retired from the race.

In all ten teams finished the race equal on laps. Twenty thousand people stood ready as the riders lined up to determine overall victory. Instead of a one-mile race off, it was determined they would go four miles.

At the sound of the pistol the fans went crazy, but the speed

Accidental Romance

was slow. The crowd egged the riders on, urging them to go faster each time they went by the grandstand, but the pace remained about the same until a mile to go, when the pace picked up considerably. McNamara was on the wheel of the leading rider, Jumbo Wells from New Zealand. Trying for a Sydney repeat, McNamara jumped with a lap to go. This time Spears was ready for it, and he clung to McNamara's wheel. Around the final turn Spears began overtaking McNamara, and both gave a mighty struggle down the final straightway. The nineteen-year-old Spears won by a wheel length over McNamara, and they covered the last mile in a little over two minutes and five seconds—nearly thirty miles per hour.

With the end of the Melbourne race, Australian six-day races had run their course. J. D. Williams had given them a great start. The New South Wales League of Wheelmen, under the leadership of A. E. O'Brien, attempted to keep them going, but they fizzled out.

Six weeks after the Melbourne six-day, Corry, McNamara, and Spears were off on their great journey to America on board the RMS *Orama*. The *Orama* was built in 1911 and had *Titanic*-like features, such as a grandiose wraparound staircase, state-rooms with magnificent skylights, and an extravagant dining room, capable of seating more than one hundred first-class tourists. Rather than taking the traditional route, going to San Francisco and then having passengers catch a train for the East Coast, the *Orama* steamed to New York via the Suez Canal and London. Spears had to pay his own way because he had passed on Chapman's offer when Grenda had gone the year before. At the time Spears's mother had thought he was too young to go off to America. The voyage took eight full weeks. For these young single men, on the verge of hitting the big-time and becoming rich and famous athletes, they must have had the time of their lives, horsing around, eating, drinking, and working out as best they could on a large steamship.

From a port along the Red Sea, Spears sent a letter back home. "We have a pair of rollers," he wrote, "but it is too hot to ride just at present. We are having a little sport on board, only I am in the bad graces of a lot of the others who say I am too big, and should be barred. Poor me! I won a pillow fight, potato race, and hop, step and jump. Mac won a euchre tournament, and Corry cleaved the Turk's head, blindfolded. Our old ship is going fine and in twenty-four hours covered 595 miles."[9]

Meanwhile, thousands of miles away, a pretty young brunette nurse with a melodic Irish accent named Elizabeth McDonough was working at the City Hospital not far from the Newark Velodrome. Elizabeth was born in Sligo, Ireland, the youngest of ten children. About the time she turned seventeen, Elizabeth's parents had put her on a boat to find a better life in the United States—all alone. According to her granddaughter, Theresa Passione, Elizabeth never saw her Irish family again. With her good looks and proper manners, she quickly secured work as an upstairs maid for a wealthy family. Not satisfied with cleaning and fussing, she enrolled herself in nursing school.[10]

The arrival of the three young Aussies made the *Newark Evening News*: "Spears is a giant, built along the lines of Grenda, but Corry and McNamara are little fellows of the Clark type. Spears is a youngster only nineteen years. Little Corry is a typical cockney Englishman. He is twenty-three years old and has been racing for five seasons in the professional class. McNamara is twenty-four years old and was the star of the past season in the Antipodes."

They expected to see many of the riders whom they knew personally, including Clark, Goullet, Grenda, and Mitten, but the four were all in Philadelphia at the Point Breeze track. The three Aussies were given a tour of the Newark Velodrome facility and told to make themselves at home and get some workouts in. They were champing at the bit to ride on the boards. But just as when Pye and Clark had arrived in the United States in 1906, they were tentative. Although they liked the sound and feel of the wood surface, the steep angle of the turns was nothing they had experienced before. There were so many new things to get acquainted with—even the most basic things such as finding their hotel. Simply getting their bearings straight in a new country with different expectations than they were used to, different lifestyles, funny accents, strange food, and all the new people was a challenge.

The next morning the trio had a big breakfast at their hotel. Cool, crisp weather greeted them as they leisurely rode their bikes out to the Newark Velodrome. There they saw some familiar faces; Clark, Goullet, Grenda, and Mitten were back from Philadelphia.

The track was much busier than the day before, with riders and trainers yelling, laughing, conversing, and moving about down in the grass, on the track, and in the stands. Frank Kramer's late arrival caused heads to turn. Corry, McNamara, and Spears were already starstruck, but when they saw the reigning American and world champion sprinter getting ready to work out as if he were one of them, it was just one more thing they had to get used to. Especially with all the people around, Corry and Spears were a little reluctant to draw attention to themselves, but McNamara threw caution to the wind and showed off his form.

With help from pacers to get him going, McNamara wound up the speed. His head down and his legs churned for all they were worth, and something went wrong. Years later Kramer called it the worst accident he had ever seen. Those who didn't see it heard it.

McNamara wrecked straight into the judge's stand at full speed. There was a big rush to the scene to help the new arrival. A huge cut on McNamara's thigh bled profusely. Some of the bystanders looked away. He was able to sit up as the muscles from the fourteen-inch wound bulged out like crimson balloons. An ambulance was quickly summoned. As he sat there, he pressed the released muscles back in place and remarked nonchalantly, "It was a bloomin' bad fall."[11]

Only his fourth day in the United States, and McNamara was laid up in the City Hospital, where doctors determined that this significant injury was such that his racing career may be limited for a long time—if not forever. Nurses dressed in white shuttled in and out of his room tending to his needs. They knew McNamara's prognosis was not good. But he cheered them up with talk in his Australian accent about growing up on the farm, cycling in Australia, and his voyage to America.

Like all nurses there, Elizabeth McDonough thought he was charming and funny, and she wanted him to get better so that he could continue the career he spoke so passionately of. The more time Reggie and Elizabeth spent together, the more a mutual fondness grew. They spoke about things they had in common, such as having grown up in a large Irish Catholic family and their arrival to this big, new, strange, and wonderful country.

After a week of lying in a rickety hospital bed with white sheets, taking rides outside in a wheelchair, and slowing putting weight on his leg again, McNamara was scheduled to be released soon. Elizabeth grew anxious that she would not see him again. But one of the last things McNamara did before he took leave from the hospital was to take her hand and ask to see her again. She agreed.

Almost immediately after his hospital stay, they started dating. Where they went and what they did can only be speculated on. But evidence of an immediate romance would later be revealed in the arrival of a little bundle of joy. In terms of "pregnancy math," the child was conceived sometime between late September and early October 1913.

McNamara was released from the hospital on or about June 18, 1913, and one of the first things he did was ride a lap at the track. The next day he rode a few more, and pretty soon he was doing two-a-day workouts. Neither doctors, trainers, fellow professionals, Elizabeth, nor anyone else could believe his resiliency. The Australians told stories about when he finished the Melbourne six-day race after getting his stomach abscess lanced. Everyone agreed that "Mac" was as tough as anyone they had ever seen and began to call him the "Iron Man."

McNamara's remarkable recovery was underscored on Tuesday, July 15, 1913—just over a month after the "bloomin' bad fall." He did not win the race, in fact he was disqualified in the final five-mile heat, but he impressed everyone, and not because he had fresh bandages on his leg. The *Newark Evening News* described him as the star of the meet: "With McNamara in the professional events last night, everything bristled. He made the racing exciting at all times and kept everybody on the anxious seat. He was always doing something and everybody was looking to him for action. Consequently, the racing was by far the best that has been seen."[12]

Spears was doing well, too, but not everyone was as impressed. About a week before McNamara's comeback to racing, Spears had won two events in a single evening. In one of the races Eddie Root thought Spears was riding him too close, forcing Root up the track embankment. But referee John Valentine saw things differently and disqualified Root. In a rage Root threw his bike at Spears. Mrs. Root wanted a piece of Spears too. As he walked his bike to the dressing room, she took a swing at him with her parasol that connected squarely on his head.[13]

McNamara was among the highlights of what was reported as a "somewhat unsuccessful outdoor season" in Newark. With the weather getting cooler and the leaves turning color, he was about to experience his first fall and winter, and his first six-day race, in the United States.

Only Ernie Pye went back home in October—for the Australian summer, not for racing. He, his wife, and child boarded a steamer from San Francisco with a final destination of Melbourne, where they were to collect an inheritance of a modest fortune from a wealthy uncle.[14] After settling up the estate, Pye and his family returned to the United States with enough assets to start what would become a very successful bicycle tire manufacturing company.

The first six-day in the calendar was inside the Boston Arena. Boston's race was a nice way to ease into the indoor six-day season because it was only ten hours a day for six days. In addition, it was a small wooden track—ten laps to the mile—and was modeled after tracks that had been built for Madison

Square Garden, so for McNamara it was great training for the upcoming New York race. Ten teams were selected to race in Boston. McNamara was probably not happy to be teamed with Spears's nemesis, Eddie Root, but he had to make the best of it. Grenda was teamed with Paddy Hehir, Corry with Martin "Grassy" Ryan, Jimmy Moran with the giant sprinter Frank Cavanaugh, San Francisco's Percy Lawrence with Philadelphia's Jake Magin, and Joe Fogler with Iver Lawson, whose brother Gussie had died two months earlier in a terrible motor-pacing accident in Cologne, Germany.

There was a lot of rough riding in the Boston race, and more than once police were called in to quell the disturbances. As a result of the rough riding, motor-pacing specialist George Cameron dislocated his shoulder and broke three ribs. Hehir and fellow Aussie Fred Keefe both broke their collarbones.

As in all four of his previous six-day races in Australia, the Boston six-day ended in a tie on laps, and five teams got set for a one-mile race off to determine overall victory. According to the *Sun*, the finish was a "complete fiasco," and riders came away very unsatisfied because the final mile was run off three times. The first was won by Lawson, but he was rightly disqualified for knocking Eddie Root and Freddie Hill off their mounts. Rather than give the race to the second-place finisher, the race was ordered to be rerun. On the second attempt Frank Cavanaugh sprinted from the gun and opened up a half-lap lead. Nobody closed on Cavanaugh to the referee's satisfaction, and again he said, "Rerun the race." The third attempt was won by Joe Fogler, with McNamara right on his wheel, and this time the referee allowed it.[15]

More than one hundred carpenters had no choice but to construct the track inside Madison Square Garden in record fashion. There were less than seventy hours from the time a heavyweight boxing match finished Wednesday night until the preliminary cycling events would begin on Saturday.

In the meantime some of the best riders in the world were

descending upon New York City in preparation for the great six-day race. Elite American trainer Dave Coburn was assigned to help the European contingent, which consisted of eight riders, including two-time Tour de France champion Lucien Petit-Breton. Like the Tour de France, any six-day victory at the Garden required some luck, and despite his many starts there, Petit-Breton never got lucky in the United States.

The favorite team on most people's list was Jackie Clark and Paddy Hehir. Both had trained diligently for New York, whether it was taking long rides or long runs into the New Jersey countryside, boxing, skipping rope, hitting the rollers, or doing dumbbell exercises.

"I am ready to start the race and in fact I have been ready for a couple weeks," Clark declared. "Everything is shipshape in my camp and I have no fear of the ultimate result. The talk about Paddy Hehir, my partner, not being able to get through a hard grind because of the injury he received in Boston is not bothering me one bit. You should see how Hehir roughs it in the training and the things he does with that injured arm and you would not think it was weak. Every precaution has been taken to assure our success and now it is up to us to ride the race. As to that I have no fear."[16]

While Clark-Hehir were two-to-one favorites, McNamara and Eddie Root were four-to-one favorites, followed by the Fogler-Goullet combination at nine-to-two. Prior to the main event, the Saturday tradition of having preliminary races was held. Ironically, McNamara had to go up against his own partner in an unlimited pursuit race, which he won by catching Root in just under twenty laps. For Reggie McNamara the big race that followed would be his very first of many six-day races inside the Garden. He would go on to win many great victories in that venue steeped in cycling history.

With his big megaphone in hand, Pete Prunty announced the teams as several flashlight photographs were taken of the thirty-four riders and their trainers at the starting line. Arthur A. Zimmerman, the man perhaps most responsible for igniting the popularity of professional cycling on three different continents, fired the gun that began the twenty-first New York City international six-day race at Madison Square Garden at one minute past midnight on Monday, December 8, 1913. After five parade laps the race was on, and thousands of fans stood up and tried to yell themselves hoarse before ten laps had been run off.

The odor of fried frankfurters and tobacco smoke as well as noise penetrated every crevice of the big building as the band inside the track proper played familiar tunes of the day. Nearly all the early arrivals who had waited in a long line for tickets went up to the top gallery. They were the younger bunch—the "gallery gods"—and expected to produce more noise and stay the entire six days if they were able to. Many brought along blankets, food, and other provisions to sustain themselves for days on end. If they ran out of food, they could rely on the Garden concessions. Below were the "rail birds," an older, more sophisticated lot who paid extra money for their seats but were just as enthused to see a rider steal a lap (popularly known as a "jam") as any teenager sitting above them.

In the first twenty-four hours of the race there were many crashes. Clarence Carmen continued on after hitting the boards three times, the last of which gave him a dislocated shoulder. In another accident Jackie Clark was knocked unconscious and had to be carried off to his training quarters. Peter Drobach, with a gash above his right ear, was able to walk away under his own power.

On day 2 Alf Grenda caught the field napping and shot out thirty yards before anyone realized a jam was on. The field strung out in a long single-file line as it clamored to catch Grenda. After several exciting laps he was caught, but suddenly McNamara took up the lead and kept the pace hot for two more minutes. The result of their efforts put one team, Keefe-Kopsky, two laps down. The thousands of fans inside the Garden had to sit down and catch their collective breath.[17]

Hehir, with his healing collarbone, went down in a heap with Drobach, Worth Mitten, and Jimmy Moran. Moran broke his

Accidental Romance

1. McNamara with his wheels. JOSEPH HORTER JR. COLLECTION.

2. Major Taylor at Buffalo Velodrome, Paris.
BUCK PEACOCK COLLECTION.

3. Floyd MacFarland, in striped shirt, with Jackie Clark, in robe, on his right. JEFF GROMAN COLLECTION.

4. John Chapman in his racing days—on rear of tandem.
BUCK PEACOCK COLLECTION.

5. Frank Kramer. BUCK PEACOCK COLLECTION.

6. Joe Fogler.
JEFF GROMAN
COLLECTION.

7. Alf Grenda.
JEFF GROMAN
COLLECTION.

8. McNamara at Newark Velodrome.
JEFF GROMAN COLLECTION.

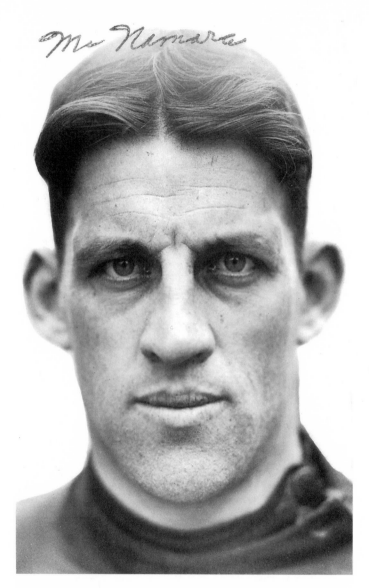

9. Reggie McNamara, circa 1914.
JEFF GROMAN COLLECTION.

Madison Square Garden

Cycle Track

DIRECTION P. T. POWERS

Saturday Night, December Ninth

NINETEEN HUNDRED ELEVEN

Commencing To-morrow Night, December 10th

AT MIDNIGHT

Nineteenth Annual

Six-Day Race

Champions From Every Country

DOORS OPEN TO-MORROW NIGHT 7 O'CLOCK

Sacred Concert By Bayne's 69th Regiment Band

OFFICIALS

BOARD OF REFEREES.

R. F. Kelsey, Chairman Board of Control, N. C. A.

D. M. Aude, President N. C. A.	Howard G. Reynolds, Boston, Mass.
C. R. Klosterman, Baltimore, Md.	Victor Breyer, Paris.
Walter A. Bardgett, Buffalo, N. Y.	Paul Thomas, Tarrytown, N. Y.

Louis Dero, Buffalo, N. Y.

JUDGES.

C. B. Ruch, New York.	E. Lee Ferguson, New York.
A. R. Cooley, New York.	F. C. Gray, Richmond Hill, L. I.
Geo. H. Muth, D. D. S., New York.	Fred. Hildebrandt, New York.
Emil Greenbaum, Brooklyn.	Sylvain Segal, New York.
C. E. Burch, New York.	J. A. Olson, Brooklyn.

TIMERS.

R. A. Van Dyke, Secretary, N. C. A.	John J. O'Brien, N. Y. A. C.
C. J. Dieges, N. Y. A. C.	John J. McHugh, Irish Am. A. C.
John P. Boyle, Pastime A. C.	Robert Stoll, New York.
Prosper Clust, Brooklyn A. C.	Dr. A. C. Griffin, C. R. C. Ass'n.
Alfred H. Seeley, C. R. C. of A.	Nelson McIntyre, New York City.
Lieut. H. P. Burchell, New York.	Chris. Dalton, New York City.

CHIEF SCORERS.

W. B. Robinson,	Howard Freeman,
10 A. M. to 10 P. M.	10 P. M. to 10 A. M.

ASSISTANT SCORERS.

Peter Wollenschlager, New York.	H. T. Mayo, New York.

Samuel Barnett, Brooklyn.

STARTER.

Hon. Thos. F. Foley.

CLERK OF COURSE.

Charles T. Earl, New York.

ASSISTANT CLERKS OF COURSE.

Frederick S. Hoeckley, New York.	H. A. Gliesman, New York.

HANDICAPPER.

R. F. Kelsey.

ANNOUNCERS.

Charles J. Harvey.	Peter Prunty.

PHYSICIANS.

Dr. Hugh M. Cox.	Dr. L. F. Sturges.

HARRY M. STEVENS, Publisher, Madison Square Garden

PRICE TEN CENTS

10. Madison Square Garden program.

11. (*Opposite top*) Goullet and Grenda at West Baden
Springs. JEFF GROMAN COLLECTION.

12. (*Opposite bottom*) Ernest and Hans Ohrt.
DENNIS HEARST COLLECTION.

13. (*Above*) McNamara in foul weather gear, 1930s.
JEFF GROMAN COLLECTION.

14. Tom Eck training
Bobby Walthour Sr.
BUCK PEACOCK
COLLECTION.

15. McNamara and
Freddie Spencer.
JOSEPH HORTER JR.
COLLECTION.

Official Program

FIRST INTERNATIONAL

6 DAY BICYCLE RACE

CONVENTION HALL
PHILADELPHIA
March 13 to 19, 1932

Under Sanction National Cycling Association

10 CENTS

16. Philadelphia six-day program, March 1932.

17. McNamara training.
PETER STEPHENS
COLLECTION.

collarbone, and for the third time since August, Hehir broke his. Both were out of the race, and their respective partners, Grenda and Clark, joined as teammates. In joining forces, the rules stipulated that the new team of Grenda and Clark would lose a lap to the field.

As hours turned to days, many attempts were made to steal laps, and some went on for ten minutes. The crowd responded to these exciting jams, in which the speed could go up to thirty miles per hour. For referee Arthur Ross and his crew it was very different. They had to have a system to determine whether a team did or did not lose a lap to the field. When big jams occurred, riders from each team would come out to relieve their partners with much more frequency. Ross had to watch for proper "pickups," in which the riders had to at least touch, usually by a forward shove. Ross had to put out fines and warnings for "wireless" pickups when they didn't touch. Ross had to know which teams were in the front and which were in the rear. Teammates shared the same color uniform, but on a 176-yard track with so many riders, at such a speed, and with so much noise, it was often difficult to sort out. Most of the time Ross's rulings were correct, but if there was any question, a rider could submit a written protest.

When seventy-two hours of racing remained—the halfway point—fifteen teams were still out on the track; eight were tied with the lead, and five were one lap down. The last-place team was several laps behind, forcing "a killing pace" at the front. It wasn't giving up. The McNamara-Root combination appeared to be the freshest of the leading group.

Despite the midweek boost in general admission prices, which had doubled, along with all reserved ticket prices, there was no noticeable effect on the size of the huge crowd. As people left the building (most of the gallery gods were only forced out during occasional "sweeps"), more would come in to keep the smoky cavernous arena packed.

According to the *New York Times*, those in the crowd were put at risk by the unsavory element of the New York underworld: "Thieves infect the Garden this year like they always have, but they seem to become more daring each year. One's watch or money is never safe there, and his overcoat is almost certain to be lifted if he takes his eye off it. Crooks have gathered up an armload of coats when spectators were bending over watching the sprint of the cyclists with the keenest enthusiasm. Complaints have been made this week of thefts and various kinds of hold-ups, but there is never anyone to be found who fits the crime."[18]

Sometimes, however, police did catch a thief. On one occasion a kindly old lady grew indignant at the way they manhandled a grossly disproportioned little man. "It's inhuman what you're doing to him," she said and started in on the police with her umbrella. "It ain't inhuman at all," said a plainclothesman. "Look, lady." He peeled off an overcoat. And another. And another. He kept going, and overcoats kept coming off like layers of an onion.[19]

Physical force was required to remove several spectators, and the police had their hands full with fights. Some hooligans threw bottles at policemen and at the track. Thankfully, no one was hurt; track attendants swept up the glass off the boards, and the race was quickly resumed.

Despite the danger, some of the riders' children were there, supervised by their mothers. Joe Fogler's little daughter, Evelyn, who would go on to become a great competitive swimmer, was there, along with Bobby Walthour's two daughters and son. Bobby Walthour Jr., who had just turned eleven, would go on to have a marvelous professional cycling career and race against many of the riders he was watching go round and round the track, including McNamara.

To make matters worse, trouble had been brewing for days between the Jimmy Kelly and the Jack Sirocco gangs. "Kelly, it is said," reported the *New York Times*, "has been disgruntled because some of his followers were not hired by Val O'Farrell, in charge of the detectives inside the Garden." In the wee hours of Saturday morning gunshots right outside the Garden, on the corner of Fourth Avenue and Twenty-Sixth Street, were fired from behind a Madison Avenue trolley car. Passengers inside dropped to the floor as return shots rang out from the sidewalk until all ammunition from the revolvers had been emptied. At least fifty shots were fired, but by some miracle, with so many people coming from or going to the race, not one person was hurt. Fearful that gun violence would spread indoors, Inspector Dougherty brought in a squad of several hundred men from police headquarters.[20]

With all the excitement off the track, fortunes turned for the worse for many riders on day 5. The reconstructed team of Clark-Grenda was unable to gain a lap to get on even terms with the leading teams. Bobby Walthour's partner was forced to quit the race with a broken collarbone. Walthour was given the standard four hours to find a new partner. Grenda began complaining about his knees, and it was suggested that Clark join forces with Walthour. Both riders agreed and immediately went to the task of getting on even terms with the leading teams. But they only did themselves in by going all out until they could go no more. They got lapped once, then twice, and then gave up the ghost, quitting the track. Walthour-Clark was not the only team showing signs of distress, and many more were forced to retire.

When 142 hours had been completed, at ten o'clock on Saturday evening, six teams were tied for first. They had gone 2,751 miles, eclipsing the record set in 1908 by nearly 14 miles. The leading teams were Magin-Lawrence, Goullet-Fogler, Halstead-Drobach, Verri-Brocco, Hill-Ryan, and McNamara-Root. So that Root could have fresh legs for the final one-mile sprint, McNamara did more than his share of riding over the last twelve hours. The other teams selected their sprinters: Percy Lawrence, Alf Goullet, Al Halstead, Francesco Verri, and Freddie Hill.

Root went off right away into the lead high up the banking. Verri was second, but he went low on the black line, with Goullet on his wheel, followed closely by the others. The speed was not great, but it was not a crawl. With a half-mile to go,

Root came down off the banking and went for broke. Goullet was ready for it, however, and went right around Verri and on to Root's wheel. With a lap to go at a terrific clip, Goullet went around Root and won with apparent ease by ten yards. Percy Lawrence made a sensational effort by coming from way back and passed Root at the tape for second place.

For all the work McNamara had done to give Root a rest, he was very disappointed. But Goullet was not to be denied the first of his many great victories inside the Garden. McNamara had not found victory, but he had found the love of his life in America. As he packed up his belongings and the Garden crowd thinned out, he shook hands with his competitors and trainers, congratulating them and wishing everyone a Merry Christmas. He and Elizabeth had many plans for the future.

5

Safe in America

If Reggie McNamara thought his trip and subsequent arrival to the United States was an exciting adventure, he was about to embark on a more thrilling one in Europe. After the finish of the 1913 Madison Square Garden six-day race, riders, trainers, referees, and company crammed into Patrick T. Powers's office at the Fuller Building to get paid. Of the $26,000 purse that was to be dispersed between the thirty-four riders, Goullet and Fogler received the lion's share; each of them earned $1,800. For second place Percy Lawrence and Jake Magin got $500 apiece, and Root and McNamara divided $750 for third place.[1] McNamara received what today would be $9,000, which would not have included his paid expenses and bonuses. Not bad for a week's work.

In addition to compensation, many of the riders settled up affairs to race in Europe for the months ahead. A large delegation was to steam for France in a few days, including part owner of the Newark Velodrome Frank Mihlon, Mr. and Mrs. Floyd MacFarland, Alf Goullet, Joe Fogler, Alf Grenda, Jackie Clark, Frank Kramer, Eddie Root, Jimmy Moran, Bobby Walthour, Lloyd Thomas, Frank Corry, Hermann Packebusch, Willy Appelhans, Andre Perchicot, Lucien Petit-Breton, Maurice Brocco, Francesco Verri, and Reggie McNamara.[2]

For some it may have been a happy trip, especially for the European riders going home with American dollars in their pockets. But for others the ocean crossing may have not been so festive. There was a general dissatisfaction among the riders with MacFarland's handling of both the New York and Boston six-day races. MacFarland was to be manager of the Newark Velodrome upon his return to the United States, and there were rumblings about a strike against him. Despite their six-day victories together in Paris in 1913 and now New York, Goullet and Fogler were not getting along well. Goullet asked Clark to be his partner in the upcoming Paris six-day race.

There were hard feelings between McNamara and Root too. "Had Root saved me on the last day, like I saved him," McNamara said, "I would have won the race. In the last half day I rode ten of the twelve hours so Eddie would have a good rest. I think there was something strange about the affair, and Root, when I asked him about the race, didn't care to talk about it."[3]

The group arrived in Paris sometime between Christmas and New Year's, in time for two weeks' preparation for the 1914 Paris six-day race at the Vélodrome d'Hiver on the corner of boulevard de Grenelle and rue Nélaton, not far from the Eiffel Tower. A permanent 250-meter track, the indoor stadium had two tiers of seats, with higher-class ticket holders in trackside seats and lower-class ticket holders in the upper seats. The entire stadium was lit with 1,253 large hanging lights.

Although McNamara did not race in the Paris six-day on this occasion, he was there rubbing elbows with the heads of state of American cycling—Frank Kramer, Frank Mihlon, and the MacFarlands and visiting other riders. He missed competing but enjoyed watching as a spectator too. The interior of the Vélodrome d'Hiver was very cold, and those riders not circling the track were huddled up in their tents at the side of the track in blankets and around stoves trying to keep warm.

McNamara was on his own until the Brussels six-day three weeks away, in February. He had time to explore and relax at corner cafés, soaking in the sights, sounds, smells, and beauty of Paris. If he found culture shock within the United States, he must have, by comparison, thought France, with its unique language, traditions, and food, more difficult to adapt to. At times the cold weather forced McNamara indoors to train on the rollers. But when it warmed above freezing outside, he bundled up for rides out on the town.

In the Brussels six-day McNamara's partner was to be Jimmy Moran, who, like Eddie Root, was another aging rider from the United States. Tall and lanky, James F. Moran possessed an incredible endurance ability. He was known as the "Chelsea Milkman" for the business he started with his brothers up in Massachusetts. Many of the riders, however, referred to him as "Piggy." Moran turned professional in 1901, specializing in the notoriously dangerous cycling sport of motor-paced racing. His first six-day race at Madison Square Garden was in 1902. Moran never had spectacular results in six-day racing until December 1908, when he was victorious, together with teammate Floyd MacFarland, at the Garden. Four months later the Moran-MacFarland team also won the inaugural Berlin six-day, an annual race that is still run today. The Americans took their victory lap in the presence of Germany's crown prince and a huge throng of spectators.[4]

Moran was first to crash out of the December 1913 New York six-day. On day 2 a trainer crossed the track without looking, and Moran rode straight into him. He flipped over the handlebars, landing hard on his left shoulder. Doctors examined him alongside the track and determined that the collarbone was broken. They ordered him off the track, but Moran pleaded to continue. His wish was granted by management, and Moran rode a little more with the shoulder bandaged up, but it was no use. He was in agony and had to quit.[5]

Whether or not his collarbone had truly been broken in New York, it had healed sufficiently for Moran to start the Paris six-day race teamed with Joe Fogler four weeks later—not good for healing a broken bone. The pair did finish, but they were way down in the standings, at tenth place.

For Moran it was one six-day race after another. But McNamara had a good amount of rest before they traveled to Brussels for the February 2 start of "De Zesdagenkoers." According to cables received by the American magazine *Bicycling World and Motorcycle Review*, the Brussels six-day was "without thrills or more than passing interest to the spectators until Thursday, when in a number of riotous sprints the contestants managed to divide the field into two divisions by lapping eight teams."[6]

In the end the winning team was Belgian Cyrille Van Hauwaert and Dutchman Johan Stol. Second place went to former Tour de France champion Octave Lapize and his fellow Frenchman Jules Miquel. The difference between second and third place overall came down to a final sprint, which McNamara lost to Lapize by just ten centimeters. The distance covered by all three teams was 2,795.7 miles. For third place McNamara and Moran split one thousand Belgian francs (US$5,000 today), and individually McNamara pocketed at least one hundred francs (US$500 today) for winning a scheduled intermediate sprint.[7]

McNamara and Moran left Brussels and arrived in Paris for some racing at the Vélodrome d'Hiver. Coming to Paris again was just a quick stop before they went to Berlin for another six-day race. It was to be Moran's fifth six-day race in as many months. Although Boston was not a full 144-hour race and he crashed out of New York, Moran would have logged five thousand individual miles of competitive racing by the time he finished in Berlin.

In Berlin, McNamara was paired once again with a veteran American six-day rider. This time it was Joe Fogler. Although they finished a disappointing fifth, the experience he acquired not only in Berlin but in all the other recent six-day races was to prove invaluable for the future. Root, Moran, and Fogler all had taken McNamara under their wing. They had all "been there, done that" in the United States and in Europe. Apart from McNamara's disappointment with Root's sprint results at the Garden, there was no question that went unanswered from the more experienced riders, and McNamara came away more relaxed and confident in his abilities.

But in just a few short months life in Europe and around the globe was about to change forever.

In the wee hours of Sunday, June 28, 1914, 147 riders of the Tour de France got under way on stage 1, a 388-kilometer (240-mile) trek from Paris to Le Havre. That afternoon Archduke Franz Ferdinand of Austria and his wife, Sophie, were murdered in Sarajevo, thus sparking the flame that was to become World War I. Meanwhile, in the United States, Elizabeth McDonough was in a Newark hospital. But rather than working there as a nurse, she was a patient, and on June 30 she gave birth to the McNamaras' first daughter, Eileen.

When Reggie left the United States in December 1913, three most likely scenarios existed: neither he nor Elizabeth knew she was pregnant; Elizabeth may have known but didn't tell Reggie; or they both knew. Whichever the case may be, Reggie continued on in Europe, racing at outdoor velodromes against some of the best competition the world had to offer. On the afternoon of April 12, 1914, he raced at Parc des Princes, an outdoor facility with a 666-meter cement track, managed by a founding father of the Tour de France, Henri Desgrange. Although McNamara competed in the Grand Prix at Parc des Princes against world-class sprinters such as Kramer, Denmark's Thorvald Ellegaard, and Italian Orlando Piani, he crashed hard to the cement in the first heat and was unable to make the final.

That morning before he crashed, Parisian spectators had come out to the start of Paris-Roubaix. There is a very good chance that McNamara, along with many of his fellow track riders, woke up early to see the 153 starters off to the "Hell of the North" road race, a field that included the eventual winner, Charles Crupelandt, as well as Oscar Egg, Octave Lapize, Lucien Petit-Breton, and Cyrille Van Hauwaert. There were a few fellow Australians in the field too—Don Kirkham, Ivor "Snowy" Munro, and Charles Piercey. Although it was a sunny day, the cobbles were tough on the riders and their bikes, just as they are today. Piercey broke a wheel, and Kirkham broke his frame. Neither rider finished, but Munro snatched thirty-seventh place.

When professional road races crossed paths with professional track racing, McNamara enjoyed the company of his fellow countrymen, especially on foreign soil. They caught up on news of their native land and spoke enthusiastically about the future of cycling in Europe and in the United States. Besides Kirkham, Munro, and Piercey, there were three other Aussies road racing in Europe at the time: George Bell, Fred Keefe, and Charles Snell.

With support from the Dunlop Rubber Company and a bicycle manufacturer named the Gladiator Company, the Aussies had a great ambition to further the status of Australian cycling in Europe similar to what they had already done in the United States several years earlier. They arrived in Europe in December 1913, about the same time as McNamara's group.

In addition to Paris-Roubaix, the six road racing Aussies, between them, competed in Milan–San Remo, Tour of Belgium, Paris-Tours, Paris-Brussels, Bordeaux-Paris, and the crème de la crème, the Tour de France. Kirkham's impressions were that road racing in Australia compared with road racing in Europe was as different as cricket was from baseball. Australians raced on flatter roads and in bigger gears. When it came to the mountains, the Europeans geared up even lower, using a reversible wheel with different-size sprockets mounted on each side of the hub. The gear change was made in less than a minute.[8] For a group not used to the landscape, culture, food, and language, they did reasonably well, and hopes were high to come back again in 1915.

In late April 1914 McNamara raced at the Buffalo Velodrome, Europe's premier outdoor cycling track. In terms of consistently attracting capacity crowds of more than fifteen thousand, it was roughly the equivalent of the Newark Velodrome. Buffalo was located at Neuilly-sur-Seine, a heavily populated suburb of Paris. The track's name came from American Buffalo Bill Cody, whose circus had performed there. Along the black line of the wooden boards, it was 333.3 meters long (approximately one-fifth of a mile), and the cream-colored railings contrasted with the well-manicured grass on the inside. Victor Breyer was the director of Buffalo and for years had been a catalyst in bringing foreign talent to Paris, most notably Major Taylor, Bobby Walthour, and Arthur Zimmerman.

On April 26 McNamara won his heat in the "Roue d'Or" over former champion Octave Lapize by three bike lengths. They were paced by pairs of men aboard tandem bicycles. In the final McNamara somehow lost contact with his tandem and placed third.

McNamara finished in the money three times in one day on May 25 at the five hundred–meter cement Hautamont Velodrome in Belgium, including taking second in a fifty-kilometer team race with another former Tour de France winner, François Faber, as his teammate. McNamara sent a letter to an Australian newspaper indicating that he had won four successive one hundred–kilometer races in Belgium and that he had more engagements in Paris in July and August. McNamara also wrote about the upcoming world cycling championships (which were never to happen) in Copenhagen, Denmark: "I guess Ellegaard will win the world's sprint championship. He is riding well again, and Hourlier, winner of the Grand Prix, has an engagement in America. Walter Rutt is also over there, and Kramer will not come to Europe for the championship, so Ellegaard will have no fear of his opposition. I would like to see Spears race in Copenhagen; I am sure he would win nearly everything. The climate and conditions would suit him there. I rode very well there in June, and got third to Ellegaard and Otto Meyer in the Grand Prix of Copenhagen, besides winning several other races."[9]

In early July, with the Tour de France under way, news of war was beginning to develop all over the world. Elizabeth may have been able to communicate with Reggie to some degree. He was always on the move, however, so it is very likely that she sent cables and letters to the office of Victor Breyer in Paris, care of Reggie, and he would pick them up when he could.

Despite the news of the war and despite traveling with an infant to a place she'd never been before, Elizabeth threw caution to the wind. Whether she decided on her own or whether

Reggie had sent her a ticket to come over to Europe, Elizabeth and baby Eileen boarded a steamer in New York bound for Le Havre, the closest port to Paris. It's not clear exactly when she arrived at Le Havre, but most likely it was near the end of July. It also remains unknown whether the one-month-old bundle of joy was a surprise to Reggie at their happy, if not also tearful, reunion.

On July 23 an ultimatum was delivered to Serbia, and so began World War I. In less than a month twenty-seven thousand French soldiers would be killed in battle—in one day.[10] All over Europe people were clamoring to read the news as soon as it came off the printing press, and wild scenes of intense excitement played out in the streets of Paris. On July 26 protesters burned a Hapsburg flag outside the Austrian embassy. This is the Paris that Elizabeth arrived in. Adding to all the excitement, July 26 was also the day the Tour de France rolled into Paris for its final day—stage 15—in its 5,411-kilometer (3,355-mile) circuit around France.

Five days after the Tour de France ended and five days before German troops marched across the Belgian border, another race took place that would be significant across Europe for years to come. It was a one hundred–kilometer team race at the Buffalo Velodrome. The field was impressive. Not only was it composed of nine starters from the recent Tour de France—Philippe Thys, Octave Lapize, Gustave Garrigou, Jean Rossuis, Firmin Lambot, François Faber, Oscar Egg, Ali Neffati, and Émile Engle; it also contained some of the best track men the world had to offer, including Edmond Jacquelin, Gabriel Poulain, Victor Dupre, Marcel Berthet, Marcel Dupuy, Leon Comes, Joseph Van Bever, Charles Piercey, and Reggie McNamara. And although the German army was mobilizing to punish France, the German rider Hermann Packebusch was also there. To be in this field was a great honor.

McNamara and Piercey were a team, so here was Australia's last time to impress the Europeans before what would be four years of war. Kirkham and Munro had done well at the Tour de

France, finishing, respectively, seventeenth and twentieth overall. But McNamara and Piercey wanted to do something special. With Elizabeth, holding baby Eileen, seated in the stands, along with thousands of other cycling fans, the two Aussies were well rested and poised for victory. They finished in two hours, twenty-nine minutes, and forty-five seconds, in front of all the other fourteen teams.[11] With everything that was going on all around them, it must have been an emotional win for the Australians. About ten weeks later the Buffalo Velodrome was torn down to make way for an aircraft factory.[12]

On August 1 American novelist Edith Wharton, who spent that summer in Europe, returned to Paris from Spain. She wrote that "everything seemed strange, ominous and unreal, like the yellow glare which precedes a storm. There were moments when I felt as if I had died, and woken up in an unknown world. And I had."[13]

The night of the Buffalo race, mobilization orders were posted. Chaos was closing in on Paris as Reggie, with Elizabeth and Eileen, and Piercey and Fred Keefe struggled to get back to the United States safely. They weren't the only ones trying to get out of France. Eighty thousand American tourists were trying to get out too.

Piercey and Keefe boarded a train from the North Station for Calais and then caught a channel steamer to Dover, England. From there they went through London and Liverpool before catching the steamer *St. Louis* back to New York. Reggie and Elizabeth took one of the last trains out of Paris from the St. Lazaire train station, where his bicycles and gear were commandeered by French authorities.[14] They arrived in Le Havre on August 8. Three days earlier French and British gunboats had sunk two German warships and captured three more.[15]

The week between McNamara's last race and boarding the train at St. Lazaire was a stressful one. More than likely, the family had difficulties obtaining tickets to get to Le Havre. Coupled with the needs of a newborn, that intensity may have been ratcheted upward a bit. To avoid a train altogether, some were willing to pay handsomely. Walter D. Hines, the general council of the Santa Fe Railroad, who was in a similar predicament, was charged eight hundred francs for an automobile to take him and his family from Paris to Le Havre.[16]

Reggie and Elizabeth secured tickets to the French liner *Chicago* and, with Eileen, boarded the same day they arrived at Le Havre, on August 8. The ship was originally scheduled to depart for New York that evening, but Captain Mace was forced to wait six days during British mobilization.[17]

As dozens of military transport vessels arrived, tens of thousands of British officers and soldiers marched ashore in their khaki uniforms. The people of Le Havre gave the good-looking bunch of men a hearty welcome. Bands turned out and played "Le Marseilles" along with English, Irish, and Scottish tunes as they marched through the streets.

For days on end those with tickets to the *Chicago*, like Reggie and Elizabeth, did not dare get out of sight of the big steamer, fearful it would sail without them. To compound troubles, waiters at Le Havre restaurants warned customers before they ordered that only gold would be acceptable for payment—no banknotes.[18] The nearly weeklong wait was not the kind of six-day endurance test McNamara enjoyed.

The *Washington Herald* reported: "At half past one on the afternoon of the 13th came the announcement that the boat would sail that night. The passengers crowded upon the decks and gave vent to their joy. Kisses seemed the most popular mode of expression. Everyone ran wild about the ship kissing everyone else."[19]

Not long after the *Chicago* got under way, however, it was halted twice by French torpedo boats. Both times officers came aboard and examined Captain Mace's papers before the ship was allowed to proceed. Finally, there was smooth sailing until the second night, when three Germans decided to gather at the bow of the ship and sing a patriotic anthem, "Die Wacht am Rhein," as loudly as possible. Captain Mace succeeded in convincing the Germans to go back to their staterooms before the assembled mob grew larger and angrier.

The *Chicago* arrived in New York on August 23, 1914. The first glimpse of the Statue of Liberty must have been overwhelming for some; perhaps there was another kissing frenzy. Whatever the case, Reggie, Elizabeth, and the rest of the passengers on board had many tales to tell about escaping from the jaws of war and returning to a land of peace and freedom.

McNamara wasted little time returning to racing at Newark Velodrome. His first race of the year there was under the lights in front of fifteen thousand fans on August 26, a ten-mile with a group of tandems out front to pace the racers. The field was big and strong and, besides Reggie, included Frank Cavanaugh, Jackie Clark, Joe Fogler, Alf Goullet, Alf Grenda, Frank Kramer, Caesar Moretti, Walter Rutt, and Robert Spears. The tandem riders paced the racers at just under thirty miles per hour, so some in the field were already gasping before the bell lap. The tandems pulled off just before the bell sounded, and the sprint began in earnest. The crowd came to their feet, and the noise increased as the speed escalated. On the backstretch McNamara went by Grenda, who had held the lead. Goullet was on McNamara's wheel, and Folger was on Goullet's, and all three were around Grenda, with one hundred yards to go. In a desperate struggle for the finish line, the front positions held until the last few feet. Goullet beat McNamara by an inch, and Fogler captured third.[20]

A few days later McNamara competed in a two-thirds of a mile race and went down with eight other riders in a heap. As the riders untangled themselves, only McNamara didn't get back on the bike. The crowd was very surprised because he was almost always the first to get up. McNamara had broken his collarbone.[21]

The likelihood that Reggie and Elizabeth talked about marriage before he went off to Europe in December had to have been great. The *Newark Evening News* had falsely reported that he and Elizabeth were married before the Boston six-day in November 1913. This report may have been generated under the direction of Reggie himself to instill the idea that they were married well before Elizabeth gave birth. But with his schedule it may have been difficult for Elizabeth to slow him down. Now, forced off the bike with no chance to earn money, and with his arm in a sling, he and Elizabeth decided to make their relationship official. On September 28, 1914, Reginald J. McNamara and Elizabeth M. McDonough were joined in matrimony in New York City.[22]

6

Politics of Racing

A month or so before McNamara first arrived in the United States from Australia, in June 1913, he had no idea about the war going on—not the war that would be raging in Europe fourteen months later but, rather, a political cycling war in America. From present times all the way back to when they raced highwheels, whether in Australia, Europe, or the United States, there was and always will be differing opinions, negotiations, and decisions about the rules, regulations, promotion, and control of professional and amateur cycling. Call it a necessary evil. The two primary factions at war during this time were divided between those on the side of the Newark Velodrome and those aligned with the Newark Motordrome, two big sporting venues that were right across the street from each other.

The Motordrome was located on the property formerly known as the Vailsburg track, and it helped put the city of Newark on the map of big-time cycling. The original Vailsburg track and stadium were constructed in 1897 with a quarter-mile board surface and large covered grandstand along the finish line and a set of open stands on either side. Over the years Vailsburg held thousands of cycling races to raucous sellout crowds, including those with great riders such as Eddie Bald, Major Taylor, Bobby Walthour, and Arthur Zimmerman. Frank Kramer won his first professional race at Vailsburg in 1900, and ten years later Alf Goullet made his American debut there.[1]

In October 1910, immediately after the Vailsburg lease expired,

John Chapman and Frank Mihlon began plans for a new board track in Newark. The location was right across the street from Vailsburg, on the north side of South Orange Avenue on Munn Avenue. Chapman and Mihlon envisioned a state-of-the-art facility in which none of the twelve thousand–plus seats would have an obstructed view. The permanent wood-surface track was one-sixth of a mile around, with wide sweeping banked turns and long straightaways. The track was perfection. According to the *New York Sun*, it was "by far the most pretentious course ever erected for the sport in this country. Bleachers are built all the way around the track connecting with each end of the grand stand."[2] The Newark Velodrome opened on a cold and windy Sunday, April 16, 1911.

In 1912 Inglis Moore Uppercu, owner of the New York Operations of Cadillac, financed a new sports arena, the Vailsburg Motordrome, that would overlap the old Vailsburg property. Rather than compete against the Newark Velodrome, Uppercu's intention for the Motordrome was to stage motorcycle races. On July 4, 1912, opening ceremonies began with eight thousand, including Newark mayor Jacob Haussling, who came to witness the high-speed excitement, noise, and smell of the motorcycles. Like the original Vailsburg, it was a quarter-mile in length, but this track was perfectly round, with sixty-degree banking that would allow the motorcycles riders to travel speeds in excess of ninety miles per hour.

Two months later, on Sunday, September 8, 1912, in front of sixty-five hundred spectators, Eddie Hasha, the national motorcycle champion from Waco, Texas, was flying down the boards at ninety-two miles per hour when he momentarily lost control of his machine. The motorcycle veered up the track incline and into the crowd, killing and maiming dozens. Hasha and his motorcycle slammed against a ten-inch wooden support beam. He fell dead into the grandstand. Parts of Hasha's motorcycle scattered in every direction. The engine and heavy back section slid down the embankment straight into the path of another rider, Jake Albright from Denver, going at a tremendous rate of speed. Albright could not avoid the wreckage and died on impact. Both Hasha and Albright's wives were in the grandstand.

The final death toll was Hasha, Albright, and six spectators, most of whom were children from thirteen to fifteen years old. In addition to the many injuries caused by the crashes, numerous other injuries were sustained in the ensuing human stampede out of the grandstand. Mayor Haussling ordered the police to stop motorcycle races at the Motordrome until his return to Newark on September 23. "In the meantime," reported the *New York Times*, "the legal department will take up the question of having Common Council adopt an ordinance prohibiting further motorcycle racing at Newark."[3]

In late October the grand jury recommended no more motorcycle racing in Newark: "The jury is thoroughly convinced that this so-called sport is of such a highly dangerous character, serves no useful purpose, is fraught with such reckless disregard and exposure of the lives of the competing riders as to render it so closely verging on criminality as to call for immediate action by the constituted authorities as will prevent any continuance thereof."[4] Uppercu and the managers of the Motordrome were exonerated from all criminal responsibilities. Because no motorcycles were allowed, Uppercu decided to enter the bicycling game and compete directly with his close neighbor, the Newark Velodrome.

Jay Eaton, a former professional cyclist, aligned with Uppercu and became manager of the Motordrome. Eaton was a savvy businessman, and two of his sons, Jay Jr. and Ray, had begun racing professionally. But Eaton had baggage. In 1900 he was caught fixing a race with fellow professional Orlando Stevens and banned from cycling for life.[5] Perhaps enough time had elapsed for people to have forgotten the incident, and somewhere along the line Eaton was allowed back in.

Not long before Eaton joined forces with Uppercu and the Motordrome, Eaton had resigned from the National Cycling Association (NCA) by affiliating himself with the revolt of amateur and Class B riders. Up until his resignation Eaton held three positions at the same time—vice president, secretary, and treasurer of the NCA. Immediately after siding with the Class B riders, he became a victim of verbal attacks by Joe Fogler and Frank Kramer, who both wanted Eaton expelled. The motion was put to an official vote and lost. Eaton could have remained, but as a point of principal, he resigned. Kramer then appointed Fogler to Eaton's former position at the NCA.

To stave off a mutiny of the Velodrome riders, Kramer called to order a meeting of some thirty riders at the Newark Velodrome. The chief complaint was that the Class B riders were making insufficient money, especially as compared to the sport's biggest stars, such as Kramer. Velodrome track management had adopted the practice of putting the best riders in separate heats so that in the final the stars would generally compete against one another. The Class B riders wanted formation of heats selected at random so that some of the big names would eliminate each other early on.

While this sentiment went over well with the riders of lesser ability, stars like Kramer, Alf Goullet, Alf Grenda, Jackie Clark, and Frank Cavanaugh opposed it. The stars asserted that the paying public came to the races for a chance to see the "big guns" fight it out in the final heat.

That evening a secret meeting, held away from the Velodrome, was called to order by Jay Eaton. His proposition was considered by the Class B riders whereby the Motordrome would compete for the paying public against the Velodrome. The situation was not new. John Chapman had promised the Class B riders be put on a salary of seven dollars per week up to fifteen dollars per week, depending on merit. But this promise never materialized. Eaton must have offered more money and promised to hold his end of the bargain that Chapman could not or would not.

Later that evening, without Chapman present because he was out of town on business, Floyd MacFarland, in an effort to sway them to the Velodrome side, addressed the disgruntled Class B men riders under the lights of the Newark Velodrome. MacFarland suggested that, instead of getting a salary, the Class B men should be put in their own races. Once they achieved a certain dollar amount, they would join the Class A group. In addition, Class B winners could race against Class A in open events.[6]

Richard F. Kelsey, the chairman of the NCA board of control, said the NCA would back the Velodrome because it held the franchise for the city of Newark. Under this condition the new Motordrome would herein be considered an "outlaw" track, and those who competed on it or affiliated themselves with it in any way would be suspended from the NCA and barred from other tracks under its control, which included every track in the country.[7]

John Chapman got back from his business trip with the bicycle racing situation in turmoil. After consulting with those he trusted most and then sorting things out in his own mind, he gave a statement to the press: "For the past two weeks or ten days there have been a number of articles published in the local newspapers about the amateur and professional bicycle riders on strike at the Velodrome. The said articles have mentioned the grievances of the riders and their demands. If this is a strike, then those interested have not gone about it in the usual manner, for I have never been approached by any rider in reference to their grievances or demands. It seems to me that if the riders are really in earnest and wanted to ride at the Velodrome with the condition changed to suit them, they would have put their proposition directly to me.

"Instead, they have proffered their services to the backers of an 'outlaw' movement and seem bent upon disrupting the National Cycling Association. This is being done under the guise of a strike designed to place the promoters of the Velodrome in a bad light with the local public.

"The prize limit in amateur races is at the present time $35 for firsts. Yesterday I conferred with R. F. Kelsey, the chairman of the board of control of the National Cycling Association, in reference to increasing the value of the amateur prizes. I proposed to put one race on each Sunday at the Velodrome with the following prize values: First, $50; second, $25; third, $15; fourth, $10; fifth, $5. Mr. Kelsey informed me that this could be done by changing the rules in reference to amateur prize values. This he has promised to do. This change in prize values is to take place this coming Sunday.

"I also intend to increase the prizes for the professionals. Each Sunday I will put on a race for the professionals with a purse of $100 to the winner, $50 for second, $25 for third, $15 for fourth and $10 for fifth places."[8]

With construction at the Motordrome to outfit it properly for bicycle racing nearing completion in May 1913, Eaton succeeded in stealing away higher-class professionals and amateurs from Chapman and the Velodrome. For the first race on Memorial Day, Eaton secured twenty-five professionals and at least twice as many amateurs. But none of the big stars crossed the line. Goullet had just won $500 in the "Newark Thousand," so he stayed put, as did Cavanaugh, Clark, Fogler, Grenda, and Kramer.

The *Newark Evening News* published photos of the Motordrome's opening day on May 31. The two-story judges' tower was smartly adorned with red, white, and blue decorations. Construction was finished, and everything was clean and new. There were no visible reminders of the motorcycle carnage from eight months earlier. Most riders thought it a little unusual to race on a track that was perfectly round—it was something they had to get used to. The scene was all set for a festive atmosphere and a great day for bike racing, but only fifteen hundred spectators showed up. Not an auspicious beginning for the Motordrome.

Conversely, on the same day and on the other side of the street, six thousand fans paid to see racing at the Velodrome. But especially considering the Memorial Day national holiday, six thousand fans did not constitute a particularly large crowd for the Velodrome.

Nevertheless, Chapman was pleased that not so many fans

changed allegiances to the Motordrome. Encouraged by the news, he went to work to secure as much cycling talent as money could buy. He sent word to Victor Breyer in Paris that he needed foreign racers quickly. Breyer sent back a cablegram indicating that he had seven riders who could come at once.[9] Chapman specifically asked for Walter Rutt, but Rutt's calendar was booked through the fall. For immediate impact Chapman called down riders from the Revere track near Boston. He coaxed Iver Lawson, the 1904 World's Sprint Champion, away from Salt Lake City with a contract.

Eaton would not give up the fight either. In addition to having some of the lesser-known Class A men, most of the Class B, and most amateurs formerly racing at the Velodrome in his pocket, he also got the most respected referee in the business, John Valentine. Valentine was known as a strict disciplinarian and a perfectionist for enforcing the rules. For the first time in his illustrious career Valentine had a few of his decisions reversed by the Velodrome management, and he quickly resigned.

And so it went for months: Velodrome versus Motordrome, Chapman versus Eaton, trading punches and squeezing out all the races and cycling talent they could while still making a profit.

With all the defections to the Motordrome, a logical conclusion could be drawn that Eaton was paying the lower rank-and-file more for their services than Chapman was willing to. But Eaton's biggest problem was star power. People did pay to see their favorites, and most of the big names stayed at the Velodrome. Consequently, the Motordrome continued to draw significantly fewer spectators compared to the Velodrome.

In late June 1913 McNamara had more or less healed from his wounds after his spectacular crash into the judge's stand when he first arrived in America from Australia. He may have been able to command a salary, a signing bonus, and potential winnings at either the Motordrome or the Velodrome. His potential winnings were probably less at the Motordrome, but his need for up-front money was high, with all the hospital bills.

In the end McNamara signed with the Motordrome. Besides, his buddy Robert Spears was aligned with the Motordrome.

A further development in favor of the Motordrome side took hold when Patrick T. Powers, a powerful New York businessman with deep pockets, together with Motordrome owner Uppercu, outbid Chapman and Mihlon for control of Madison Square Garden the first week of December for the 1913 six-day race.[10]

For years Powers had managed affairs at the Garden six-day race, until the control was wrested away in 1912 by Chapman and Mihlon. According to the *Newark Evening News*, Powers resented the treatment he had received at the hands of Chapman and Mihlon and "expressed a desire to square accounts" for having been "frozen out" the year before.[11]

A gentle breeze drifted in one large window and out the other of Powers's office, located on the eleventh floor of the Flatiron Building in New York City. He leaned back in his leather chair with a broad grin, and he gazed out at Madison Square Garden below. Powers juggled his many different sports and entertainment business interests. Besides cycling, he also had been president of the Eastern Baseball League. He was finalizing details of the Greater New York Fair and Exposition, which was to be held the entire month of August 1913.

"It is a little too early to talk of the six-day grind just now," said Powers, "but you can say that we are going to have as good a race as was ever run in the Garden. My plans are all mapped out and when the time comes, the information regarding them will be given out. I am going to manage the race absolutely. Mr. Uppercu has turned the matter over to me and everything is to be referred to me. Uppercu did not go into the matter blindly. In fact I can truthfully say that I tried to dissuade him, but after he had examined my reports on the past races that I conducted we came to an agreement and once more I find myself in the six-day game.

"When it comes down to the question of the NCA prohibiting riders from competing in our race, why, the thing is a joke. There is no such thing as the NCA. The organization is Richard

F. Kelsey, Frank Mihlon and John Chapman. It is known as such the world over and Mr. Kelsey will find out very soon. Why, the men in the NCA are not sportsmen. Kelsey does as Chapman and Mihlon tell him and I believe the foreign racing associations are aware of this fact.

"It is going to be a fight, but in my opinion, a short one. We will have an organization the world over that will take the place of the NCA and its arbitrary policies. One that will be world-wide and representative. I will have all the foreign riders I desire for the long grind, and in fact, I might add that we could get many more than are needed. Our race will be as good as any I have ever run and I believe that we will be able to smash a few records when the time comes."

Powers was just warming up. "How I was put out of the cycling game is an interesting story. It goes to show the class of men at the head of the organization that I believe will be wiped out of existence," he continued. "When Madison Square Garden was sold I secured a five-year contract with the persons who were to build a new Garden. When the purchasers of the old building failed in an attempt to secure a plan for the erection of an office building, the Garden was allowed to stand. I have built up the six-day race at considerable expense and have even gone to much trouble in getting vetoed by Mayor McClellen an ordinance prohibiting the race. The fact that the race was run and was a big success proved that the grind was popular. Chapman and Mihlon ran a race for ten percent of the profits.

"As I had always considered myself an associate track owner in the NCA, it is needless to say that the trick Kelsey turned on me in giving the New York franchise to someone else hurt. Last year I had lunch with Kelsey and gave him a check for $50 for the New York franchise. This was a year ago last January. The annual meeting of the NCA was to have been held in February and I presumed that I would get the franchise as usual. I was led to believe by Kelsey that there was no doubt about my getting the franchise and he left me. In April that year I got a letter from Kelsey to the effect that Chapman had protested against a franchise being awarded to me and that the matter would come up at the annual meeting. They surprised me because the annual meeting, when the franchises are awarded was to have been held, as I said, in February, and I always got a notice to be present.

"Just when the meeting was held I have no knowledge, but I was informed some time during the month of April that Chapman and Mihlon had been awarded the New York franchise. I received no notice from Kelsey to attend the meeting, and even though I was vice president, and even to this day, I have never heard from him nor have I received my check for $50 back.

"Since Kelsey has been in charge of the NCA the doings of that body have never been conducted in accordance with the corporation laws of New Jersey and it is a question in my mind whether there is any such thing as the NCA but it is apparent that he does as Chapman and Mihlon say. They dictate the policy of the organization and it does not represent what it was intended to when organized. There are no sportsmen in it. It is to be a fight from now on, and you can say a survival of the fittest."[12]

On July 31, 1913, a month after Powers's publicized rant, the two warring factions agreed to meet at the Woolworth Building in the office of Uppercu's attorney, Henry Amermen. An agreement was drawn up to pool the interests of both parties. According to the *Newark Evening News*, Uppercu "declared he entertained the suggestion of entering into a peace agreement because he believed it to be for the best interests of the public, the riders and promoters. He had found, he said, that the public would not support the so-called 'outlaw' meets on the Motordrome track, in spite of the fact that some very famous riders were competing there."[13]

Uppercu invited Mihlon to see the Motordrome for the first time. Although it was still considered by many to be the finest motorcycle racing track in the country, it would effectively be closed down. There remained uses for the Motordrome, but the Velodrome was tailor-made for cycling, and it had larger seating accommodations. The NCA would continue to operate

Politics of Racing

but not as it had in the past. Certain corrections needed to be addressed. They were confident all would work out.

Among the most interesting absentees from the proceedings was the chairman of the NCA board of control, Richard F. Kelsey. Kelsey claimed he had not heard about the meeting until the next day. John Chapman was not present either. But he knew more about the affair than Kelsey because he was offered $20,000 to relinquish his interest in the Newark Velodrome.[14]

"I am very well satisfied with the new turn of affairs," said Chapman, "as I was taken care of financially. I wasn't asked to remain with the interests here and I didn't ask to stay on. I didn't take part in any of the conferences looking to a consolidation, and in fact it was Floyd MacFarland who told me most of what I know of the affair. I would not care to work for the interests now in the game as I don't believe in laboring to advance the interests of a man who had taken money from me through an outlaw movement . . . I don't harbor any ill feeling against Floyd MacFarland for the part he played in the affair, as I don't think MacFarland did anything that was not fair and above board."

With a wink and a nudge it was reported that "the fine hand of MacFarland can be seen through the entire proceedings." MacFarland was good friends with Pat Powers and was employed by Mihlon. When Powers and Uppercu gained back control of the six-day race, Mihlon was ready to quit. There was much speculation that it was MacFarland who had broached the subject of consolidation. The outcome couldn't have been better for MacFarland; he would take over Chapman's duties as manager of the Mihlon tracks, not only in Newark but also in Boston, New Haven, and Philadelphia. In addition, he became Powers's assistant in managing the upcoming six-day race in December.[15]

As management and owners sorted out who would get what parts of the mine, the riders were left to fight out who would get the shaft. Kramer, Fogler, and the other Velodrome riders felt they had sacrificed a great deal in sticking by the Velodrome and were not about to let a bunch of "outlaw" yahoos back into the fold.

Fogler was defiant: "We have notified Chairman Richard Kelsey of the National Cycling Association to take no action on the reinstatement of the Motordrome riders until he hears from us . . . if these 'outlaws' are to be put on an even footing with us, there will be trouble. They have taunted us with remarks that we would be out in the cold and that there would be no quarter if they were in control. Well, we have the upper hand now and they will have to take their medicine, bitter as it is."

Many discussions and meetings took place to arrange out how the Motordrome riders would get back into the NCA. Payment of fines was the most obvious answer to the Velodrome riders. A reporter asked a group of the Motordrome riders if Uppercu was going to pay their fines for them or whether they would get stuck with the bill. Some smiled and laughed, and one shot back with: "Forget it. You don't suppose we're dropping any good money unless we have to, do you?"[16] Whether or not the Motordrome riders did pay any fines was not known, but everyone moved on.

The bike war was finally over. On August 17, 1913, in one of the first competitions with all the riders at the Velodrome, a symbolic race of pride took place between the star of the Velodrome riders, Frank Kramer, and the star of the Motordrome riders, Reggie McNamara. The race was a five-mile open, and the field was crowded. Although Kramer and McNamara weren't even competing for first place—because it was already a foregone conclusion—all eyes were on them. With a lap to go, Kramer and McNamara were fighting for fourth place. On the backstretch McNamara went right around two riders to lead out the final sprint for fourth place. Kramer was three wheels back and went right after McNamara, catching his wheel on the final turn. Kramer came around McNamara on the straightaway, and side by side they churned their pedals with their entire power. The referee declared Kramer the winner. Many in the stands protested that McNamara had won by six inches.

7

The War Years

Although McNamara and his young family were in Europe just as hostilities got under way and escaped with little more than the clothes on their back, they spent the war years comfortably in Newark and peacefully in the United States. It was a wonderful time; he and Elizabeth were newly married with a cuddly baby daughter to care for and play with. Elizabeth didn't have to work anymore, and during this time Reggie brought home roughly $4,000 per year, or close to $100,000 in today's money. They welcomed their second child, Regina, on February 9, 1917. For so many other professional cyclists, however, things were not so cozy during these traumatic years. For some their lives and families were torn apart.

Walter Rutt, a German sprinter who bore a close resemblance to Frank Kramer, had many plans ruined. Rutt was a very popular rider in the United States. He had won the six-day inside Madison Square Garden on three occasions: 1907 with Johan Stol, 1909 with Jackie Clark, and 1912 with Joe Fogler. In addition, he took second place twice, in 1908 with Stol and 1910 with Clark. Rutt had come to the United States with the full intention of beginning racing in the spring of 1914. He planned to return to Europe in late July to defend his world champion sprint title at the Ordrup Track in Copenhagen.[1]

After the political battle from the year before, cycling in America was showing signs of a comeback. Having Rutt, the 1913 world champion, race against Kramer, the 1912 world champion, didn't hurt either. Paid attendance on any given race night or day at the Newark Velodrome, which included standing room only tickets in the infield, was topping fifteen thousand at times, and fans were getting turned away at the ticket gate for seated accommodations. With Germany's declaration of war, Rutt found himself in a tough spot. Some years before World War I, while racing in Australia, he had received orders to return to Germany for mandatory service to his country. But he refused to go. Because the crown prince of Germany was a big cycling fan, Rutt was given a release from service provided he promised to take up arms in the event he was ever called. Rutt remained in the United States more than a month after hostilities broke out.

Late August of 1914 was McNamara's first racing in the United States since returning from Europe and Rutt's last racing before he left.[2] Six weeks later, on October 17, the *Newark Evening News* carried a photo of Rutt in his German army uniform. A letter to his good friend and trainer, Dave Coburn, was sent from Rutt's parents' house in Düsseldorf. "Dear Dave, On my way to the front. I am in charge of a car and ordered to headquarters. In one day I had my uniform, car and papers. Tomorrow morning I leave for Cologne. Goodbye and best wishes. Walter Rutt."[3]

Dave Coburn also received a letter from Englishman Tommy Hall, who had met Rutt on his way back to Germany: "Rutt said that he hoped you, Clark and all of his friends would forgive him for leaving so impromptu. I argued with him against going to war, as did Mrs. Rutt, who did not want him to volunteer. I told him if he was a single man it would not be so bad, but being a married man, he should think about his family. Who would look after his wife and boy if anything happened to him? Nothing could stop him from enlisting. His wife's family, Mrs. Rutt, Oscar, his son and I saw him off at the station and wished him Godspeed. I can tell you, Dave, that I have seen some heartrending sights watching the German reservists, who have made Denmark their home, return to join the army, saying goodbye to their wives and children. I certainly wish it was over, but it looks as if it would take a long time. It appears as if Belgium will be wiped off the map."[4]

Since the war began, the first American six-day to happen was the Boston ten-hour-per-day race, which started on November 2, 1914. It adopted the "Berlin" system of scoring, whereby points would be given for a daily series of sprints. Rather than have the race come down to one final sprint at the very end and also eliminate any rumors of "combinations" or "teaming," in which one team or individual would help another team or individual for side money, the Berlin system was a great improvement. Depending on how it went over in Boston, the idea might be implemented in New York too.

The result was a smashing success not only in terms of fairness and producing a clear winner on the merits of each team but also because it created a more exciting race to watch. The Boston Arena was packed all week, but especially on the last night, despite the doubling of prices. On the last night, according to the *Boston Daily Globe*, "a record crowd occupied the building. At 8 o'clock only standing room was left and late comers poured into the oval. Men were packed 30 deep around the inside of the fence. It was safe to say that 40 percent of those in the oval heard, but never saw the men whirling around the bowl."[5]

Three teams were tied for first at the end: Alf Goullet–Freddie Hill, Peter Drobach–Iver Lawson, and Reggie McNamara–Jimmy Moran. Each team had a local Massachusetts rider: Hill from Boston, Drobach from South Boston, and Moran from Chelsea. Utilizing the Berlin system, five heats were set up for the final, and Goullet won all but one, thereby clinching the overall victory for his team. McNamara rode in all five heats for his team as well and scored enough points to take second place overall.

Floyd MacFarland was manager of the twenty-second annual New York six-day race at Madison Square Garden in 1914, and for the first and only time, in an unwelcome break from tradition, it was run entirely in November—starting only a week after Boston. In addition to going with the Berlin system, Mac-

Farland took on another innovation by giving extra prizes for special sprints during the week.

Despite the war raging in Europe, MacFarland was able to secure a number of European riders, including Belgian Victor Linart, who was at home in Antwerp when a terrible German bombardment began. Only days earlier Linart had sent his wife and children to the safety of Opp Zoom, Holland. With his home and city in ruins, Linart rode his bicycle about eighty miles to Ostend, where he took a refuge boat to Folkstone, England. "The Germans put me in shape for the six-day race," he wrote to MacFarland. "I was one of the last to leave Antwerp, and I was chased all the way to Ostend by Uhlans and scouts on wheels. It was a hard ride, but I won."[6]

News of former six-day riders engaged in the war came pouring in. Had it not been for the war, at least a few of them would have raced in the New York six-day. "One favorite is missing and he, Walter Rutt, the German, is at the present time in a hospital with catarrh of the lungs," reported *Bicycling World and Motorcycle Review*, "contracted from exposure while doing military duty for his country during the war now raging on the continent. Other riders that have competed in past races have been captured, killed or wounded in battle. Among them are Lapize, Brocco, Perchicot, Pouchois, Berthet and Van Hauwaert."[7]

Of the thirty-six riders to compete in the 1914 six-day race at Madison Square Garden, ten were from Europe: four Frenchmen, Émile Cousseau, Marcel Dupuy, George Parent, and George Sérès; two Danes, Norman Anderson and Norman Hansen; two Italians, Vincenzo Madonna and Francesco Verri; Oscar Egg from Switzerland; and Victor Linart from Belgium.

At the start no rider got a bigger reception than did the diminutive Belgian motor-pacing specialist Victor Linart. According to Ernest Hemingway, Linart's nickname was "the Sioux" for his Native American–like profile. Linart had replaced Maurice Brocco as the crowd favorite—especially among the "gallery gods."

Most of the Europeans had little time to prepare for the six-day, and the media's predictions of poor showings came true. Before six hours of racing had elapsed, the team of Parent-Cousseau called it quits, and Linart-Madonna were out before twenty-four hours.

The continuous 142-hour race stopped on Saturday night with five teams tied at 2,758 miles and one lap, beating the previous New York record by more than 7 miles. The Garden was filled to capacity on the last day—a vast chain-smoking rollicking mass of humanity.

All week McNamara had worked hard to become the fan favorite—the "bearcat." On day 5 he and his partner, again Jimmy Moran, had nearly succeeded in lapping the entire field in what was the longest jam in recent memory. But the team of Alfs—Goullet and Grenda—were not to be denied. With the Berlin system in place, they cranked out sixty-seven points in the final series of sprints. Second place went to Peter Drobach and Iver Lawson, with sixty-one points, and McNamara-Moran third, with fifty-three.

The war continued to rage in Europe, but in the cold New Jersey spring of 1915 it was business as usual, and the best from America and Australia were out training for opening day of the outdoor season at the Newark Velodrome.

America's top trainer, Jack Neville, switched allegiances from Frank Kramer to Alf Goullet, and Goullet's trainer, Maury Gordon, crossed over to Kramer's camp. Neville had been with Kramer for fourteen years. Behind Goullet's coup was a quarrel with Floyd MacFarland. Joe Fogler advised Goullet that the best way to get even with MacFarland was by going after Kramer's scalp and winning an American sprint championship title.[8]

Gordon, Goullet, and Grenda went west to Baden Springs, Indiana, to train and soak in the baths there. "I believe my trip to West Baden will do me a lot of good," said Goullet, "and in fact upon my return I shall be able to get in condition very quickly. While there I expect to do some road work, as both Grenda and myself have arranged to take our road wheels along with us."[9] McNamara, Clark, Frank Cavanaugh, and many other riders competed in roller races at Miner's Empire Theatre in Newark to keep fit. With several amateur riders Bob Spears went south to Savannah to train outside in the warm sunshine.

The ageless Frank Kramer was unsure about the upcoming 1915 season. "I'll be either very good or very bad this season," he offered. "I feel fine in every way and the rest I have had this winter has done me a lot of good. . . . In former years I was always able to tell pretty well just how I would ride during a season, but I am surely up in the air now."

On Sunday, March 28, blue skies prevailed enough for some twelve thousand fans to brave the temperatures in the midforties at the Newark Velodrome. Kramer gained the first notch on his fifteenth straight title by beating out Goullet and Francesco Verri on the one-mile open. McNamara took second place in the B. M. Shanley Jr. Handicap.

The sunshine was short-lived, however, and manager Floyd MacFarland's next big meet was delayed to Sunday, April 18. Although it was MacFarland who laid out the schedule of races, when the program was handed to him, he was surprised it was so long. In all there were to be thirty-two heats, plus finals, in one day of racing.

Besides getting the venue cleared of snow, MacFarland had been hard at work trying to secure services of top European sprinters, sending letters and cables to Paris and elsewhere. Italian sprinter Caesar Moretti confirmed his pending arrival to America from war-torn Europe with the sprint champion of Denmark, Thorvald Ellegaard. They were to sail on May 1. In the letter Moretti confessed to his getaway from Italian army officials by disguising himself as a waiter on a dining car.[10]

The afternoon before Sunday's racing, MacFarland socialized at a local sportswriter's office—probably with the *Newark Evening News*'s Howard Freeman—where they laughed and joked. From there he went to the Newark Velodrome to check on things. Upon entering the grounds, he was annoyed. MacFarland took exception to advertising signs put up by David Lantinberg, who sold confections and refreshments at the Velodrome. As Lantinberg continued to install the signs along the track's guardrail, MacFarland approached and requested that Lantinberg remove the signs. Lantinberg simply ignored Mac-Farland and continued his work.

But MacFarland would not let up, and in short order an angry exchange of words was enough to catch the notice of several people nearby. Lantinberg was a small man, weighing no more than 110 pounds, whereas MacFarland stood six foot four and weighed nearly twice as much. In some unnecessary combination of trying to be funny and to teach Lantinberg a lesson, MacFarland picked up the smaller man and carried him at arm's length as if he were a child. Lantinberg resisted violently. From his work with the signs Lantinberg held a screwdriver, and in his fury he took a strike at MacFarland's head. MacFarland turned his head to avoid the blow, but in doing so, the point of the screwdriver entered his temple, just above the left ear. MacFarland fell down senseless.

Riders, trainers, and spectators rushed to the scene. Lantinberg's anger subsided as quickly as it had been provoked, and he helped Alf Grenda, the biggest man around, lift MacFarland into his own vehicle. Lantinberg went off at full speed to Newark's City Hospital. Lantinberg was arrested at the hospital, and the police detained a dozen witnesses at the Velodrome. Meanwhile, MacFarland never regained consciousness and died at nine o'clock that evening. At his bedside were his wife, Elenora, Frank Kramer, and Frank Mihlon.[11]

McNamara, who did not witness the scene, gave an account to a Sydney newspaper. In the letter he wrote, "Kramer, who had been a close personal friend of MacFarland for over twenty years, was terribly upset at his tragic end."[12] "MacFarland's death was a terrible shock to everybody in Newark," said John Chapman. "You would think someone of national importance has died. MacFarland was one of the most popular men in Newark and he will have the biggest funeral in the history of the city."[13]

The *Newark Evening News* gave a tribute: "There is something poignantly tragic about the death of Floyd A. MacFarland—

something strange and weird and depressing. It tugs at the heartstrings of his friends and those who were not his friends as they realize that the thing which brought him success—his aggressiveness, his dominating personality—should bring the chill blackness of death at the very noonday of his career. It is the grim irony of fate that burned into the consciousness of even the callous."[14]

In June, Lantinberg was acquitted of charges of manslaughter.[15] He and his wife, Mary, continued their business at the Newark Velodrome and at six-day races in New York and Chicago. By 1924 the Lantinbergs had catered for other events in Madison Square Garden, including the National Democratic Convention.[16]

Like the Lantinbergs, normal life went on, the European war went on, and cycle racing in America went on. Almost immediately after the tragedy, "Colonel" John Chapman was announced as MacFarland's successor.

The Berlin six-day scoring system, newly instituted in the United States, seemed to suit McNamara's style of racing. His consistently high placings were good, especially considering how many other teams were competing, but he hadn't come away with a six-day victory since arriving in America. He hoped all that would change when it was announced that his new six-day partner, instead of a grizzled American veteran such as Fogler, Moran, or Root, was his young Aussie traveling partner, Bob Spears.

McNamara and Spears had become good friends, and in 1915 they were scheduled to compete as a team in November's Boston race as well as New York in December. But the hex continued as they took second place overall in both races due to rule infractions. In Boston they had five points taken away because of a faulty pickup, the method in which riders trade places on the track. Each team member was supposed to at least touch the other, but mostly, the incoming rider got a big shove from the rider going in for a rest.

In New York, in an effort to prevent Oscar Egg from passing,

Spears grabbed his arm and nearly shoved Egg off his mount. Egg, the big rider from Switzerland and current world record holder for the unpaced hour, at 27.4 miles, was a great favorite among the crowd, who booed and hissed Spears with great gusto. The McNamara-Spears team was penalized eleven points for the foul, and the overall win defaulted to the second-place team of Alf Grenda and Freddie Hill. When Grenda and Hill went out to parade around the track for several victory laps, they were booed and hissed because of what Spears had done. Spears refused to come out for his second-place parade laps with McNamara. But when McNamara came out, all by himself, he was given the greatest cheer from the packed house of more than ten thousand fans inside Madison Square Garden as if he were the true winner.[17]

McNamara's perseverance would not be denied, however, and he got his first American six-day victory in February 1916 in Chicago. At first McNamara and Spears did not want to come to Chicago because the race had been sanctioned under the auspices of the Twentieth Century Cycling Association, in direct opposition to Chapman and the National Cycling Association. But the Chicago promoter Packey McFarland was persuasive; he was able to get not only McNamara-Spears but also eleven other teams, all members of the NCA.

Packey McFarland was Chicago's most famous boxer. To this day he ranks as one of the best prizefighters never to have won a world title. McFarland had retired from the ring in 1915 and hoped his entrance into the cycling game would help boost both his image as a promoter and his bank account.

More than twelve thousand people crammed into the Chicago Coliseum on Wabash Avenue before the fire marshal was forced to close the doors. Most had come to see McFarland's boxing exhibition, which made for a unique and exciting start to a bicycle race. The *Chicago Tribune* reported: "When Packey McFarland crawled through the ropes to box three rounds with Ever Hammer, the local lightweight, the building echoed and reechoed with cheers. As the pride of the stockyards, who is considered Chicago's premier boxer, took off his bathrobe, the band played 'The Wearer of the Green,' and another cheer went up."[18]

Like Boston, Chicago's race was not a continuous 142-hour six-day race but, rather, a 12-hour-per-day affair. The pistol cracked at one o'clock in the morning of February 4, 1916, and the twelve teams went round and round the ten-lap-per-mile track as the band played "America" and the thousands of fans stood up in respect.

By day 4 six teams were tied on laps. Team partners Frank Corry and Iver Lawson were two laps down, and they made several desperate attempts to gain the laps back. But seeing Corry falter, McNamara jumped the field, and there went another high-paced dizzying chase seconds after Corry gave in to his fatigue. Spears was ready and came out to relieve McNamara. Other teams started relief work as well. The crowd stood in disbelief that such a high pace could be maintained for so long. When the dust finally settled, most believed Corry-Lawson had lost a third lap in the melee, but the referee ruled that no team had gained any lap due to faulty pickups.[19] Perhaps McNamara and Spears were thinking to themselves, "Here we go again."

Not many in the Chicago Coliseum were surprised—or disappointed—that the "Kangaroo" team, as McNamara and Spears were called, won the final series of Berlin system sprints. They collected seventy-two points, whereas the team of Philadelphia's Jake Magin and San Francisco's Percy Lawrence finished second overall, with fifty-six points.[20] Tied with the exact mileage, McNamara and Spears finally got their overall victory together.

Going back to Newark, McNamara and Spears knew that by having ridden in the Chicago six-day, they would have to atone for their defection from the NCA. The pair spent more than an hour behind closed doors with John Chapman. McNamara and Spears wanted reinstatement, but they didn't want to pay big penalties. The figure came up at $150, not necessarily "chump change" in those days, but for McNamara and Spears, who had just cleared more than $1,000 each in Chicago, it wasn't too bad.

The War Years

Back in the fold of the NCA, McNamara and Spears immediately went to work at the Newark Velodrome to prepare for the fast-approaching outdoor season. But before everything got back to normal, word on the street was that the two were considered "double-crossers" by other professionals who had also raced in Chicago and joined the outlaw movement against the NCA.

On their way to the Newark Velodrome, McNamara and Spears confronted a group of outlaws and asked if they had uttered the distasteful remark. Collectively, they had nothing to say, and then they were questioned individually. No evidence came forth, only expressions of surprise that some person or persons would call Spears and McNamara double-crossers. Just as all appeared to come to a satisfactory conclusion, up walked Californian Willie Hanley, who immediately confirmed the rumor.

Up went McNamara's fist to Hanley's jaw, and the battle began. Not only was Spears a big man, but he was also an experienced boxer who had fought professionally on more than one occasion. He had his hands full, but he was dishing out some good licks.

Jack Neville, who witnessed the encounter, saw that despite being considerably outnumbered, McNamara and Spears were holding their own. But eventually, superior forces began to prevail. In support of McNamara and Spears, Neville heaved pretzel bowls that proved such effective ammunition that many from the outlaw contingent were driven to cover.

McNamara continued with Hanley, but Spears pushed him aside and engaged Hanley, remarking that Reggie's punches were missing too much. Someone had rushed to the Velodrome and made a call to the police, who arrived in record time, coming in patrol wagons, on motorcycles, and by horseback. According to the *Newark Evening News*: "A roll call disclosed that there were no casualties and few injuries. There was a mouse on each of Hanley's eyes and Frank Cavanaugh and McNamara each sported a lump on his left cheek. Cavanaugh sustained his injury ducking behind a motorcycle as he rushed to get beyond the wild paths of crockery. After being treated by the Red Cross surgeon, Hanley was decorated with the iron cross for bravery and made no further mention of the double-cross."[21]

McNamara wasn't seriously injured in the fight, but a broken collarbone he received in Boston almost kept him out of the December 1916 six-day race at Madison Square Garden. The prize money from the year before had jumped up considerably. The winners in the Garden six-day the previous year, Grenda and Hill, had split $1,500, and this year's team was to receive $5,000. The $1,250 that McNamara and Spears split for second place had gone up to $3,000. For that kind of money five weeks of recovery from a broken collarbone was going to have to be enough time to heal. McNamara was in.

Once again, he was partnered with his buddy Bob Spears. By day 2 McNamara and Spears had become the crowd favorites at Madison Square Garden, whereas the team of Alf Goullet and Alf Grenda became the villains. The crowd stood up every time McNamara came out on the track because they knew he'd soon be going at breakneck speed. In the day's sprint for points, McNamara beat Goullet four times, winning the first heat, the third, the seventh, and the ninth. Spears won the second heat, and by most accounts he beat Grenda in the fourth heat by a wheel length, but the referee saw it differently. When Pete Prunty raised his megaphone and announced Grenda had won, the crowd "hissed and booed like a lot of wild men."[22]

According to the *New York Times*, the pickpockets, coat stealers, and gangsters were no longer a factor, and the only thing missing at this year's race was fresh air: "Through the thick haze of tobacco smoke it was almost impossible to see across the arena. The mixture of stale blue smoke, boiling frankfurters, and fragrant mustard created an aroma entirely new and lasting. The band was still among those present, but was quite ignored. Numerous vocalists tried hard to attract attention but all the musical art was lost in the riot of yells which greeted the sprinting cyclists."[23]

The next day McNamara again won four heats and came in second in another. The only reason his team didn't catch up with Goullet-Grenda was that Spears did not do so well in the sprints, failing to place in any of his three heats. On day 4 Grenda's tire tore off its rim, and he flipped over the handlebars. He came up with a broken collarbone and was forced to abandon the race. Goullet was given four hours to secure a new partner, but he was unable to, and just like that, he was out of the race too. In the first sprint of the night McNamara crashed just after he crossed the line a winner, and there were concerns that he may have rebroken his collarbone. Spears was having a rough go of it, too, and his legs from all the miles ridden and lack of sleep were starting to wear on him. He had talked about quitting so that McNamara could team up with Goullet, but Spears stayed on.

With Grenda-Goullet gone, it seemed likely that McNamara-Spears would supplant them as the leading team. But the team of Eddie Madden and Eddie Root took the day's sprints and edged ahead on points, with six teams still tied for first on laps. Madden was a twenty-one-year-old youngster from Newark, and the grind did not seem to affect him as it did the other riders, whose eyes were bleary and bloodshot. Riders were falling off their mounts from a combination of a lack of sleep and exhaustion. Madden suddenly became the crowd favorite, and McNamara started getting booed.

But Madden and Root didn't bother McNamara so much. "I fear Egg more than any other rider in the race," confessed McNamara. "Once he gets going he is hard to catch. Dupuy can also go some. They gave us a merry chase on Thursday night and they'll not get away again if I can help it."[24]

With less than two hours left in the race, wherein the last series of sprints would resume, McNamara aggressively went after and won a fifty-dollar premium offered by a fan in a box seat. Then what McNamara feared would happen did happen. No sooner had McNamara won the sprint than Oscar Egg flashed down from high off the banked curve. The *New York Times* reported: "As all the riders had slowed up after the sprint, Egg was half a lap ahead before the others realized the peril that threatened them. Egg was bent far over his handle bars and his legs were working like two piston rods, in the greatest outburst of speed of the race. After he kept up the killing pace for a couple laps, his teammate, Dupuy, took up the whirl and increased the lead to three-quarters of a lap. Over the big arena, fast filling with spectators, spread a realization that the race bade fair to be settled right then, and the crowd started a riot of noise. Men and women stood on chairs and waved their arms wildly as the riders went pell-mell around in the frantic chase of the flying riders in the red and white jerseys."[25]

Oscar Egg and Marcel Dupuy won the overall race by a lap and brought down a huge payday. Madden and Root took second overall on points. McNamara and Spears split $2,000 for third place overall.

Egg, who from 1912 to 1922 went back and forth between the United States and Europe no less than ten times, answered the call of the Swiss Ministry for all reservists of the Swiss military. Egg left New York in February 1917, and when he returned nine months later, his wife, who had remained in New York, presented him with their one-month-old daughter, Ester. He was overjoyed.

Despite the war, Egg competed in a number of races in Europe. In Italy he won two road races and was on the verge of winning Milan–San Remo when he punctured a tire a half-mile from the finish. According to Egg, there was not much money for the riders in Europe because the bulk of the receipts went to the war effort. Egg's traveling partner, Bobby Walthour, had just recovered in a Paris hospital from a near-fatal skull fracture he received crashing on the cement track at Parc des Princes stadium. From the United States, Mrs. Walthour had sent message after unreturned message to find out her husband's condition. When he appeared at their Newark home, his wife "couldn't have been more surprised if a ghost had crossed the threshold."[26] Egg had trouble securing a passport, purportedly because the Swiss army was mobilized for border patrol. After weeks of delays, however, he was finally able to obtain passage.

The War Years

While Egg and Walthour were coming over from war-torn Europe, many riders in the United States, including McNamara, were training for Boston's six-day race, which was to begin on November 4, 1917. The day before the start, most of the riders were testing the newly built track inside the Boston Garden. McNamara had just paced the big Canadian Willie Spencer and went up to the top of the embankment with one foot out of the pedal for a rest. He got within a foot of the rail, which put him in impending danger of going over a twelve-foot drop to the cement floor below. He righted himself a bit too much, however, and fell in the opposite direction. McNamara went all the way down the steepest angle of the track. He fell fifteen feet before he struck his face against a post on the inside of the track.

He broke his jaw and his nose and fractured his skull. According to the *Newark Evening News*: "The impact knocked out several teeth and cut his face from his mouth to below his left ear. At no time was the rider unconscious and when placed on the operating table at the hospital he requested the doctors sew him up quickly, as he wished to rest before starting in the races that night."[27]

An old joke among the riders was that the best day of a six-day race was on the seventh day. For Bob Spears in Boston the seventh day may not have been the best, but he did get sweet revenge. During the final series of sprints at Boston, Spears and his partner, Willie Spencer, were victims of a four-team combination against them that eliminated any chances of victory. Spears and Spencer were considered the most dangerous team because they were both such good sprinters—probably the two best in the entire field. During one of the blatant combinations, which the referee was apparently ignoring, Jake Magin made the mistake of telling Spears he was "yellow." Spears bided his time but finally confronted Magin at the Colonial Hotel after the race—on the seventh day. When Magin refused to take back his words, Spears unleashed his fury on the poor fellow. The one-sided fight started in the mezzanine lobby, took a detour through the main dining room, and went right on through the kitchen. Every time Spears beat Magin to the ground, he helped him back up and smacked him down again. Both were arrested, but only Spears spent the night and most of the next day in jail.[28]

Spears was released from jail and helped McNamara back home to his wife and children in Newark. But before they got to McNamara's home, they spoke with sportswriters. Despite his jaw, smashed in three places, and a broken nose, among the more serious injuries he sustained in Boston, McNamara declared he was feeling great. Why not? Only his face was damaged. Nobody would be surprised if he worked out in his basement on the home trainer that evening. The only thing he complained about to the reporters was his difficulty eating because his jaw was wired shut.

In his condition, however, no amount of optimism was going to convince him to race in the big six-day race in New York; not even the Iron Man of cycling could heal that quickly. But with his face and head swathed in bandages, McNamara attended the Garden as an interested spectator, where he was mistaken for a soldier just back from the front. The team of Alf Goullet and Jake Magin won the 1917 race at Madison Square Garden, a great financial success for promoter William Wellman, who cleared more than $7,000 for himself. Immediately after Goullet was paid his share of the winning purse, he enlisted in the navy at a New York recruiting office. He signed up as a regular with the United States Aviation Corps, and in January 1918 he went to Pensacola, Florida, for training. Goullet's brother Ernest had been badly injured in the war and was back home in Australia. The cyclist, who was perhaps the greatest rider of all time, was determined. "I intend to work hard," he said, "and I feel certain that I will master the aircraft. I'd like to be in the flying squad that first sails over Berlin."[29]

The United States did not declare war on Germany until April 1917. Large numbers of American soldiers arrived at the western front in the summer of 1918 and played a vital role in the Allied victory, which followed on November 11.

Over the course of the war many inaccurate reports were generated about the status of professional cyclists who had competed at the Newark Velodrome and six-day races in America. In various newspaper accounts, for example, the Belgian brothers Marcel and Lucien Buysse, Belgian Cyrille Van Hauwaert, Frenchman Gabriel Poulain, and German Walter Rutt were all presumed dead. In fact, they all lived through the war, and most of them continued their cycling careers to some degree afterward. But many professional cyclists, fighting on their country's land and for their country's freedom, made the ultimate sacrifice. Among them were three Tour de France champions—François Faber, Octave Lapize, and Lucien Petit-Breton.

Faber, who won the 1909 edition of the Tour and competed in the New York six-day in 1908, was killed on May 9, 1915. He was mortally wounded, presumably after climbing out of a trench and running toward a hailstorm of German machine-gun fire, four days after he first received news of the birth of his daughter. His body was never recovered.[30]

Lapize won the 1910 Tour de France and raced at the Madison Square Garden six-day race in 1911. After training as a fighter pilot, Lapize went to the front in February 1917. About five months later, on Bastille Day, his plane was shot down by German aircraft. He survived the wreck but died two days later in a hospital.

Petit-Breton had back-to-back Tour victories in 1907 and 1908. Although he competed at the Madison Square Garden six-day races five times—in 1903, 1904, 1906, 1907, and 1913—he never placed any better than sixth. During the war Petit-Breton was assigned to ferry officers to the front in his automobile. On December 20, 1917, he crashed into a horse-drawn cart driven by a drunken butcher. He was ejected from his car and killed.

McNamara had brothers and sisters involved in the war too. Leo, one of his younger brothers, served as a gunner. His unit embarked from Sydney in October 1915 to Egypt. For his service he earned three Western Front Medals: the 1914–15 Star, British War Medal, and Victory Medal. His unit returned home on

April 13, 1919. Patrick McNamara enlisted in 1916 and served as a driver for the Fourth Battalion. Patrick returned home a week after Leo. Reggie's younger sisters Eileen and Kathleen both enlisted in October 1918 as nurses. They joined late, so neither saw any action nor experienced hostilities.

8

The Prodigal Son Returns

Seven years had gone by since McNamara was in Australia. Seeing his parents and siblings, whom he missed, was a great incentive to lure him back. But while the war raged and with most business profits stretched to the limit, promoting professional cycling in Australia was not a high priority. Because most Australian cycling celebrities, like McNamara, took shelter in the United States, it was even a thornier proposition to promote races—especially on a grand scale.

But after the war, in August 1919, plans were hatched for professional cycling to boom once again Down Under. Ernest J. Ohrt, who was managing the San Francisco Velodrome, proposed to have several riders from America go out and help revive Australian cycling. "No doubt Fred Keefe told you," Ohrt wrote to the *Sydney Referee*, "of the preliminary arrangements with Mr. George Dowsing to bring three teams with such star riders as McNamara, Corry, Spears, Willie Spencer, my brother Hans (who is the big star at the 'Frisco track) and myself as sixth man. Mr. Dowsing leaves here tomorrow in the *Ventura* for Sydney, and is willing to invest between three and five thousand dollars in the way of transportation, advertising and incidentals for the proposed Sydney and Melbourne six-day races. If he receives full cooperation from the League of NSW Wheelmen and an assurance that fifteen additional teams can be got together in Australia for the races."[1]

Once again, however, Sydney's main event, the six-day race,

was scheduled to take place at the same time as the December six-day race at Madison Square Garden in New York City, forcing riders to choose one over the other. In McNamara's case there was only one logical choice.

A year earlier the Garden six-day had begun just three weeks after the cease-fire was declared, so it was a time of great celebration in New York and all over the world. During the war the outside of the Garden was kept "in a gloom of Fuel Administration darkness," but now it was lit up like a Christmas tree. Throughout the December 1918 six-day race, management allowed convalescing soldiers and sailors in for free. Anytime a new group arrived in uniform with crutches, bandages, and slings, they were given a rousing ovation.

Among the fifteen teams to start, Bob Spears was to partner up with Alf Grenda, but Spears got the Spanish flu, so Freddie Hill was substituted in his place. McNamara teamed up with Jake Magin, who, with Alf Goullet, had won the previous year while Reggie's broken jaw was healing. Frank Kramer wanted to give six-day racing one more try, and he teamed up with a talented French sprinter, Marcel Dupuy. Promoter Jimmy Johnson took out a two-week $100,000 blanket policy that protected the riders against injury or death. After McNamara's experience in Boston the year before, he refused to race without insurance protection. Between loss of potential prize money and hospital bills, McNamara's losses may have exceeded $5,000.[2]

In their light-blue jerseys McNamara and Magin had a great start and monopolized the twice-daily sprint points. During the sprints Kramer complained that he was being pocketed and threatened to quit the race unless referee Richard Kelsey called for interference. But the pocketing continued, and the crowd, typically strong supporters of McNamara, began to boo and hiss him, and Kramer, as the underdog, became the newest fan favorite.

From early in the race McNamara and Magin stacked up sprint points, making it clear that they would need to be lapped if they were going to lose the overall victory. On day 2 Kramer

The Prodigal Son Returns

set out to do just that. The old warhorse showed that he still had endurance in his legs, and nobody could question his sprint. His chrome-plated frame glistened from the electric lights above as he started a jam, and the crowd came to their feet. The field was after him, but he had caught them napping, and before anyone knew it, he was a half-lap in the lead. Dupuy came out in relief of Kramer, and he gained more ground. At just the minute he was going to catch the riders at the rear of the pack, there came a loud report from the tire of Willie Hanley, the same man who had been in a fistfight with McNamara. According to the rules, any lap gained during an accident or equipment failure would be nullified, so the Kramer-Dupuy effort went for naught.

The next day, just as the night series of sprint points were completed, there was a jam that lasted nearly thirty minutes. When the smoke cleared, six teams had been lapped, including the Kramer-Dupuy team. Kramer quit the track and announced that he had had enough. Dupuy fumed at Kramer's lack of moxie, as he was given the standard four hours to find a new partner. "What's ze use, ride two, three days and out he go."[3]

Of the eight teams tied for the lead on laps, McNamara and Magin continued to rack up sprint points and held a comfortable edge. Magin strongly denied rumors suggesting they were working in "combination" with other teams. "Just figure it out yourself," Magin said from the cramped and smelly confines of their bunker at the side of the track, "why should McNamara and I go in combination? We have been riding strong all week. Why should I give up any of my prize money away? It is hard enough to get it, let alone split it with anyone."[4]

Lines wrapped around the building with people hoping to buy tickets to the final series of sprints. Many were turned away at the gate. The *New York Times* reported from inside: "Over the noisy multitude hung a smoky screen which looked as if it had lately been imported from the western front. The few whiffs of fresh air which managed in through the cracks immediately frightened and blew out again."[5]

As Alf Goullet, winner of the 1913, 1914, and 1917 New York

grinds, made his way through the crowd, many spectators recognized him and shook his hand and slapped him on the back. Goullet was all smiles amid the packed house. He had only four months remaining to serve out his first lieutenant's commission. With the riders lined up and ready to go for the first of the fifteen-lap (one-and-a-half-mile) sprints, Goullet stepped up to the starter's podium. There was a brief moment of hesitation while the whole of the Garden held its breath. Goullet's pistol cracked, and the trainers shoved their riders forward. The massive Garden crowd went berserk as the colorfully clad riders went round and round the yellow pine bowl.

McNamara and Magin clinched their overall victory by winning the first, second, third, fourth, eighth, tenth, fifteenth, and twentieth sets of sprints. It marked McNamara's first six-day victory at the Garden, but there were plenty more to come. During the 142 hours they covered 2,447 miles and rang up 1,197 points, compared with the second-place team of Frank Corry and Eddie Madden, with 912 points, followed by the distant third-place finish of Alf Grenda and Freddie Hill, with 581.

The next day the riders gathered at 152 Market Street, the offices of the Cycle Race Association, where they were paid. McNamara and Magin received their bonus cash and split their $3,000 first-prize money. The pair also signed a six-week agreement for easy money to appear at various theaters around town to ride onstage on the training rollers.

The following spring during the 1919 outdoor season, attendance records were broken at the Newark Velodrome. Unless the weather was bad, no less than fifteen thousand fans paid their way through the turnstiles. By all accounts McNamara enjoyed a very good outdoor season. He took third place in the "all-around" competition to eventual winner Goullet, who came back from military service as if he had never gone away. McNamara had many great victories, including one with Alf Goullet in a team race. He was rarely paired with Goullet, but together they took home $150 each by winning a 100-kilometer race (roughly 62 miles) in front of a sellout Labor Day crowd.

No race was ever closer than when McNamara won another race in July "by a distended nostril."

Whereas the all-around competition tested a variety of skill from speed, stamina, and strength, the people paid to see the "heavyweights" of cycling—the pure sprinters. At thirty-eight Frank Kramer was getting old. Many eager young riders—including Bob Spears, the Spencer brothers from Canada, and Jay Eaton's son Ray—wanted to replace him on the throne that he had held for nearly two decades.

Willie and Art Spencer were big kids from Toronto with a lot of raw talent. In late May Willie had lost the first heat in a best-of-three-heat race. In the second heat Willie appeared to be a sure winner until he looked over his shoulder to see Kramer gaining rapidly. Rather than taking a straight line to the finish, Spencer veered left and "inserted a switch so wicked Kramer could not avoid it."[6] Both were sent flying and Kramer, although badly cut up and bruised, was able to get up and walk around. Spencer was fined $100, was suspended for two weeks, and received a large splinter in his back.

Only a few days later Kramer, bandaged heavily from the previous accident, lined up to race against Willie's brother, Art, in a semifinal of a quarter-mile championship race. The gun fired, and Spencer went just a few feet and stopped. He claimed his foot strap had broken. Referee Caufield refused to run the race over and gave the signal for Kramer to finish. As Kramer circled around toward Spencer, Spencer grabbed Kramer's bike and, in a rage, brutally threw the aging champion to the track. Kramer's head hit heavily, and he was knocked unconscious for fifteen minutes. Even those closest to Art, including Willie and their trainer, Fred Bullivant, were shocked by Art's actions. He was arrested at the Velodrome, placed under a $500 bail, and pleaded guilty to disorderly conduct.

Kramer refused to press charges against Art and was back to training on the bike and working at his favorite pastime, golf, within a week. In July, Art Spencer was allowed back to race at the Newark Velodrome. The crowd gave him an icy reception.

But when he and Kramer shook hands, it seemed to everyone that all was forgiven.

Yet Kramer, or "Big Steve" as he was nicknamed, had more bad luck. In August he fractured a rib from a crash up north at the Providence track. He did not realize he was injured until days later, when he took a hefty swing at a golf ball and dropped to his knees in pain.[7] Because of the rib, he was forced to cancel several races, including some against the eventual winner of the 1919 national sprint championship, Ray Eaton.

With the outdoor season ending, it was time, once again, for McNamara to prepare for the six-day season. He had heard from Ernest Ohrt about the racing revival in Australia. On one hand, he wanted to go, especially to see his family. But on the other hand, he was reigning champion of the greatest bicycle race in the United States, if not the world—the New York six-day. He and Magin would be paired up again.

McNamara made a deal. He would go under the condition that he would not race in the Sydney six-day race but would compete in other races. The conditions were met, and McNamara and his old buddy Bob Spears left New York for Australia right after the six-day race at Madison Square Garden.

With Prohibition going into law on January 1, 1920, people all over the United States went looking for an excuse to drink legally while they could. In New York City a perfect place to imbibe was the six-day race, which began on December 1, 1919. Madison Square Garden reached a critical point of ten thousand spectators; fire marshals and police worked together to keep the place from being dangerously overcrowded.

By Thursday, day 4, twenty-five thousand people tried to get inside the Garden. The *New York Times* reported: "What was probably the greatest crowd that ever tried to see or fight its way into a six-day race stormed Madison Square Garden last night and made it necessary to call out the police reserves of two stations to maintain order among the thousands who clamored for admission for hours after the doors had been closed by order of the Fire Department. Promoters of the race could not remember when there has been such a crush."[8] One spectator climbed up a steel girder and made his way onto a beam, where he had a spectacular view of the track directly below him. He defied all attempts by the police to bring him down and remained on his lofty perch until the end of the race, when, presumably, he was arrested.

Paired together were Alf Goullet and Eddie Madden, who stacked up sprint points from beginning to end, much like McNamara and Magin had done the previous year. The best team since 1913 had been Goullet and anyone else, and this year proved no different.

Twelve thousand people were packed into the stands like sardines on the final day. Eight teams were tied at 2,501 miles and one lap going into the final series of sprints. Goullet and Madden did not have to work very hard because of the great lead they had established. The two teams riding for second-place honors were McNamara-Magin and Marcel Dupuy with Oscar Egg. In what may have made up somewhat for the pairing of him and Kramer the year before, Dupuy got a gamer in Egg. Egg was the current unpaced hour record holder, and he was riding into form. He dominated the sprints, and Egg-Dupuy took second place overall by a slim margin.

More than $100,000 in revenue was generated for the race. With expenses estimated at $65,000, the promoters made a fabulous profit. Of the $25,000 share of prize money and bonuses, Goullet pulled down $4,000. McNamara received $1,500 for his share of the third-place prize money.

McNamara said his good-byes to his wife and little daughters before his journey back to Australia. Eileen was now five and Regina two. Why the entire family did not go along for the journey is not known. But the last time they were separated by an ocean, a great war had broken out. Although he had earned what in today's money would be $25,000 at the New York six-day, perhaps they were trying to save money and had debts to pay off.

He did have a traveling companion, however—Bob Spears. They took a train to San Francisco and boarded the ss *Ventura*.

They possibly spent Christmas Day in Hawaii. McNamara and Spears were not among the first-class passengers to arrive in Sydney on January 6, but it probably did not stop them from having as good a trip as they did when they came to America six years earlier. When Spears and McNamara walked down the gangplank of the *Ventura*, each made a beeline to their respective homes. So much had happened over the years Reggie was gone. Surely it was a joyful reunion with his parents and brothers and sisters.

A group of cyclists had arrived from America one month before McNamara and Spears, including Alf Grenda, Frank Corry, the Ohrt brothers (Hans and Ernest), Willie Spencer, and Charles Osteritter, the former amateur American cycling champion. Leading up to the eight-hour-per-day six-day race that was to begin on December 30 at the Sydney Sports Ground, there was much racing. On a typical afternoon in Sydney, it was not unlike a Newark Velodrome crowd with fifteen thousand people present. Although the stadium could hold many more, the races were successful.

When the mayor of Sydney fired the gun to start the six-day race, it began to rain and didn't let up for three days. But by day 4 the sun stayed out for the remainder of the race, which was won by the team of Spencer and Osteritter. The *Referee* claimed that Spencer's sprint in front of a mob of thirty thousand fans for the overall victory "was one of the finest sprints Australia cycling enthusiasts have seen since the visit of Major Taylor. Spencer outclassed the opposition to win very decisively by half a dozen lengths."[9]

Just as the six-day race was ending, the *Ventura* arrived at dock in Sydney. Bob Spears, in a newspaper article he wrote seventeen years later, remembered McNamara was sick.[10] There were also reports that McNamara looked gaunt.

Both Spears and McNamara had a few weeks to prepare before another series of races at the Sydney Sports Ground took place. Spears won the coveted "Sydney Plate" against a terrific field that included Corry, Grenda, Hans Ohrt, McNa-

The Prodigal Son Returns

mara, and Spencer. The next week promoters set up a special match race between Grenda and McNamara. McNamara won in straight heats.

But McNamara was unable to race again in Australia because of a disastrous health problem. If the following newspaper account is true, it must have been a sudden appendicitis attack—possibly during a long training ride shortly after the race against Grenda: "They found the body on the roadside eventually, and much to everyone's amazement the 'corpse' started to breathe. Not only breathe, but it gave instructions. Reggie was emphatic that they get him to the hospital immediately. 'Can't,'" his rescuers replied. 'The nearest one is fifty miles away.' 'Take me there,' demanded Reggie. 'Don't let the amateurs chop me up.'"[11]

They got him there as quickly as they were able, and McNamara had emergency surgery at St. Vincent's Hospital, just south of Sydney. After the operation the doctors were in awe at how McNamara had been able to race at cycling's highest level with an intestinal "growth" that had spread to the point where it would have incapacitated most other people. The doctors advised McNamara never to ride again.[12] Whether this was cancerous would be difficult to say, but McNamara would be stricken by stomach problems for years to come. After about two weeks he was released from St. Vincent's. He went back to the family farm, where he recuperated for another four weeks before steaming back to America, again aboard the *Ventura*.

Bob Spears did not go back to the United States with McNamara. Rather, he left for France with Hans Ohrt, Ernest Ohrt, and Ernest's wife, Florence. Because Spears had been racing so well during his short stay in his home country, he was convinced that he should take a shot at a world title. The world champion sprint title was last earned by Walter Rutt in 1913. The host city for the 1920 world championship was to be Antwerp, Belgium.

Right before their departure, Ernest Ohrt was interviewed. He had nothing but kind things to say about Australia and how he, his wife, and brother were treated there. But he did make some surprising comments. Ohrt said he would like to come back to Australia "and reorganize the game, which is twenty years behind the times and run in a very lax manner. Those running the show are no doubt good business men and give the riders fair treatment, and make good on all obligations, but they lack entirely any showmanship or entertaining ability. They go on week after week, their show as flat as can be, and never attempt to introduce a novelty. They go on running cycling meetings like laying endless lines of railroad tracks; the same thing all the time."[13]

Not surprisingly, Theo O'Halloran, the secretary of Carnivals LTD, the organization that had promoted the recent cycling events, did not take kindly to Ohrt's remarks. "Having gone to some pains to state that he does not want to knock Australia," O'Halloran wrote, "he forthwith proceeds to knock the company which was the means of providing him with the finest honeymoon trip he ever dreamt of, and also placed him in a position of earning more money than he ever got out of the bike game in his life. . . . We are pleased to know that Ernest Ohrt is coming back as a manager, not as a rider. His remark that all is wanted is that the sport should be run in a clean manner, comes well from one who was fined more times than any other rider during the season that just ended. And so he is coming back to put the bike game on the high plane as it is in America and Europe? Who put the bike game on the high plane in America? Was it Ernest Ohrt? Or was it Jackie Clark, Ernie Pye, Alf Goullet, Paddy Hehir, Alf Grenda, Reg McNamara, Bob Spears and a host of other Australians who have been the big draw-cards on the American tracks?"[14]

To accommodate larger football crowds, the track at the Sydney Cricket Ground was torn down shortly after the season ended. The track had been there for twenty-four years—since about the time Zimmerman had first visited Australia. It was the sign of the times for cycling in Australia. Although all sides, from Ohrt to O'Halloran, wanted to see professional cycling prosper in Australia, it remained a breeding ground for America promoters.

Not only did Spears win the 1920 world title in Antwerp, but he was also victorious in the coveted Grand Prix of Paris. McNamara arrived back in America and completely ignored the doctor's advice; he was racing at the Newark Velodrome in April 1920. McNamara also made a further commitment to the United States and became an American citizen.[15]

9

Training Old School

Legendary coaches such as Vince Lombardi and Bobby Knight would have agreed that success comes not from the will to win but, rather, the will to prepare. No matter the sport, preparation takes effort; it takes time and requires adaptability. It necessitates acquiring knowledge; it requires sacrifice and responsibility. Perhaps above it all, it involves a passion and a love for the game. Today's cyclists have an arsenal of resources at their disposal to prepare for the rigors of competition. There are books and websites dedicated to nutrition, strength conditioning, stretching, cross-training, performance peaking, and so on. There are cyclometers, heart rate monitors, and power meters. Much knowledge can be gained about speed drills, distances, watts, thresholds, ratios, percentages, and averages. Wading through it can be quite a task. To sort it all out, today's professional cyclists have teams of experts whom they can trust.

Compared to today, professional riders such as McNamara had to rely on unscientific methods. Although there did not exist the amount of information available today, trainers and professional riders knew the fine line between being overtrained and being underconditioned. They knew that proper rest and nutritious foods were vital. They knew that taking "dope," drinking, and smoking were not good for them over the long haul. But having this knowledge, just as today's athletes do, they sometimes strayed from what they knew was right.

One of the earliest aerobic-oriented coaches in the United

States was Tom Eck. Eck, originally from Canada, trained cyclists such as Jack Prince, a top professional rider from the high-wheel bicycle era. Eck also trained Jimmy Michael and Bobby Walthour, two of the best motor-pace riders of their generation. In 1915, after more than two decades involved with cycling, Eck switched to coaching at the University of Chicago, where he trained athletes such as famed long-distance American runner Joie Ray, who in 1925 set the indoor mile record at four minutes, twelve seconds.

Tall and lean, with a droopy white mustache, Eck was one of the first to reject the ancient English tradition of training. He had read all the old books. The English method taught that waking up very early in the morning was important. Drinking a glass of sherry with an egg in it followed by a three-mile walk was also part of the English technique. Eck had tried these methods himself and got headaches from the sherry, and he thought the walk was too long on a virtually empty stomach. The English tradition held that no vegetable was good—they made you soft. "I thought I would try some vegetables with my meals," said Eck, "and I added potatoes, corn, cabbage, turnips, carrots, cauliflower, onions and any vegetables I liked or those that agreed with me. I began to find out that I perspired more freely; my skin was taking on a better glow and color. I cut out the old ale and other stimulants."[1] Eck also embraced fruit as well as meat but only in small portions.

Although Theresa Passione was the youngest of McNamara's four grandchildren, she remembers that her grandfather loved steak. That must have been so especially during six-day races, when there was food aplenty and it was on the management's dime. McNamara did not likely heed Eck's notion of eating meat in small portions. The *Brooklyn Daily Eagle* once reported that after waking up after a few hours of shut-eye, McNamara's first words were "Bring me a steak." Nor was McNamara too picky about it either. Jimmy Moran once ordered a steak and raised an awful howl because a vein ran through it. He refused to eat it. A little while later Joe Fogler came in, and he was given the same steak Moran had refused. Fogler inspected it and smiled, shoving his plate away as if they were kidding him. The steak was put in the steamer to keep warm. A few hours later, in strolled McNamara, and he ate it. Jack Neville asked him whether he enjoyed his meal, and McNamara replied that is was "the best steak I ever ate in my life."[2]

To feed the riders and staff for a six-day race required several truckloads of provisions. A typical grocery list included 250 chickens, 500 lamb chops, 200 sirloin steaks, 200 dozen eggs, 3 barrels of spinach, 50 cans of asparagus, 50 cans of peas, 2 barrels of lettuce, 200 bunches of celery, 2 barrels of apples, 50 pounds of prunes, 200 gallons of milk, and 25 pounds of coffee. As part of their head trainer duties, Jack Neville and Charley Stein were in charge of inspecting the food as it arrived.

They also made their typical run on local drugstores. Willie Ratner of the *Newark Evening News* copied one drugstore shopping list: "Alkaline tablets, oil of wintergreen, zinc ointment, bunion pads, a gallon of arnica, ten gallons of witch hazel, one gross kidney plasters, two boxes of mustard plasters, two boxes of joint ease, five pints of bay rum, five pints of Florida water, thirty cakes of soap, one pint of aromatic spirits of ammonia, sixty eye cups, five quarts of eye wash, twelve hospital size rolls of adhesive tape (1,000 yards), 250 square yards of assorted bandages, six pounds of Vaseline, three pints of mercurochrome, thirty face sponges, three ounces of Squib's mixture, one dozen bottles of magnesia, ten pounds of cotton, one quart of peroxide, fifteen pounds of Unguentine, one case of vichy water, two dozen bottles of pluto water, six ice bags, lanoline, dyspepsia tablets, collodion, tarrants, ten gallons of alcohol, pint of camphorated oil, glazed cotton, coconut oil, cocoa butter, twenty gallons of olive oil for food and rubbing, bicarbonate of soda, gallon of vinegar, ten pounds of rock salt, Noxema, two gallons of ether to wash bandages and grease spots off riders, glycothymotine, colorless iodine petrogen, colet [cloth?] for rubbing, two thermos bottles to a man, a dozen nose atomizers, 200 tongue blades for applying ointment on bandages, a dozen pair of medical shears, half a dozen tweezers, needles and thread for stitching wounds and thirty combs."

Reviewing the extensive list, Ratner asked Neville, "What's the white iodine for?"

"White iodine," he answered, "Ha ha. That's the greatest cover up in the world. There's nothing like iodine for bad knees. You know bad knees put more riders out of a race than anything else. Regular iodine is brown and if we painted a rider's knees with that the rest of them would see it and know they had gone wrong in the knees. And they would immediately give him 'the works.' They'd hand it to him so hard they'd put him out of the race before the iodine had a chance to take effect. But the white iodine you can't see anything. Get me?"[3]

Eck also thought massage was very important. He claimed to have started the practice in 1883, when "a rubbing board in a dressing room was unknown. I erected the first one in use at Lynn, Massachusetts, when Jack Prince was champion of America, and I was the first to massage an athlete after his work." Neville and Stein thought they had perfected massage with olive oil, a practice that had been handed down by Eck.

Neville seemed to get the best out of each and every rider, and doctors marveled at what they could do. For road rash (or track rash) they had a special therapy. "Drop in some day and you'll enjoy watching us give some of these birds a bath," offered Neville. "Imagine a boy with raw spots all over him getting a bath of hot water with the rock salt and bicarbonate of soda! Just think of that! They holler and kick a little, but we hold them in. And three of us rub him good and hard. That softens the muscles, takes out soreness and puts pep into them again."

Eck thought that because all athletes are different, there was not one system of training that could be applied to all athletes. He encouraged each person to study themselves and formulate individual methods suited to them. In short, relative to the times, Eck was a modern thinker.

Most riders were unable to afford a full-time trainer. But two of the best and wealthiest bike racers in the game, Alf Goullet and Frank Kramer, could afford the best training money had to offer. Neville took care of Kramer for nearly fifteen years until their well-publicized breakup, when he switched to Goullet in 1915. Upon hearing the news that Goullet had "stolen" Neville from him, Kramer hired Goullet's trainer, Maury Gordon.

Neville could get quite excited when defending his clientele. On one occasion at the Newark Velodrome, in a close race that was called a dead heat between the big Italian sprinter Orlando Piani and one of his riders, Willie Spencer, Neville ran up to the officials in disbelief. "And to strengthen his complaint," reported the *Newark Evening News*, "Neville rushed back to the trackside and brought Piani, hand in hand like a lost child." Despite the fact that he and Spencer had already shaken hands after the dead-heat decision and to keep Neville happy, Piani good-naturedly agreed to have the race rerun. But the referee stuck to his decision. After ten more minutes of arguing, Goullet had to come out and take Neville away from the scene, "and from then on everything was quiet—except Neville."[4]

The typical professional bike rider would hire a trainer for two to four weeks to help prepare for the outdoor season in the early spring. The same would occur in the fall as preparation for the indoor six-day season. A week or so before and during six-day races, one trainer helped a large delegation of riders. Dave Coburn, for example, often trained all the European riders who came to race at the Madison Square Garden six-day.

If McNamara had a trainer working with him throughout the course of his career, or even a large part of it, it remains unknown. McNamara did, however, solicit the tutelage from trainers such as Neville for at least a short period. The two went to Europe together in 1925. McNamara was known as one of the best in home trainer "roller" competitions of the day, so there can be no doubt that he owned a set of rollers himself. Most likely, it was down in the basement of his Newark, New Jersey, home. Sometimes he traveled to warmer climates, such as Miami, to train in the off-season. On at least one occasion he joined the Newark Velodrome Trainers' Association on a trip to Staten Island. Late in his career it was noted that McNamara did not like to train outside of competition. This in fact may have been true because by the 1930s six-day races in the United States were not isolated to just Boston, Chicago, and New York in the winter. They were held all over North America nearly year round, including Cleveland, Detroit, Kansas City, Los Angeles, Milwaukee, Minneapolis, Montreal, Philadelphia, Pittsburgh, San Francisco, and Toronto. Europe was no different. Besides Berlin, Brussels, and Paris, there was Amsterdam, Breslau, London, Marseille, and Stuttgart. McNamara put in an enormous number of miles during this period—mostly in competition. In a six-day race each competitor rode at least 1,200 miles, and McNamara rode in about 120 of them. By easy math he rode more than 150,000 competitive miles, and half of these miles he rode from 1928 to 1935. Although it never hampered the longevity of his career, perhaps McNamara's worst decision was to race and train his way out of injury, which he did time and time again.

In February 1915 Jackie Clark hired Fred Bullivant to prepare him for the outdoor season for another shot at the American sprint title. The year before, Clark had started out the outdoor season well. He led Goullet, Kramer, and Walter Rutt in the sprinter's points table for the national title. But in the latter half of the season he began to falter and rode inconsistently. The *Newark Evening News* claimed Clark's poor showing was due to "sickness and a laxity of training."[5] By bringing on Bullivant, Clark expected to turn things around.

Clark was short in stature and had a tendency to put on unwanted pounds. Bullivant put him to work. In a room "heated to suffocation" Clark put on several heavy sweaters and rode a home trainer twice a day, one hour at a time. Perspiration fell to the floor in great beads, and a big puddle had to be mopped up at the end of each hourly session. Bullivant had him skip rope, counting to three thousand. Clark ran out on the roads, and he wrestled and boxed with Bullivant and two other heavyweights at a local gym.

In 1922 the *World* published an account of Vincent Markey, who had only three weeks left to keep fit for the upcoming six-day race. Markey and Joe Kopsky signed up as partners for the December race at Madison Square Garden. With the weather too cold to train outside on the roads, he needed a home trainer with which to ride indoors. Markey went to a sporting goods store in Newark and tried to finagle a lower price. Once the salesman realized Markey was never going to afford the machine, he made him another offer. Markey could use the one in the store as much as he wanted as long as he rode it in the store window. After his training was done and the six-day race was over, the salesman let him have it for free. He rode himself "blue in the face while thousands blocked traffic as they tried to crowd toward the window to see Markey do his spinning."[6]

Unfortunately, and not surprisingly, Markey had overtrained. "Why he was nothing but skin and bones," said Joe Fogler after Markey quit before the first twenty-four hours. "He rode in a little hot window while training and he didn't have anything left."

With their fixed-gear bikes modified to ride hills, many riders would take to the roads to train in the fresh air. But even back then, cyclists had to be cautious around vehicles and traffic. In 1917 Alf Goullet was hit by a car coming around a corner at high speed.[7] Although he wasn't seriously injured, it served as a warning to those training on the open roads.

McNamara likely endured the same type of workouts that Clark, Goullet, or any of his contemporaries did—hiking, running, riding on the roads, riding on the rollers, jumping rope, boxing, or even throwing a medicine ball back and forth to a partner while riding. He certainly never stooped to the desperation of Markey. Although not much is known exactly what McNamara did for workouts, whatever he did, it worked for decades. In the latter part of his career, an article from the *New Yorker* claimed that whether McNamara worked out by taking long walks with the family Scottish terrier or if he rode for many hours on the bike, he always made sure to get eleven hours of sleep at night.[8] In the winter of 1926 Goullet was trying to extend his career into his midthirties, but he knew he was done when he couldn't keep up with McNamara's road workouts. It was then that Goullet knew it was time to hang up the racing shoes.[9]

McNamara liked to help younger riders when he could with advice on training and racing. He even helped a fellow Aussie, Harris Horder, without knowing it. "I learned from watching Reggie McNamara," said Horder. "There's a lot of little things that you've got to know and take advantage of—and Mac knows them all. The idea is to ride into your bicycle, down in your handle bars. But keep your chest expanded all the time. . . . Oh there are dozens of things, little things, but mighty important things you pick up from a master like McNamara."[10]

Long before McNamara turned professional, performance-enhancing drugs were used in cycling. They were legal but frowned upon. Unlike today, at least in the infamous case of Lance Armstrong, drugs were not used as part of the training process to build up and peak for a grueling event such as the Tour de France. Most whispers about drugs were during six-day races, when they were used to keep the riders awake and to keep them going.

On December 15, 1900, the sports page headline for the *New York Herald* read: "Drugs a Factor in Six Day Contest." It was the fifth day of the race, and supposedly all eight remaining teams took pills made of one or a combination of strychnine, digitalis, cocaine, arsenic, and nitroglycerin. "No trainer would admit that he was using drugs on the men in his charge," reported the *New York Herald*, "though each trainer was emphatic that all the contestants, excepting those he was concerned in, were kept on the track by the liberal use of the pill."[11]

In the race one rider generally not considered to be taking "dope"—and it was called dope in those days too—was Harry Elkes. But the same could not be said about his partner, Floyd MacFarland, who was having great difficulty just standing when he wasn't on the bike. Apparently, MacFarland's condition was justly improved on day 5 by the use of "the little white pill." In front of fifteen thousand spectators, who together made the girders of Madison Square Garden shake, the team of Elkes and MacFarland won.

The next year's six-day race at the Garden, in December 1901, was won by the team of Bobby Walthour and Canadian Archie McEachern. French cycling promoter and editor of *Le Vélo*, Victor Breyer, who had made the trip to New York with the other Europeans, claimed that for trainers to administer drugs on day 2 was "nonsense" but suggested that by day 5 it would be the norm. But at the end of the race Walthour denied the rumors. "McEachern and myself took no drugs," he said, "all reports to the contrary notwithstanding. Coffee was our strongest stimulant."[12]

Among the regulars at six-day races in the Garden were Christy Mathewson, among the first five inductees into the Baseball Hall of Fame, baseball giant Babe Ruth, and New York Giants coach John McGraw. In an article for the *New York Times* Mathewson marveled at how Frank Kramer, at thirty-nine years of age, could still compete in cycling at such an exceptional level. Mathewson, Kramer, McGraw, and others had been out to the Polo Grounds together to look at the possibilities of installing a cycling track inside the grounds. One of the participants at the roundtable discussion was Arthur Irwin, who spoke up: "I remember how the trainers threw pills at the riders for the last lap. They were dynamited with dope. Remember that, Frank?" Perhaps not wishing to elaborate on the subject, Kramer simply replied, "Yes."[13]

Kramer had not forgotten about drug use in cycling from years earlier, and apparently it had continued. Alf Goullet claimed that his perfect six-day partner was fellow Aussie Alf Grenda. While Goullet was high-strung, Grenda didn't seem to care about anything—as long as he got his share of food. In January 1915, just a few weeks after Goullet and Grenda won the six-day together at Madison Square Garden, Goullet hired Jack Neville away from Kramer. In 1893, long before Kramer and

Goullet, Neville had first trained his brother, Speck, a famous road rider of the time. According to Goullet, Neville's favorite motto was "Keep 'em clean and healthy."[14]

Considering one of Neville's first training recommendations for Goullet, no more persuasive argument can be made for the motto. In early March 1915, in preparation for the outdoor season, Neville traveled with Goullet and Grenda to West Baden Springs, Indiana. Waiting for them at West Baden were the "miracle" mineral waters in which they would rest, relax, and rejuvenate.

The *Newark Evening News* reported on the supposed more sinister nature of their visit to West Baden: "Goullet may not be as good as he was last season and his chances may go a-kiting also. He competed in three six-day races last winter. These long grinds affect riders in various ways. Six-day races have improved riders, but they also have put riders out of commission for the outdoor season. But Goullet, with his usual thoughtfulness, took the precautionary measure of going to West Baden Springs to boil out and rid himself of the six-day 'candy' that has proved disastrous to the hopes of many a rider. In six-day races the riders—all of them—take strong stimulants in the form of strychnine, digitalis, nitroglycerin, and other drugs and, unless this 'ammunition' is removed from their systems before the start of the outdoor season, their riding is likely to be bad."[15]

In 1921 an attempt was made to create an ordinance by which there would be "better" enforcement against the "unlawful use of drugs" at six-day races in Madison Square Garden. John Chapman, the promoter of the races at the time, flatly denied any use of drugs during six-day races. According to the ordinance, any promoter "consenting to, allowing or permitting" drugs in a bike race was subject to fines and imprisonment.[16]

Willie Spencer, who had become a cycling promoter after his retirement from professional racing, used kerosene—but quite by accident. According to the *Newark Evening News*, Spencer was known as the "kerosene fiend."[17] One can only speculate about Spencer's use of kerosene, but he may have used it on his skin as an antiseptic for cuts and scrapes. The newspaper may have made mention of it because of its offensive odor. But five days after the "fiend" comment, it was reported that Spencer "drank copiously from a mug containing kerosene that was mistaken for water and the unfortunate victim was so busy icing his esophagus and other innards the rest of the evening, he had no time for racing."[18]

In 1927 Howard Freeman of the *Newark Evening News* drew a sketch of a thin Jack Neville with hand in pockets and a long cigarette stuck in his mouth. An accompanying article featured Charlie Winter, a young rising star from the Bronx. Freeman's Neville sketch had a balloon quotation comparing Winter to Reggie McNamara. "If that boy isn't a second McNamara," Neville purportedly said, "I don't know my digitalis."[19]

In a videotaped interview of an aging Sammy Gastman, a six-day rider and motor-paced specialist from the 1920s, he claimed that Piet Van Kempen and all the Belgians used to drink a concoction made of Coca-Cola, Cognac, sugar, and ether: "You could smell [ether] all over the place, oh sure." Gastman said that Van Kempen kept ten bottles in his tent—all different colors.[20]

Not much was known about McNamara's drug use. In 1967 René de Latour wrote an article for *Sporting Cyclist* in which he claimed that during a six-day race in Paris at Vélodrome d'Hiver, McNamara had numerous pills contained in unmarked vials. De Latour said it was "useless to ask Mac what they were. But I guess Mac knew what he was doing."[21] Although it would be impossible to prove one way or another whether McNamara ever used drugs to enhance his six-day performances, it was a likely scenario. Given the longevity of his career and the long life he lived, if he did take them, they must not have taken too much of a toll on his body and mind.

Tobacco smoke at indoor six-day races in Chicago, New York, Paris, and elsewhere penetrated the riders clothing and lungs. Rather than fight it, McNamara chose to join the smokers. Several reports indicate that McNamara enjoyed a good cigar. Given his longevity in a competitive aerobic sport, it is likely he only smoked them occasionally. Although a good nicotine buzz could be had from chewing at the end of a cigar, the smoke was not deeply inhaled into the lungs like with cigarettes.

One drug that McNamara did abuse, however, was alcohol. McNamara only drank beer, but he consumed a lot of it. The earliest he admitted to having a problem with alcohol, which he deeply regretted because it would be the last time he saw his parents, was on his trip back home to Australia in 1930. "I was drunk the whole way over on the boat," he said. "They even threw me in jail in Dubbo for creating a public disturbance."[22] After his trip to Australia, his addiction to alcohol only got worse. Any lack of natural cycling talent McNamara may have had, he more than made up for with his gift of will.

10

Let the Roaring Twenties Begin

In January 1920, while Reggie McNamara and Bob Spears were off to Australia on a steamship, the Roaring Twenties and a great era of prosperity began. Although John Chapman could not have predicted how professional cycling would flourish in America, he did notice the demand for ticket sales—especially at Madison Square Garden six-day races—was going up. Chapman thought, "Why just December?"

The idea of two New York six-day races in one year was a novel one. Chapman and his fellow promoter Charles Hanson put a plan in motion for the first ever spring six-day at the Garden. They enticed riders with the highest prize money yet offered—$50,000. Had McNamara not been recovering from appendicitis surgery back home in Australia, surely he would have loved to compete.

The governor of New Jersey, Edward Irving Edwards, fired the starting gun on March 8, 1920, and the band struck up the strains of the Prohibition anthem "How Dry I Am." The first night was not a sellout. But by the end it was very successful, much like the typical race held in December—stuffed to capacity. New York loved its cycling, and New Yorkers loved to boo the foremost oddsmaker favorite, Alf Goullet.

Days before Goullet and his partner, Jake Magin, sealed their overall victory, a cordon of police stretched around the outside of the building to fend off a crush of people trying to get inside. Goullet-Magin rode 2,379 miles and two laps and dominated the points, with 1,238. Freddie Hill and Harry Kaiser were second, with the same mileage and 573 points. The week of racing was a phenomenal financial achievement for Chapman and Hanson: total gross receipts came to $118,000. Goullet and Magin split the first-place prize money of $5,000 plus expenses, special bonus money, and premiums (or "premes") donated by fans.[1]

McNamara also missed an exciting opening day at the Newark Velodrome, which was another strong indicator that professional cycling in America was not going away anytime soon. On Sunday, March 28, 1920, a record crowd of more than twenty thousand people that included Newark mayor Charles P. Gillen, cheered on the old, Frank Kramer, and the young, Bobby Walthour Jr., to great victories. Kramer, starting in his twenty-first year as a professional, won a special one-mile invitation race over five riders, including Art Spencer. As the son of one of the greatest cyclists of all time, seventeen-year-old Walthour tried to live up to great expectations. Nearly his entire professional career Walthour Jr. was referred to in newspapers as "the son of the famous Dixie Flyer." On this day—opening day—he did live up to expectations and won the half-mile amateur handicap.[2]

McNamara's first competition, in direct contrast to the wishes of the doctors in Sydney, was at the Newark Velodrome on Sunday, April 25, 1920, against Oscar Egg in a two-mile paced match race. Oscar Egg won in two straight heats. The result would be a typical one for McNamara in the months to come. Perhaps contemplating the doctor's advice, the thirty-two-year-old McNamara seemed to be at the crossroads in the career he loved. Many had written him off as a "has been." In early October 1920 the *Newark Evening News* reported on his struggles: "He has overcome not only the physical waste due to his years of hard racing, but also the devastation due to numerous bad accidents he has suffered, as well as sickness. In the matter of accidents Reggie has suffered greater misfortune than any rider of this or any other period, with the possible exception of Fred

Hill, and last winter he was not expected to survive an operation performed in a Sydney hospital."[3]

But on October 10, at the Newark Velodrome, McNamara broke out of his slump in record fashion. Because of the high pace set by Goullet and McNamara, the crowded field of twenty-five starters in the twenty-five-mile open race was reduced to eight by mile 15. McNamara took more than two minutes off his own former world record, going the entire distance in just over fifty-one minutes and twenty-five seconds. But the victory was controversial. Although McNamara had a good lead rounding into the final straight, Goullet and Ray Eaton were coming on fast. Whether the suffering of going nearly thirty miles per hour for the entire race made him change his line or if it was done deliberately so that Goullet could not pass, nobody knew. Goullet, to avoid McNamara's "switch," was forced to go up the track embankment, and in doing so, his rear tire rubbed the front tire of Ray Eaton. Eaton crashed hard to the boards. Goullet stayed upright but was slowed enough for McNamara to cross the line in first place. The referee made no move to disqualify McNamara.

Whether he deserved the victory or not, McNamara's form was coming around just in time for the December six-day race at the Garden. Also in his favor was the fact that he was paired with one of the gamest riders of all time—a rider with a style very similar to his own—Oscar Egg. The pair became the favorite in a somewhat depleted field because of a competing "outlaw" six-day race in New York that had been run at the Twenty-Second Regiment Armory at Broadway and 168th Street two weeks earlier. Alf Goullet, who was no fan of John Chapman, along with other great six-day riders, crossed the line of the National Cycling Association in another "bike war," and his team took second place at the armory.

But the field for the Madison Square Garden six-day race in December 1920 still had some fantastic riders too, including the gallery favorite, Maurice Brocco, who was paired with American Willie Coburn. The winner of the 1920 Giro d'Italia, the wild-haired Gaetano Belloni, was teamed with sprinting ace and fellow Italian Francesco Verri. Bob Spears, recently back from his sensational European invasion, was with San Francisco native Percy Lawrence.

Before the race at the Garden was twenty-four hours old, one team created a spectacular commotion by stealing not just one but two laps in front of eleven thousand fans. The *New York Times* reported on the crowd's lunacy when Brocco and Coburn stole their second lap: "The crowd to a man, and to a woman, too, gave itself up to one of those demonstrations of approving acclaim which are characteristic of the annual race. This outburst, however, in the volume, completely overshadowed anything in the memory of the oldest race attendant. Hats and coats were thrown indiscriminately through the smoke-laden air and newspapers, programs and anything else that happened to be within reach and movable were sent in showers from the gallery occupants while the standees in the arena infield danced several jigs and jazzes in the outburst which transformed the Garden into a bedlam."[4]

In the first few days of the race McNamara's stomach ailment had come back to haunt him, and Egg was involved in three crashes, one requiring medical attention. Despite the bad luck, they refused to give up. The pair put in a number of "all-out" assaults with the intention of gaining the lost laps back. But because McNamara-Egg was the strongest team not in first place, Brocco and Coburn shadowed them closely.

On day 4 a half-dozen spectators sitting in the most expensive box seats along the finish line began yelling at the riders, calling them "tramps," "work-dodgers," "loafers," and other unmentionable names. Had the riders known these men hailed from the New York underworld, they may not have dished it back at them with such gusto and humor as they usually did. Although drinking was illegal, it was clear that all the men had been hitting the booze heavily. Shortly after their arrival, a drunken argument began among themselves, and then there were gunshots.

Writing about the incident seventeen years later, Bob Spears remembered the chaos. In the confusion all of the riders took cover. Spears got off his bike and climbed into the balcony. "A bike fan hid me behind his overcoat—not much protection when bullets were about," he began. "Then a bullet whistled over my head and I fled to greater safety—to an underground basement. The rest of the riders scattered to safety, and it took them an hour to get them together. Belloni, the champion road rider of Italy, took a lot of persuading to return to the track. He wanted to leave there and then."[5] Calm was restored, however, and all returned to normal.

Although neither the McNamara-Egg team nor any team made laps up on Brocco-Coburn, McNamara hogged the headlines on day 5 for a circus stunt he performed. Rounding the banked turn at full speed, a sure winner for a thirty-six-dollar preme offered by a spectator, McNamara's tire suddenly peeled off its rim. In his predicament he showed quick thinking and superb balance skills. With his right hand on the handlebars, he reached down with his left and pulled up the tire and inner tube before they could get tangled up. McNamara amazed everyone by riding on his rim to win the thirty-six-dollar preme.

As more and more people could afford mass-produced automobiles and have telephones in their home, indoor plumbing, and electricity, the economy continued its growth, as did the popularity of professional cycling in America. In February 1922 John Ringling, of Ringling Brothers and Barnum & Bailey Circus, along with Inglis M. Uppercu, put up the capital to complete the construction of a brand-new open-air velodrome stadium in New York at Broadway and 225th Street—right along the Harlem River.[6] Although the New York Velodrome and the Newark Velodrome were separated by not much more than twenty miles, the two facilities survived and thrived harmoniously for years to come.

With the two outdoor velodrome stadiums operating from late spring to early fall and Madison Square Garden hosting two six-day races in the spring and winter, cycling was becoming a year-round sport. The original Madison Square Garden, located at East Twenty-Sixth Street and Madison Avenue, was in operation from 1879 to 1890 and hosted the inaugural six-day race in 1881. The second Madison Square Garden was built on the same site in 1890 and closed in 1925. The man with the most at risk in building the third incarnation of the Garden, located on Eighth Avenue between Forty-Ninth and Fiftieth Streets, was Tex Rickard.

Rickard was a visionary. He was born in Kansas City, Missouri, in 1870. The family moved to Sherman, Texas, when he was four years old. In 1895 Rickard went to Alaska to strike it rich. He quickly achieved that goal when he and his partner, Harry Ash, staked gold claims and sold their holdings for an astounding $60,000. With that money the pair opened the Northern Saloon, and Rickard promptly lost everything to gambling. A few years later, in Nome, Alaska, Rickard met Wyatt Earp, a fellow boxing enthusiast. Rickard had promoted boxing matches in and around Nome. Earp had officiated a number of boxing matches, including the infamous heavyweight match he botched between Bob Fitzsimmons and Tom Sharkey in San Francisco on December 2, 1896, at Mechanics' Pavilion. Rickard and Earp were friends for life.

In July 1920 Rickard signed a ten-year lease on Madison Square Garden with the owners of the property, the New York Life Insurance Company. There had been rumors that the Garden was to be torn down, but Rickard promised changes and improvements that included the accommodation of more seating. Rickard also promised that events that had been there before, such as the dog, poultry, motorboat, automobile, and horse shows, would continue. Six-day races would go on as they had for years—but now they'd be held twice a year.[7] In 1924, with help from Wall Street millionaires, Rickard began to build up financing for construction of the new Madison Square Garden.

During the course of Rickard's plans for Madison Square Garden, as promised, not only did the six-day races continue at the Garden, but they thrived. Never before had fourteen thousand fans been able to see the bike race at once, but after Rickard's new configuration for the March 1922 edition of "the grind," they could.

As usual, Patrick Mulvey, a burly man born in Ireland who used no blueprint drawings, built the track. The first one he built was at Madison Square Garden around 1910. According to the *Newark Evening News*, Mulvey was purported to be the "only man in the country—the only man in the world—who knows how to put up a bike track the way it should be put up."[8] Joe Fogler came up with the idea of making a collapsible, portable track, but Mulvey was never able to accomplish this—he always made the tracks from thirty-five thousand square feet of new spruce lumber. Mulvey said that 84,480 eight-penny nails were put into the track surface and 2,200 sixteen-penny nails were used for the framework. From start to finish, and with a full crew of sixty carpenters, the job took sixteen hours.

As was his custom, McNamara was the first to come out to the track hours before the start of the race. In the relative quiet McNamara could breathe easily and hear the whir of his tires, pressurized at 120 pounds per square inch, as they rolled smoothly along the board surface. Because every track at Madison Square Garden was built new, each had its own nuances and idiosyncrasies. McNamara came out to test for any dips or bumps and to see how the banking was at high speeds.

McNamara and his fellow Aussie Alf Grenda competed against each other for more than a decade on three different continents, but never had they been six-day partners, until now. Besides the McNamara-Grenda combination, the oddsmakers' favorite teams were Alf Goullet with American Eddie Madden, Oscar Egg with Ray Eaton, and Maurice Brocco with Belgian Charles DeRuyter.

After much negotiation Alf Goullet was not only reinstated back into the National Cycling Association, but he signed a two-year deal to compete at the Madison Square Garden six-day races, the Newark Velodrome, the New York Velodrome,

18. McNamara
pumping up tire.

19. Bobby Walthour Jr.

20. (*Opposite top*) Gaetano Belloni.
JEFF GROMAN COLLECTION.

21. (*Opposite bottom*) McNamara
with Regina and Eileen.
JOSEPH HORTER JR. COLLECTION.

22. (*Above*) McNamara signs autograph
at Madison Square Garden.
JEFF GROMAN COLLECTION.

23. (*Opposite top*) Alf Goullet and Cecil Walker.
PETER STEPHENS COLLECTION.

24. (*Opposite bottom*) McNamara and
Harry Horan on their way to Berlin.
JOSEPH HORTER JR. COLLECTION.

25. (*Above*) McNamara and Horan in Berlin.
PETER STEPHENS COLLECTION.

26. (*Left to right*) Mrs. Giorgetti, Franco, Eileen, McNamara, and Elizabeth, March 1926, at Madison Square Garden. JOSEPH HORTER JR. COLLECTION.

27. (*Opposite top*) Elizabeth, Regina, and McNamara. JOSEPH HORTER JR. COLLECTION.

28. (*Opposite bottom*) McNamara, circa 1929. PETER STEPHENS COLLECTION.

29. McNamara in pinstripes.
JOSEPH HORTER JR. COLLECTION.

30. (*Opposite top*) McNamara with Eddie Seufert
(*standing far left*) and champion greyhound "Dark
Hazard." PETER STEPHENS COLLECTION.

31. (*Opposite bottom*) McNamara surrounded by
younger riders. PETER STEPHENS COLLECTION.

32. Ref McNamara and Torchy Peden. JOSEPH
HORTER JR. COLLECTION.

33. (*Opposite top*) McNamara with Rosemary
and Ken. LORI MCGOWAN COLLECTION.

34. (*Opposite bottom*) McNamara Christmas.
JOSEPH HORTER JR. COLLECTION.

35. Grandson Joe's
first bike.
JOSEPH HORTER JR.
COLLECTION.

36. Alf Goullet at
102 years of age.
JEFF GROMAN
COLLECTION.

and all other velodromes within its control, including Boston, Philadelphia, and Providence. Figures were undisclosed, but certainly it was a pile of money.

At just past midnight on March 6, 1922, heavyweight champion of the world and one of the 1920s greatest icons, Jack Dempsey, fired the gun that began the long journey round the one-tenth-of-a-mile highly banked wooden saucer. Ray Eaton flashed ahead and led the first lap of the snakelike procession. The huge crowd took several minutes to simmer down until an hour later, when Willie Hanley, the same person McNamara had traded punches with seven years earlier, shot out from the pack and quickly gained a half-lap lead. Hanley was soon caught, however, and the group went back to their normal pace.[9]

Perhaps suffering from sleep deprivation, Patterson McNutt, a sportswriter for the *World*, compared the dyed-in-the-wool six-day bike fans to the Utopia found in the 1921 Jack Barrymore film, *The Lotus Eaters*. "In that picture not even father worked unless he was so inclined," wrote McNutt. "Except for the thirty-odd riders in the six-day race there are no workers at the Garden. Some of those filling the seats are classed as nuts, cuckoo birds, saps and eggs, but apparently not one among them could be justly accused of ever having had a callus on his hands or a brain cell that ever suffered from even passing a thought."[10]

On day 2 Grenda took off on a flier. With McNamara's help the pair soon gained half a lap. The jam was unlike any the cycling-mad fans had ever witnessed and was sustained for twenty-five minutes. Once the dust settled and the referee tallied the laps of all the riders, an announcement was made that the two teams of McNamara-Grenda and Brocco-DeRuyter had each gained a lap on the field. This announcement was followed by a great storm of boos and catcalls that rained down upon the track. The referee's decision held that with the exception of the two teams now leading the race by one lap, all other teams had made faulty pickups.[11]

A few days went by, and the McNamara-Grenda and Brocco-DeRuyter teams remained in the lead. Grenda was interviewed in their tiny headquarters below the track while eating one of his many large meals. "Barring mishaps," he said, "McNamara and I should win this race. We are one lap ahead of the best teams in the race. Brocco and DeRuyter, who are on even terms with us, are not a formidable combination and we do not fear them. If we hold that lap until the last hour there will be no question about the winner of the race." He was asked to rank the top riders in the race. Without hesitation he ranked Goullet as the all-time six-day rider in the world and McNamara as second. He also gave kudos to Ray Eaton, Oscar Egg, and Eddie Madden. Sportswriter Robert Boyd asked Grenda where he belonged in that group. When Grenda shillyshallied, Boyd suggested that maybe he was somewhere near the talent of Eaton, Egg, and Madden. With a mouthful of steak the tall Tasmanian looked up and offered, "Yes, somewhere thereabouts."[12]

On the final day, in front of the capacity crowd of fourteen thousand spectators, the pair of Aussies held on for victory. It was McNamara's second six-day win at Madison Square Garden and the third for Grenda. The surprise of the race came in the closing hour, when the team of Harry Kaiser and Fred Taylor gained a lap, making it three leading teams on laps. Although their final sprint-point tally was not enough to overtake McNamara and Grenda, they did manage to steal second place overall away from Brocco and DeRuyter.

Shortly after their victory in New York, McNamara and Grenda boarded a steamship for Europe, where they competed as a team in the Paris six-day at the Vélodrome d'Hiver. It was the first time McNamara had been in Europe since 1914. Considering the short time for recovery, a five-day transatlantic voyage, and little time for preparation, they did remarkably well.

Whereas Madison Square Garden's track was newly built for each six-day event, the 250-meter track at the Vélodrome d'Hiver near the Eiffel Tower was a permanent structure. The team of Dutchman Piet Van Kempen and Charles DeRuyter led nearly the entire race on points over McNamara-Grenda and the team of Belgian Émile Aerts and Frenchman Georges

Sérès. On the morning of day 6, for fear that the other two teams were too close, Van Kempen and DeRuyter went on an all-out assault to gain a lap. With the Vélodrome d'Hiver's track, which was about twice as long as the one at the Garden, it was no easy task. Unfortunately, not only did they fail to gain the precious lap, but they exhausted themselves to such an extent that they themselves were lapped. Now hopelessly behind, they abandoned the race.[13]

Several hours later Aerts and Sérès put in the same kind of effort and succeeded in gaining a lap from McNamara-Grenda and the rest of the field. The great crowd went berserk in the melee of the French-Belgian victory. When they took their laps of honor, it was a scene of great emotion. McNamara and Grenda had to return to America satisfied with second place overall.

On May 30, 1922, the New York Velodrome opened its doors for the first time. Fully fourteen thousand cycling fans were present, including Babe Ruth, who fired the starting gun at a special three-way match race between Ray Eaton, Alf Goullet, and Orlando Piani. A total of $250,000 had been spent to bring the project to completion. The designers showed enough foresight for the mammoth facility to incorporate boxing matches, football games, ice skating races, and hockey games. "But," reported the *New York Times*, "it is as a cycling landmark that the New York Velodrome is destined to fulfill its greatest mission."[14]

If Yankee Stadium was "the house that Ruth built," then the Newark Velodrome was certainly the house that Frank Kramer built. Nineteen twenty-two was Kramer's "farewell" year, his twenty-third as a professional. Approaching his forty-second birthday, he knew it was time to hang up the racing shoes. The list of his accomplishments was astounding: two amateur national sprint titles, eighteen professional national sprint titles, and a world title. He only competed in the Grand Prix of Paris twice, in 1905 and 1906, and he won both times. Kramer was independently wealthy and had amassed a fortune worth about

$4.7 million in today's dollars. For Reggie McNamara and all the riders and fans, Kramer was an inspiration.

He would ride twice more: once at the New York Velodrome and once at the Newark Velodrome. Both tracks were one-sixth of a mile in length, so he decided to try to break the one-sixth-mile world record, held by Albert Krebs, of 15.4 seconds—more than forty miles per hour.

On Tuesday, July 25, under the lights at the New York Velodrome and the threat of rain, ten thousand fans came out to see the old warhorse race in the state of New York one last time. As he straddled his bike, the band stuck up "Auld Lang Syne" and stood up, taking their hats off. Kramer acknowledged the ovation with a broad smile. Alf Goullet paced him for four laps, gradually winding him up to full speed. The gun was fired when Kramer, all by himself now, hit the starting line for one more lap around. Kramer flashed around the track, negotiating the distance in sixteen seconds—not quite a record.[15]

The next day the sun came out, and long before the pistol fired for the first race, twenty thousand spectators crammed the Newark Velodrome for one last chance to see Kramer ride. When Kramer came out the final time in his white silk jersey with an American flag stitched in it and black shorts, his reception was five minutes long. Not only did the fans crane their necks to get a look, but so, too, did the riders. Ray Eaton and Bobby Walthour Jr., neither of whom was born yet when their fathers first competed against Kramer, were there, as was Alf Goullet, Alf Grenda, Art Spencer, and of course Reggie McNamara.

Maury Gordon, Kramer's trainer, held him up one last time at the starting line as photographers shot historic images. Grenda readied himself to pace Kramer, as Goullet had done the night before, and off they went into the early evening to a thunderous cheer. Grenda peeled off after his pacing job was done, and Kramer took center stage. Furiously, he pedaled with his old snap as he hunched over his Pierce-Arrow one last time. As he fairly flew around the track, the sight evoked a raw emotion that caused lumps in throats and dampened eyes. When it was announced he had equaled Krebs's world record, the entire crowd burst into an unbridled frenzy, with hats and programs flying in every direction.

Several minutes later Kramer and a group of people gathered near the announcer's stand. Unable to compose himself and speak, Kramer handed track announcer Willie Sullivan a written statement. "I want to thank you for your interest shown in me and your appreciation of my efforts in the last twenty-seven years. I'm only sorry that I am not fifteen years younger, so that I might continue to entertain you. However, I have no alternative, and must bow to Father Time."[16]

McNamara and everyone there knew they had witnessed something special that day, like Babe Ruth calling his shot to center field or Joe DiMaggio's streak or Willie Mays's catch. Although Kramer was an all-time great and should be immediately recognized as one of the iconic American sports figures of the 1920s, on par with Babe Ruth and Jack Dempsey, he is little known today.

McNamara knew he could not last forever in a growing sport that had young riders working hard for a chance to earn a good living. He wasn't much younger than Kramer; he was almost thirty-six. Although McNamara had no immediate plans for retirement, had he known his six-day results over the next two years, he may have reconsidered.

McNamara and Grenda were paired again at the December six-day grind at Madison Square Garden. Frank Kramer, refereeing his first six-day race, peered through spectacles at the judge's stand. On day 2 in the smoky sold-out arena, McNamara and Willie Lorenz locked handlebars and went airborne right in front of Babe Ruth and his wife in trackside box seats. Five other riders went down as well, including Harry Horan, who took the most extraordinary fall. Horan went up the fifteen-foot embankment and smashed against a steel wire guarding the fence; he was tossed back to the track and then rolled to the bottom. Excitement ran high in the Garden as trainers, doctors, and riders sprang into action.[17]

McNamara had cuts on his legs, head contusions, and a badly injured shoulder. Two riders, including Lorenz, were forced to quit from their wounds. McNamara and Horan kept going. Because of his injury, McNamara was unable to compete for the overall victory, which went to the worthy team of Gaetano Belloni and Alf Goullet. The Aussie-Italian combination made history in the thirty-third New York City six-day race because Belloni, the winner of the Giro d'Italia in 1920, became the first ever Grand Tour champion to also triumph at the Garden. McNamara and Grenda took fourth.

In February 1923, according to the *Chicago Tribune*, McNamara and Grenda refused to ride together in the six-day race at the Chicago Coliseum. Originally thought to be a great team together was a pair of Chicagoans, Carl Stockholm and Ernest Kockler, but they also refused to ride together. Dealing well with this situation, promoter Paddy Harmon made everyone happy by offering Kockler to team with Grenda and Stockholm to team with McNamara.[18]

By day 5 McNamara and Stockholm were in third position with the most sprint points of any team,[19] but they were one lap up on the two most formidable teams of Alf Goullet with Bobby Walthour Jr. and Maurice Brocco with Oscar Egg. All McNamara and Stockholm could hope for was to steal a lap in the final day, but they could not manage it. If McNamara's multiple crashes, including one on day 6, had anything to do with their failure to close the gap, it was not mentioned in the newspapers. McNamara suffered his worst finish ever to a six-day race, taking eighth place. All week long the crowd favorite was the young Bobby Walthour Jr., but he and Goullet could not overcome the lap gained on day 6 by Brocco and Egg.

McNamara teamed up with a young American from Newark, Harry Horan, in the next month's six-day at Madison Square Garden, and they only managed fourth place. Then McNamara was paired with Grenda once again at the Paris six-day in April 1923 but with another poor result—seventh place. Rounding out a year of poor six-day race results, McNamara again got fourth place with Harry Horan in November 1923 at Chicago.

With one more six-day race remaining in 1923, the December classic at the Garden, McNamara was hoping to turn around his string of lackluster performances. He did not give in easily. For the first time McNamara was paired up with dark-haired Piet Van Kempen, from Holland.

Just before the American team of Ernest Kockler and Percy Lawrence stole a lap from the field on day 4, McNamara and Van Kempen, riding in their purple-and-gold uniforms, had been in a tenuous lead on points. Kockler shot out, and after ten laps he had gained three-quarters of a lap. When Lawrence came out in relief, they began losing precious ground. Kockler had to come back out on the track with only a minute's rest. Fifteen minutes of wild riding was stopped when Van Kempen and Piet Moeskops collided. According to the *New York Times*, in "one of the most unusual decisions ever rendered in a six-day race," referee Frank Kramer made the announcement that Kockler and Lawrence had lapped the field. The crowd, twelve thousand strong, had already been in an uproar from the jam, but when the announcement came that a lap had been gained, a tidal wave of disapproval was voiced by nearly everyone in the Garden.[20]

For the final hour of the race fourteen thousand people flocked to the Garden, including some who were able to gain admission from a ticket counterfeiting operation. Hundreds of police officers were posted outside and inside, and the doors were closed.

Kockler and Lawrence had staked everything on the gained lap—they had no interest in scoring sprint points. With so many good teams one lap down, it was a dangerous game they played. But they succeeded in keeping on high alert and corralled the numerous attempts to gain the lap. McNamara and Van Kempen scored second overall; Reggie had finally made a decent finish.

Alf Goullet and his partner, Italian sprinter Orlando Piani, finished in a surprising sixth place. Goullet had been on a tear of late, and most thought his would be the winning team. "It was so hot in the Garden all week," said Goullet, "and the riders perspired so much that they did not have any strength left in the final hours. Manager Chapman came to me shortly before the finish and told me there was only fifteen minutes left. I told Chapman that my rear wheel was tied to the track and I just couldn't go. . . . I think Ernest Kockler and Percy Lawrence deserve a lot of credit for winning. They lapped the field on Thursday night, and held the margin to the finish. I rode a race and won with Kockler in Chicago. He is not flashy, but he is a good strong athlete."[21]

Despite the counterfeiting operation, 100,000 legitimate tickets had been sold at the Garden during that week of racing. If only the Garden had been larger, John Chapman and Tex Rickard knew many more tickets could have sold. With the 1920s well under way, an investment in cycling, if done correctly, was going to pay off.

11

The Italians Are Coming!

What bike fan doesn't love *Breaking Away?* With its terrific cast of Dennis Christopher playing the protagonist, Dave, and Daniel Stern as Cyril, Dennis Quaid as Mike, and Jackie Earle Haley as Moocher, the movie is staged as a rivalry between hometown post–high school age kids, the "Cutters," and college kids going to school at Indiana University in Bloomington. Writer Steve Tesich won the 1979 Academy Award for Best Original Screenplay, and the movie received nominations in four other categories, including Best Picture.

In the movie nineteen-year-old Dave is obsessed with two things: racing his bike and anything to do with Italy. As he prepares to race the "Cinzano 100," a road race in Bloomington, he speaks Italian and plays Italian opera records, to his father's chagrin. In pursuit of a pretty college girl, he pretends to be an Italian exchange student. His obsession is discernible by his great respect for the Italian riders on Team Cinzano. When he first finds out that the riders on the team he idolizes were going to be in Bloomington for the race, his cry of "The Italians are Coming!" could be heard far and wide. But his fixation is U-turned during the race, when one of the Italians on Team Cinzano purposely puts his pump into Dave's spokes, causing him to crash. As they ride ahead and chuckle to themselves, Dave is left behind, bloodied at the side of the road.

Reggie McNamara was not necessarily obsessed with Italian cyclists, like Dave, but he did have a profound respect for the

Italian riders of his generation. One of the treasures contained in McNamara's scrapbook, saved by his great-granddaughter, Lori McGowan, is an essay he wrote called "The Race Is to the Swift—Sometimes." It was probably written in the late 1930s, hammered out by McNamara on a mechanical typewriter that occasionally dropped an *e* or an *a* a half-line low. It is the only piece of evidence found that McNamara may have intended to write an autobiography. Whether the essay was ever published, until now, remains unknown. In its near entirety it reads:

> It is one of the peculiar facts of geography that there are more Italians in New York City than there are in either Venice or Florence, and—according to some notions—probably more than there are in Rome itself. And it is one of the particular facts of the professional bike game that practically all these metropolitan sons of Italy are rabid rooters at the race track.
>
> These Italians and their American children have a way of picking their own favorites. Brocco, Linari, Verri, Belloni and other notable riders have shared the loud and eloquent cheers of their countrymen, and I came in for a share of it when I found myself teamed with any of them.
>
> The great single favorite of all was Franco Giorgetti,[1] whose consistent success and constant popularity with the crowd influenced the point of view of the management of Madison Square Garden and others directing the Six Day business. Little Franco, properly handled, could always be well exploited to the best possible advantage of the box office. It meant a profitable race if Giorgetti's team was among the leaders going into the last days, and Franco himself was just the kind of rider who belonged up front.
>
> Yet, if he were badly teamed, it might mean he would be out of the race, the Italians would be outside the arena, and the management would be out of pocket. This provided a problem which called for certain shrewd pairing before a big race and for some considerable strategy in keeping all the teams fairly evenly matched—yet not too dangerously on a par with each other.

The Italians Are Coming!

This was probably the only real discrimination ever observed in setting up the teams. Of course, it was quite possible—like the seeding of ranking tennis players for the rounds of a championship tournament. Abused, this same practice might easily have horrified those who habitually look for skeletons in the sports' closet, but it was innocent enough from the angle of bike riding, where competition makes the race and an even chance to win is the best guarantee for each team giving its utmost to claim first place at the finish.

The teaming of little Franco with me never seemed to appeal over much to the strategists arranging the Six Day race in New York and other large cities. While it assured Giorgetti a probable high place at the finishing gun, both in points and position, it made the prospect of a runaway race dangerously impossible. I say this only on the basis of demonstration, for we have been teamed on occasions and the effect of the pairing made things pretty discouraging for all the other riders.

Yet it is true that much also depends upon little things in a race. Nothing, however sure, is ever in the bag in the bike game. While I could count on Franco to hold his own, and he could depend on me, the pair of us could not feel absolutely sure just because we shared the colors. There is always the chance of just a little slip making a big difference.

In 1925, in the December race at the Garden, Franco and I were teamed, and we rode steadily to an expected victory—until the last hour of the sixth day. In the jams and sprints of the final hour, certain victory became tense uncertainty. For five days the mingled appeals and compliments of the gallery had shouted Giorgetti on to glory, with similar words of praise and urging for me, if only for the sake of my being Franco's partner. For five days we had ridden ourselves weary, leading in every jam and pushing the pace all the way.

Going into the final hour, we held the advantage of one lap, a slim lead at best, but with a top-heavy total of accumulated points from the earlier sprints. We slackened in vigilance only because of the unremitting strain of leading the race, and the cheers that celebrated us throughout the week began to betray notes of impatience. Other teams began pressing, and, while Franco and I held our slim one lap advantage, point totals of the other riders began to pile up. The partisan audience began to fear defeat for their favorite, and it became difficult for me to believe our supporters entirely in their shouts to me.

Here was the dilemma. If we attempted to break from the field, it might be an invitation to disaster, so our team was content to hold its place and its one lap margin safely, with victory coming closer every minute. It was one of those unexplainable discriminations of prejudice on the part of the audience that I should be held somehow to account while my partner was excused for it. But to the wider crowd, the policy we pursued was sound and strategic. It seemed to be the way to win the race, and that was our object.

The pace of that last half hour was furious with reckless riding. With points jumping from one to ten for the final sprints, it looked as if the finish would be close enough to allow almost anything to happen. Franco and I rode desperately now, with every hazard focusing directly on us. One to the other, we passed the pace of the mad sprints between us, holding fast to the advantage of our one lap lead, with Debaets and Goosens pressing us and points piling up higher for the other teams.

The field was another two laps behind Debaets and Goosens, but some of the teams were taking sprint after sprint and threatening to steal enough laps to pull up even with us and take the victory away from us. The safe margin of our point total continued to slip as others continued to climb upward. But Franco and I knew better than to jam for another lap for fear of a possible spill which would deprive us of winning the race itself.

I counted the minutes as we sped around the big saucer, and my heart pounded with the combination of excitement and exertion as I listened for the final gun to mark the end of the six days' riding. And, when at last the pack of us rode down across the black line for the last time in the race, I was satisfied that Franco and I had ridden our best race together through the last day. Together we were happy in the realization of a successful, if desperate, coordination.

But our sense of achievement was short. The decision of the judges was temporarily withheld, and that meant trouble of some sort or other. When it was announced, we heard that we were to be deprived of the victory. On the basis of what the judges ruled were faulty pick-ups in the final sprints, our team was penalized two laps.

The news came to me like a flash of lightening [*sic*] out of a clear sky to be followed by a deafening roar from the crowd, which thundered its combined shock and disapproval. Complaints avalanched in the shout of vocal protest from the grandstand and gallery, but the decision of the judges remained firm. Penalized by two laps, our team was rated in second place instead of first.

Debaets and Goosens, with 2,294 miles and nine laps, and with a point total of 306, were declared the winners. Giorgetti and I were credited with the same mileage and eight laps, although we had actually covered 2,295 miles, with a total of 541 points. Four laps behind us by actuality, but only two laps behind us in the technical ruling, Walthour and Spencer finished, with a point total lacking only four of 1,000 points. It had been a thrilling finish, if technically disappointing and fairly outrageous to the Giorgetti fans.

They acted bitter at the outcome, and gave only a reluctant recognition to Debaets and Goosens as they took the winners' bow in a circle of the track. And when, to accept our second place award, Franco and I took our turn around the boards, only a deep silence greeted us. Then it rose to assail us like a great wave, the first shout of audible repudiation, and a deep answering groan echoed it. Our sweat turned cold in our bodies as this sound increased to a thunderous boo.

This made the fact plain to us: we *had not won* the race—we *had lost* it! Our errors had betrayed our supporters. That was the tragedy of the 47th International Six Day Bicycle Race at Madison Square Garden, and it burned deeply into my sensitive nature. For the first time in my long career in sport, I had been deliberately hurt by my friends whom I had hoped to please. Many times I have been physically injured and painfully hurt on the track—but this was a different and worse kind of wound.

That experience served but to determine me that my wound must heal, just as physical injuries suffered on the track had mended. But it is only too true that, while a bone may be re-set in five or six weeks and lacerations may be stitched into scars, an injury to the spirit goes too deep for a quick and easy recovery.

Yet I knew one certain way to accomplish that recovery, and that was to ride again and win, and win so decisively that every last doubt in connection with the unfortunate 47th Race finish should be erased from my own mind and memory of the indignant fans at the Garden.

So ride I did, teamed with Bobby Walthour Jr., at Chicago, the following February. We rode as no team has ever ridden before or has ridden since. Franco Giorgetti was teamed with Freddie Spencer, and this pair were of the same mind as ourselves. Franco had his grievance to settle as well as I, so his team went out from the opening gun to win, and they pressed with exactly the same purpose as drove us forward.

Bobby and I worked together in almost mechanical perfection, and by one o'clock on Friday morning, drawing toward the climax of the race we held a lead of six laps over the field. During the early morning sprints for special premes, shortly after one o'clock, Bobby spilled at the edge of the track and piled into the fence. He had to be carried to his cot for emergency medical attention, and I took my place on the track to protect our team's lead against a mounting effort by the field to overtake us.

Every other team knew that Bobby was badly hurt, and it was a question whether he would recover sufficiently to be able to resume his place in the grind. They all concentrated on me, and I had to run the gauntlet of the toughest competition ever stacked against leaders of any race. During a long series of sprints, as riders of each team relieved each other in a constant drive to cut down our lap advantage, without respite I kept on the track with never a moment when my heart was not hammering against my ribs like a machine gun.

I lost all notion of time as hour by hour the morning sprints piled up on me. But I kept riding as I had never ridden before, remembering the rebuke of the Italian fans in New York and determined that I would not surrender even one lap to the team of Giorgetti and Spencer which was pressing me so desperately. Finally, as I was about ready to collapse, good old Bobby appeared on the track and took over the lead from me. It was two o'clock in the afternoon. I had held our lead against all comers for thirteen hours straight.

From that point on, our slogan in action continued to be "Carry On," and we pedaled on through the sprints to the final hour holding our lead to win at the finish with a victory that has never been matched in many a long year since. Walthour and I won that race with a staggering point total garnered in the sprints and by a margin of six laps!

The proof of this race, established in spite of almost insurmountable handicaps, convinced bike fans everywhere in the world that the Iron Man had not begun to gather rust. It also convinced the promoters that I had set my cap to win the March race at Madison Square Garden. It was not surprising then that I was teamed with Giorgetti for this race. We won that race, riding as we had three months before, and with a margin of three laps.

This was additional proof of the fact that we were a winning combination, and the sons of Italy were once again reestablished in the host of our boosters. A comparison of results from those three races, the two in New York and the one in Chicago, led the sports writers of the nation to acclaim Franco and me as the greatest riders in the Six Day business. That was good news for the Italian fans in New York, but it was even better news to me. You see, I had counted the Chicago race as the big test between the two of us, and I had the facts of that result to make it entirely clear to me just how the two of us stood on the basis of that record. . . . When I started out by saying that there were more Italians in New York City than in either Venice or Florence, I was not trying to explain how Fiorello H. La Guardia got the votes that elected him mayor for two successive terms. I was remembering all too vividly the numerous occasions when I was cheered in dialect—and the one terrible night when it seemed every Italian-born metropolitan from the Bronx to the Battery gave me the kind of cheer that is particularly associated with the former.

I have ridden in Italy on many occasions and have met thousands of Italians on their home grounds. At Rome, in 1927, after the race at Milan, I made a pilgrimage to Rome to be accorded an audience by Pope Pius in the Vatican. There were, in fact, two audiences, for both of which I felt deeply honored as a member of the Church and a citizen of the world.

The first was formal in every respect, and my wife, and our two daughters and I treasure that experience. The second was unique. I saw His Holiness alone, and we had quite a conversation—on the subject of bicycle riding.

Then I went to see Il Duce. Benito Mussolini proved to be just as rabid a bike fan as any boy on the bicycle path at Central Park. He wanted to know the secret of successful racing. He asked me directly how to set new records on the track. I tried to tell as fully as I knew. He seemed to understand. "I see," he said. "The secret of your victories lies in the good fortune you have had in always riding with Italian partners."

He knew all the Italian riders by name, and he recited them in a way to indicate that he followed the races as enthusiastically as all the grandsons of the Caesars. He had me almost believing that my mother had brought me up, back on the farm in New South Wales, on a diet of macaroni. "I have found Italians excellent partners," I told him.

Then he mentioned the inevitable sore spot in my racing experience. "Tell me, how did you lose with Giorgetti in New York, a year ago in December?"

I was proud of the answer I gave him. I am still proud of it,
I guess. It sounded almost like a proverb as I said it. "You see,
Duce, the race is to the swift—sometimes."[2]

It is quite possible that McNamara was working on an autobiography, although the account printed here is the only mate-
rial related to such a project that is known to exist today. In
the mid-1930s, when he was nearly retired from professional
cycling for good, McNamara was hospitalized while purportedly working on his memoirs at a friend's house in Denville,
New Jersey, near the scenic ninety-nine-acre Indian Lake in
the Adirondacks. The lake was far from the many distractions
of city life—a perfect setting for writing a memoir. But his stay
was rudely interrupted by a bout of internal bleeding, possibly brought on by long-term alcohol abuse or blunt trauma or
both. McNamara was close to death and rushed to the hospital. But once again, the Iron Man confounded doctors and survived another close call.[3]

12

Mac Strikes Gold

Up to this point in his career McNamara was better known for his Iron Man durability, already an aging star in a young man's game. But for the next two and a half years, from December 1924 to April 1927, he was to set the six-day world afire. When his streak came to an end, he would always be able to go down as one of the greatest cyclists of all time—despite six-day racing's forgotten history in America. But before the streak began, McNamara was not riding well. Perhaps it was the Chicago six-day race of January 1924 that snapped him out of his funk.

Tom Eck, the running coach at the University of Chicago, fired the starting gun that sent fifteen teams away at the Chicago Coliseum. Among the favorites were Oscar Egg with Alf Grenda; Kockler and Stockholm, who had repaired their relationship and become the "Chicago Team"; and McNamara with Piet Van Kempen.

McNamara and Van Kempen began stacking up sprint points ahead of the other teams and led for the first three days. Whispered rumors began to circulate that the race was fixed and the riders were on the take. The theory was that any bet on McNamara and Van Kempen was a sure winner and any bet on the Grenda-Egg combination was a losing proposition.

But those rumors were loudly quashed when Egg shot out from the field in a terrific burst of speed at midnight in the race's seventy-second hour. Grenda and Egg performed a perfect pickup, and the tall Tasmanian tore around the wooden saucer and increased their lead. When the dust settled, referee Kramer ruled that the Egg-Grenda combination and the team of Eddie Madden and Belgian Maurice Declerek had gained a lap. The ruling caused widespread dissension among the riders and the fans. Kramer was suddenly the most unpopular person inside the Chicago Coliseum. Van Kempen and the normally mild-mannered McNamara were both hot. They, along with two other riders, Dave Lands and Willie Coburn, deserted the track and went down into the dressing room. Kramer sent notification to the pouting riders that if they didn't soon return to the track, they would be suspended.

The quartet remained in the dressing room, and Kramer, who was not only the referee but also the chairman of the board of control of the National Cycling Association, which was affiliated with the Union Cycliste Internationale, suspended each of them from competing professionally anywhere in the world for six months.[1]

McNamara returned home to Newark with his tail between his legs and was unable to compete at the spring six-day race at Madison Square Garden. The potential loss of earnings weighed heavily on his mind, and one can imagine that his wife, Elizabeth, gave him a deserving dose of guilt. Some consolation was that he was able to spend more time with Elizabeth and his daughters, Eileen and Regina, now nine and six years old, respectively.

McNamara served out his suspension, which was reduced to three months, and he competed at opening day ceremonies at both the Newark and New York Velodromes. Newark opened on Sunday, April 27, with more than fifteen thousand fans, and Babe Ruth fired the starting gun before nine thousand fans at New York. Had there not been threatening skies at the New York Velodrome, thousands more would have gone through the turnstiles. McNamara didn't do so well at Newark, but in New York, just before the rain came, he won the five-mile open against forty-five starters. And so it went with McNamara's outdoor season—the usual ups and downs. When the six-day racing started that winter of 1924, he was happy to be off suspension and back at Madison Square Garden. With Van Kempen and McNamara paired up again, they had a shot at redemption for having been thrown out of the Chicago race.

During the week of racing, a constant rain came down outside, making it nearly impossible to air out the old building. A great haze of blue tobacco smoke draped over the building in unusual thickness—even for a six-day race—and irritated the eyes of riders and fans alike. But that did not stop thousands of fans and the many famous people who were lured by the fascination and history of the race, including Ty Cobb, Babe Ruth, Knute Rockne, and Will Rogers. For Cobb it was his first six-day race, and he was given a tour of the riders' training quarters, which generated much interest among the riders, trainers, and cooks.

In their usual team style over the course of the week, McNamara and Van Kempen rang up more sprint points than the other teams. The lead on laps, however, yo-yoed for the entire contest. Oscar Egg and his partner, Costante Girardengo, the 1919 and 1923 winner of the Giro d'Italia, led on Monday. McNamara and Van Kempen led on Tuesday. The team of Gaetano Belloni and Charles DeRuyter led on Wednesday. On Thursday it was the youthful combination of Italian Franco Giorgetti and Bobby Walthour Jr., who were locked on laps with McNamara–Van Kempen.

The blond-haired Walthour was a big favorite at the Garden, a reminder of the days when his father had earned his great six-day victories there. On day 5 Walthour was on the flat of the track, coming out in relief of Giorgetti. His pedal accidently carved into the banking of the track, causing him to swerve suddenly. He went down hard. A great hush came from the crowd, and hundreds of infield spectators rushed to the scene, nearly causing the railing to give way. Walthour was carried to his cot. When he came out shortly thereafter and remounted his bike, the great throng of eleven thousand cheered him on.

Mac Strikes Gold

The thirty-seventh international six-day race at Madison Square Garden came down to the two leading teams on laps. The fans, who came in great droves to witness the final hours, were disappointed that no great effort was made to gain a lap on the final day; it seemed that the riders were satisfied that McNamara–Van Kempen would win and Walthour-Giorgetti would take second. According to the *New York Times*, "There was not even as much as the suggestion of a jam" in the final hours.[2] The final totals were 2,368 miles and five laps, and McNamara-Van Kempen scored 1,057 sprint points versus 543 points for Walthour-Giorgetti.

Although Alf Goullet's original partner, Harry Horan, was forced to abandon the race with a broken collarbone, the greatest of all six-day riders resembled a "pathetic figure" in the race. Goullet and his reconstructed teammate, Alex McBeath, finished far down overall. Little did most people know that Goullet had been suffering from an acute attack of appendicitis during the race but refused to quit. Several days later he collapsed and was rushed to the New York Hospital, where an emergency operation was performed. "Guess I will need a rest after this," he said from his hospital bed. "I am going to take a trip to Europe next month, a pleasure trip, and will be back here in March and will team up with Horan in the next race."[3]

Reggie McNamara, who was three and a half years older than Goullet, was regarded as "beyond his best riding age,"[4] but little did anyone know that his streak had just begun. He went home to his wife and children, and after his first good rest in a week, they all went to Catholic Church services.

McNamara had first met Bobby Walthour Jr.'s father during the six-day race at Madison Square Garden in December 1913. Eleven-year-old Bobby Jr. and his two sisters had been there under the supervision of their mother. It remains unknown whether McNamara and Bobby Jr. first met then, but certainly young Walthour would have remembered meeting many great riders. A little more than eleven years later, in February 1925, both McNamara and Walthour must have been thrilled to be paired together at the Chicago six-day race. Walthour would benefit from McNamara's experience and wisdom, and McNamara had the added benefit of youth and vigor on his team.

On day 1, before the race at the Chicago Coliseum was two hours old, McNamara and Walthour appeared to have the magic. Gaetano Belloni tried to sneak away from the field. Having none of it, McNamara went to the front of the chase. When the field caught a rider, it would typically slow down to catch its collective breath, but McNamara steamrolled ahead and quickly gained a quarter-lap advantage. Walthour came out in relief on McNamara and set a furious pace and gained further. After ten laps or so, McNamara came back out to finish the job. But Walthour's arm got caught in McNamara's shirt during the pickup and landed heavily on the boards. The crash stopped them from gaining the lap, but Walthour was unhurt.[5]

In much the same fashion as the recent six-day race in New York, there were many lead changes in Chicago. But late into Thursday evening, McNamara and Walthour gained a lap when it mattered the most. According to sportswriter Walter Eckersall, the pair stole the lap in "the wildest riding ever seen in a six-day bike race in Chicago. The riders took all sorts of chances, but the real riding of the jams was done by Walthour and McNamara, the former especially."[6]

On February 12, 1925, McNamara and Walthour took a victory parade around the track with their bikes adorned with flowers. McNamara's ten-year-old daughter, Eileen, came out on the track and congratulated both her father and Walthour. Posing together for a photo that appeared the next day in the *Chicago Daily Tribune*, they were sitting and smiling atop their bikes, with their trainers holding them up, and Eileen was right in front, soaking up the fun.

With only two weeks since the finish at Chicago, the riders were at it again at Madison Square Garden. Although Goullet had promised to be back for the New York City six-day to race as a teammate with Harry Horan, he and his wife were aboard a ship coming back from their European honeymoon adventure. McNamara was substituted in Goullet's place, taking the young Horan under his wing.

Walthour Jr. was paired up with fellow youngster Freddie Spencer, from Plainfield, New Jersey. Their combined age was only forty-one. Spencer preferred training on the hills around his home to the track. He and Walthour were both talented sprinters who had plenty of stamina in their legs and lungs. Among the European teams were Swiss ace Oscar Egg with Maurice Brocco; Gaetano Belloni and Franco Giorgetti as a formidable Italian combination; and the Belgian racers Harry Stockelynch and Alphonse Goosens.

The March 1925 six-day race was scheduled to be the final one in the old building. Tex Rickard was busy getting the new Madison Square Garden ready for the next bike race that December. After ceremonial introductions sixteen colorfully clad cyclists went away on a rolling start at one minute past midnight, on Monday, March 2. The riders leaned into a new turn about every five seconds as the field snaked its way around the track at twenty miles per hour. There was the usual hubbub of activity inside the track, with trainers all about, in and out of the riders' tents at the side of the track. Every tent was bedecked with two flags representing the country of each teammate.

The old Garden's concluding event proved to be a difficult one. Franco Giorgetti was forced to retire after sliding down the steep banked track and catching a two-and-a-half-inch splinter in his side. The big sprinter from Holland, Piet Moeskops, sustained a fractured rib and was also forced to quit the race.

Among the twelve thousand spectators was Col. Theodore Roosevelt, the eldest son of the former president of the United States, sitting in the best box seat near the finish line. Both he and his sister Alice had attended six-day races before. For Theodore this was the first one he had been to since he was a student at Harvard.[7]

Another figure of prominence—sitting with Tex Rickard in his box seats—was Alf Goullet, who had recently arrived back from his European honeymoon. No doubt there was some discussion about the design of the new Madison Square Garden building and how it would favor cycle racing. Goullet was introduced to the great crowd as the "king of all six-day riders." Although Goullet was often booed in the Garden because any team with him was always the preeminent favorite, he was given a rousing ovation when he stood up in acknowledgment. Goullet then offered a $100 preme to whomever would win a one-mile sprint. Walthour and Egg went after the cash, but it was won by a Belgian, Maurice De Wolfe.

By day 5 they had gone twenty-one hundred miles, and three teams were in the lead on laps: Walthour-Spencer, Stockelynch-Goosens, and McNamara-Horan. The overall race came down to points, and Bobby Walthour Jr. and Freddie Spencer took it, with two hundred more points than McNamara-Horan. For Walthour it was his sixth six-day race. He had been on the winning team three times, taken second twice, and was forced out once due to injury. Spencer was escorted back to his Plainfield, New Jersey, home by the town's mayor and was given a noble welcome.

As historic as the last six-day race at the old Garden was, the first six-day in the new building was even more memorable. In December 1925 tickets for the first event to open the new Garden, located at Eighth Avenue between Forty-Ninth and Fiftieth Streets, were in great demand. All the way to the 1960s the arena would be witness to many great boxing matches, hockey games, and basketball games, but the first event it would host—sporting event or any other—was cycling.

Nor was it any six-day race either because it was the very race McNamara wrote about, the one in which the crowd turned on him and his partner, Franco Giorgetti. In addition to provoking his disgust, then compelling him to dominate a subsequent six-day teamed with Walthour, the race marked the beginning of the end for Alf Goullet. On day 4 a capacity crowd tested the limits of the new building as thousands were left outside in the rain trying to obtain tickets. Goullet was in the race but in an unfamiliar position—far back in the standings with his Aussie partner, Cecil Walker. "It's the youngsters," said a veteran six-day fan, "they've gone crazy."[8] The fan was referring to an apparent change in six-day racing. It was a different game than Goullet was used to—less strategy and more aggressiveness.

The young Walthour-Spencer dynamic duo were paired again and always in the mix. The only "old man" in the race doing well was McNamara, and he and Giorgetti were tied on laps on day 4 and into day 5 with another young team, the Belgian combination of Gérard Debaets and Alphonse Goosens. On the fifth night there seemed to be a "lull before the storm," while another sellout crowd grew impatient, longing for a jam. But the riders went on, unmindful of the multitudes, and conserved their energy for what would be a thrilling finish.

Before the final night three teams hopelessly behind were requested by the race management to leave the track, including that of Alf Goullet. It was sad for the fans to see their "Goullie" in a bad way. "This doesn't mean I'm through with six-day riding," he said. "On the contrary, I'll be back winning again in another year. . . . I just couldn't get started this year. I didn't feel like myself, although I have no alibi to make. It's just a case of not being good enough. But I'll be back."[9]

Although McNamara and Giorgetti did not enjoy the outcome—being booed vociferously—promoter Tex Rickard loved the aftermath. About 120,000 people had passed through the turnstiles, and the estimated Garden receipts for the six-day race were $300,000 (more than $4 million in today's dollars). Rickard was happy that the sport of cycling was going to continue to be a bright feature twice a year at Madison Square Garden.

Almost immediately after the Garden race, McNamara traveled to Europe to race in the Berlin six-day at the Sportpalast stadium. McNamara and his American partner, Harry Horan, spent the first day in second place overall to the Italian team of Franco Giorgetti and Costante Girardengo. But on the second day Girardengo crashed and was forced to abandon with a broken collarbone.

Girardengo's departure from Berlin put McNamara-Horan in

first place, and Giorgetti teamed up with a German rider, Rieger, whose teammate had crashed into Girardengo and was also forced to abandon. The next four days it was a seesaw battle on sprint points between Giorgetti-Rieger and McNamara-Horan.

On the afternoon of day 5 nine of the original fourteen teams were still fighting when Debaets and McNamara fell down in a big tumble. McNamara survived the scare with just scratches, but Debaets's injuries were serious enough to force him out of the race.[10]

The Berlin race was held under the direction of Walter Rutt, who was now permanently retired from racing. Sportpalast could hold ten thousand people, and at no time was there less than a capacity crowd for the entire six days. To meet the demand of the final day, prices were raised to a point that people were paying the equivalent of $25 American (or $325 today) for gallery seats.

Going into the final hour, McNamara-Horan and Giorgetti-Rieger were nearly deadlocked on points and laps. Because Rieger was German, his team was the natural fan favorite. A series of fifteen sprints was the last shot at getting points. McNamara displayed his true grit when he, "alone, had garnered six first places. The crowd soon woke up to the fact that McNamara and Horan were riding in almost super-human style, considering the tremendous amount of jamming they had done all week long, and soon everyone in the place were with the American riders."[11]

The *Newark Evening News* featured photos with a big head-line in the front page of the sports section: "Newark Team Wins Berlin Six-Day Race." McNamara was no longer considered Australian in his adopted city of Newark, New Jersey. With his victory in Berlin, McNamara had won six-day races on three continents. Horan, who had served in World War I for eighteen months, was the hometown hero in South Orange, New Jersey.

According to the *New York Times*, the German press pro-claimed McNamara as the world's greatest rider.[12] "After the victory," said Horan, "we were dined and wined for several days. Wherever we went Mac and I were recognized. Our bills in restaurants were all paid in some mysterious manner, it seems.

Mac Strikes Gold

We were guests wherever we went. The Germans couldn't have treated us better were we native sons."[13] With little time to spare, they collected their significant prize money, bonuses, and expenses, and the two boarded the ss *Olympic* at Cherbourg with Franco Giorgetti so all three could all make it back in time to race in the Chicago six-day.

An assembly of thirty or so of the best cyclists on the world, along with trainers, mechanics, and racing officials, boarded a train at the Meeker Avenue Station that would make its way to the Windy City in twenty-six hours. During their journey Horan delighted everyone with stories about the Berlin race. "One night," he said as more people leaned in to listen and laugh, "the management announced a preme in German, of course, and the crowd gave a great hurrah. I thought it must be for something worthwhile so I gave a chase for it and won. Then I discovered it was for a great, big pudding made by a prominent chef in Berlin. When they brought the pudding down to us, Mac and I presented it to Mrs. Walter Rutt, but it was so big and hard to handle, it couldn't even go into a taxicab, so Mrs. Rutt left it at the Sport Palast, and the riders finished it."[14]

To make the race as competitive as he saw fit, John Chapman arranged the pairings of the Chicago race. Harry Horan was teamed with Chicago native Ernest Kockler, Giorgetti was teamed with Freddie Spencer, and McNamara was teamed again with Bobby Walthour Jr. Walthour was referred to as the "blushing bridegroom" because he had recently returned from his Miami honeymoon with the former Miss Margaret Murray; as his parents had done decades earlier, Walthour and Murray eloped.[15] European teams included Oscar Egg with Frenchman Pierre Sargent, the Belgian team of Alphonse Goosens and Harry Stockelynch, and the German team of Richard Golle with Werner Meithe.

On day 1, February 15, 1926, things looked bad for the McNamara-Walthour combination in Chicago—they were three laps down on the Belgian team of Stockelynch and Goosens. The Chicago race was unlike any other ever seen before. Riders stole laps across the board, and team placings went up and down like a roller coaster.

On day 4 McNamara and Walthour took the lead, and Goosens-Stockelynch plunged all the way down to fourth place, eight laps down. Walthour in particular was riding recklessly, and he crashed several times in front of his new wife, Margaret. In one relief of McNamara, Walthour pushed him so hard that both crashed. It was reported that Walthour thought "nothing of cutting down in front of another rider, giving him maybe half an inch, or shoving a rival out of the way, knocking him down, or going down himself."

In attendance was University of Illinois halfback Red Grange as well as former Chicago mayor William Hale Thompson, who was promptly ignored because of a jam, and McNamara's youngest daughter, Regina, smiling, clapping, and rooting for her father.

McNamara and Stockelynch, a noted hothead, nearly came to blows. Stockelynch crashed uninjured, but when McNamara came around, the Belgian made a move to throw his bike at him. Stockelynch complained to the referee Frank Kramer about McNamara. But Kramer said McNamara would never do such a thing deliberately. Stockelynch alleged that he would settle accounts later. Kramer warned that if he did that, he would get kicked out of the race and suspended from racing.

Partly due to Walthour's reckless abandon, he and McNamara shot up the leader board six laps over the second-place team. But Walthour's rough riding eventually got the best of him on Friday at three o'clock in the morning. Walthour was working his way through the field, and in his attempt to get around a couple riders, he went high up the banked turn and crashed into the railing. The angle of the track was so steep that Walthour tumbled down, head first, without ever touching the track.

After he regained consciousness, track physicians worked on Walthour's face for two hours. He took three stitches on the chin and three stitches to his upper lip, and it was feared he had a broken nose.[16] With thirty hours left in the race, there was serious concern about whether Walthour would be able to reenter the race. As McNamara went round and round with other teams trying get laps back, Walthour sent word to McNamara that he thought he would be able to resume in an hour. McNamara told the attendant: "Tell him to take six hours if he likes. I can hold off this crowd."[17]

Not long after Walthour's accident, in consideration of rider safety, Frank Kramer made a bold move. He gathered all the riders together and said that instead of relief riders coming from the inside, they would now come from the outside as high up the track as possible. For some time the riders couldn't get the hang of the new way, and there was danger of more severe falls than ever, but Kramer's new rule ended up being a good one.

Six hours after his bad smash-up, Walthour resumed riding with his face almost completely covered with bandages. He got a standing ovation when he came back out on the track. The gameness of his team was something to admire. In thirty hours they had only lost one lap, and they won the overall race by five laps. McNamara's status as an Iron Man was confirmed. The *Newark Evening News* reported: "Riders will readily admit that McNamara is super-human. Even in spills and smash-ups on the track in which Mac may figure, the old-timer comes up smiling. While others are carried off and need medical attention, Reggie picks himself up, brushes the dust off his arms and legs and walks, or sometimes mounts his wheel and rides back to his cot."[18]

McNamara had won two in a row—in Berlin and in Chicago—and he had been robbed of another victory in the Garden with Giorgetti, the one they had been booed for losing. To stir things up, John Chapman put McNamara and Giorgetti together again in March for the spring six-day at Madison Square Garden. Since December, four months earlier, McNamara's schedule had been nonstop racing and traveling—to and from Europe. He arrived in New York with little rest. But he and Franco Giorgetti had a great incentive to prove to the New York crowd that they deserved the win. Instead of the typical black jersey McNamara and his teammate would usually wear, they opted for the colors of the Italian flag.

During the week more famous people came and went than maybe had ever been to a single six-day race, including the Marx Brothers, Douglas Fairbanks, Mary Pickford, Red Grange, Theodore Roosevelt Jr., and William Fox of the Fox Film Corporation.

Nearly from the gun, McNamara and Giorgetti went all in and lapped the field in a sensational jam that ended with a nasty crash on the backstretch. But their lead didn't last long in this day and age of six-day racing, in which stealing laps happened all the time. On day 3 they got the lead back, and Bobby Walthour, who still had scars from getting his face smashed in Chicago, fell and broke his collarbone. Walthour's teammate, Harry Horan, was unable to find a new partner in the four hours allowed, and he was forced to withdraw.

With each successive night the crowd inside Madison Square Garden grew bigger and bigger, until day 6, when eighteen thousand cycling-crazed lunatic fans were yelling themselves hoarse, throwing paper, and drinking illegal booze that had been snuck in, nearly all of them rooting for the team of McNamara-Giorgetti. The two teammates must have enjoyed the moment, looking at each other and shaking their heads, realizing what a fickle bunch of fans these New Yorkers were.

McNamara-Giorgetti led nearly the entire race, and in the final hour they stamped an exclamation point by pilfering another lap, winning over the second-place team by two laps. The minute the race was done, Giorgetti rushed over to McNamara and kissed him on the cheek. One sportswriter commented, "I would have kissed McNamara too, if he had carried me on his handlebars for six days and six nights to win a race."[19]

A week later McNamara was the guest of honor at Newark's Krueger Auditorium, on the eve of his departure for Paris to race in another six-day at Vélodrome d'Hiver. Three hundred friends were there, including Frank Kramer, who gave a short history on six-day racing, George Chapman, Sammy

Gastman, Eddie Madden, Harry Horan, Willie Hanley, Alf Grenda, Freddie Spencer, Bobby Walthour Jr., Willie Coburn, Joe Kopsky, Tony Beckman, Vincent Markey, Frank Cavanaugh, and Jack Neville. McNamara was given a gold card case and a watch.

McNamara's win streak of three six-day race victories in a row came to an abrupt end at Paris. The same partner he had won with in Berlin, Harry Horan, was injured after only thirty minutes of riding. McNamara was forced to go alone for four hours while French doctors tended to Horan. It was feared Horan had sustained a broken collarbone, but he did come back out to the track and got a standing ovation from the huge crowd at the Vélodrome d'Hiver.[20]

On day 3 the race was stopped for more than an hour when fights nearly broke out between the riders because of collisions caused by rough riding. Trainers rushed out to separate riders. Whether McNamara was involved in the fisticuffs is not known, but it would not be surprising. McNamara-Horan were in virtually last place—fourteenth—but they fought their way back, finishing fourth place overall.

That December, McNamara had a last chance to get four six-day victories in 1926. He thought his odds were good teaming with Franco Giorgetti again in Chicago's October six-day. But Giorgetti complained bitterly about the rough riding and threatened to quit the race. He blamed Alphonse Goosens most of all but also called on John Chapman, the promoter, to do something. Giorgetti did not race in his usual aggressive manner, whereas his partner, McNamara, did. On day 5, when they were just one lap down, Frank Kramer, perhaps taking a directive from Chapman, pulled Giorgetti out of the race for "poor riding." McNamara ended up with Goosens as a partner when Goosens's teammate and fellow Belgian, Harry Stockelynch, failed to respond to treatment after an accident. McNamara-Goosens finished a respectable third place overall.

For the New York race in Madison Square Garden, McNamara, back in his traditional black jersey, was paired with a big, square-jawed Italian, Pietro Linari. Like most Italian professionals, Linari had road racing experience. He had won Milan–San Remo in 1924 as well as two stages of the Giro d'Italia in 1922 and 1925. Linari was familiar with New York crowds—he had competed in the December 1925 grind at the Garden. Surely Linari felt confident, having one of the best six-day riders in the business as a partner.

After nearly a year off the bike Alf Goullet was back with a great young teammate, Freddie Spencer. But for Goullet, who was only thirty-four—three and a half years younger than McNamara—it was to be his last race ever. "I left my race on the road," Goullet said. Leading up to the six-day, Goullet forced himself to keep pace with McNamara on training rides on the roads in and around Newark. He knew then it was time to quit, but he had to try one more race. Unfortunately, Goullet failed miserably in his comeback attempt. By day 4 he and Spencer were in last place—sixteen laps down from the leading team. Perhaps because years earlier he had projected McNamara's demise, only to see him come back stronger than ever, Howard Freeman of the *Newark Evening News* was cautious about Goullet. "In fact we will never predict that any rider is through," he wrote, "for that may start 'em on another epoch of successful six-day racing days, and one cannot tell how a rider's family feels about these extended racing careers. Goullet does not believe that he has reached the end of his racing days, and he is always smart in assaying his own physical worth."[21]

While Goullet-Spencer faltered, McNamara-Linari rose to the occasion. In an odd way the race was a passing of the torch from a younger Goullet to an older McNamara. Goullet used to dominate six-day race after six-day race, especially in the Garden, and he was always booed and hissed because the big crowd thought someone else should win for a change. In this race, however, Goullet was cheered by the twenty-three thousand fans, while McNamara was jeered because now he was the new general.[22]

There were several lead changes, but McNamara-Linari

were always in the lead or close to it. Other teams fighting as a front-runner were the Giorgetti-Belloni Italian combination, the Belgians Goosens-Stockelynch, and the Americans Winter-Stockholm. In the final hour of racing the four teams were deadlocked on laps. McNamara and Linari had stacked up a large amount of sprint points, so if the four teams ended in a tie on laps, McNamara-Linari would win. But rather than go conservatively, the team in black rode "as if their very lives depended on the result."

The final hour was marred by many crashes. Stockelynch went down with cuts and bruises to the face, arms, and legs. The doctors were concerned about internal injuries. Goosens made an attempt to keep going without Stockelynch, but it was no use; he retired from the race. With Linari making a relief of McNamara, they accidently bumped too hard, and both went down, taking Charlie Winter down with them. Winter was fine and got up quickly, but McNamara and Linari were both stretched out unconscious. The emergency gong rang out, and the crowd was hushed. With painful effort McNamara raised himself to a sitting position. He was able to get up and limp off in search of a new bike. When he straddled his new mount, the crowd was overjoyed with happiness—again showing their fickle nature. Linari was helped to his feet, and the doctors had a very limited time to bandage up his left shoulder before he was out in relief of McNamara. Thereafter, the crowd really got behind the riders in the black jerseys.

The first people to greet McNamara after he crossed the line a winner were his wife, Elizabeth, and eldest daughter, Eileen. McNamara and Linari made the traditional victory circuit "amid the most thunderous round of applause which ever greeted a winning cycling team."[23] At the finish line they were presented with roses and posed for a scrum of photographers, with Elizabeth and Eileen holding most of the flowers and their trainers holding the riders upright on the bikes.

One of the flashlight photographs appeared in the *Newark Evening News*, and the caption read "The End of a Perfect

Week." For McNamara not only was it that, but it was the end of a perfect year—Christmastime notwithstanding. In 1926 he won four six-day races in Berlin, Chicago, and New York, twice, making him one of the elite players in the cycling world. His career number of six-day victories climbed up to eleven, which was only one away from Goullet's world record of twelve overall victories.

Howard Freeman wrote once again about his intension never to write a rider off: "A couple of years ago we stated in this column that Reggie McNamara, the gent of iron, was through as a six-day rider. Reggie had made a dismal showing in a Chicago six-day race, which inspired us to write of his passing and we garnished his obituary with a lot of pathos. We had hardly gotten the words out of our typewriter when Reggie won the New York six-day race, which started the best six-day spree any rider ever went on. He followed the New York triumph by winning a six-day race in Berlin and one in Chicago. By that time we were convinced that we could not comment expertly on these bike riders any more. The Iron man made us look foolish and then proceeded to rub it in by winning several more six-day races. In fact, if memory serves us, he had lost but one six-day race since we announced that he was absolutely through and positively finished as a grinder."[24]

13

Rusty Iron

Taking into account his share of the six-day win in the December race with Linari, along with his other great string of six-day victories, McNamara was becoming a wealthy man. Frank Kramer and Alf Goullet were independently wealthy after retiring permanently from professional racing. If McNamara had plans to do the same, he was on the right track. He loved cycling, and now cycling was loving him back with great motivators—money and fame. But later in his career that strong motivation may have propelled him beyond his capabilities.

In 1926 the greatest and most famous athletes of the day were earning fabulous money. McNamara's $75,000 in earnings that year (about $1 million today) was listed alongside figures for many notable athletes, including Babe Ruth, whose baseball salary for the year was $52,000. Ty Cobb and Tris Speaker reportedly drew $60,000 and Rogers Hornsby $40,000. Football star Red Grange pulled in $50,000, and golfer Walter Hagen received $75,000. French tennis player Suzanne Lenglen earned $50,000, and jockey Earl Sande's 1926 income was estimated at $100,000. Gertrude Ederle, the first woman to swim across the English Channel, received approximately $75,000.[1] It was quite possible that McNamara, who would turn forty in November 1927, was the highest-paid professional cyclist in the world.

Despite his wealth, fame, and advanced age, McNamara was a very likable character and still one of the "boys." In late February a photographer captured McNamara, along with Bobby

Walthour Jr., Alex McBeath, Willie Grimm, Otto Petri, and Harris Horder, at South Mountain Reservation, "training" in the snow for the upcoming six-day race at the Garden. They were running and wrestling, and someone had brought a snow sled, which inevitably led to sled versus bike races. Despite the snow, the riders picked up a good amount of work on the roads and at the Newark Velodrome.

On one afternoon twenty-five or so riders, in the presence of several newspapermen, did a series of stunts around the track for a motion picture cameraman. When the cameraman had to tend to a mechanical problem, the riders started clowning around. Harris Horder pushed one of the riders, Alfredo Dinale, into an unsuspecting Alphonse Goosens. Goosens flew back and landed into a large ice-covered puddle, and everyone roared with laughter. But then the ice gave way, and Goosens went headlong into three feet of water; McNamara hurried forward and pulled him out of the freezing water. The normally mild-mannered Goosens rushed at Dinale, who had had nothing to do with the incident, and tried to choke him. While the riders pulled Goosens off Dinale, Harris Horder made a getaway to the exit area of the stadium. When Goosens learned of the party responsible, reported Willie Ratner of the *Newark Evening News*: "Out of the Velodrome and up South Orange Avenue ran Horder with Goosens after him, and twenty bicycle riders following Goosens to prevent him from tearing Horder to pieces."[2]

In the spring of 1927 McNamara was paired with Franco Giorgetti at Madison Square Garden for the third time. If McNamara were to win, it would be his twelfth six-day victory and would tie him with fellow Aussie Alf Goullet for the highest number of six-day wins.

Charlie Chaplin was supposed to fire the gun to start the race, "but he forgot his baggy trousers," and Harold Lloyd, another comedic actor, was put in as a substitute. Nearly from the gun, the stout-hearted Giorgetti went to the task of stealing laps, and Madison Square Garden went into an uproar. Willie Ratner, sportswriter for the *Newark Evening News*, from behind the WMSG microphone, perhaps the first radio broadcast of any cycling event in the United States, said simply, "Looks like a big week, boys."[3]

The high-speed action started by Giorgetti resulted in one of the riders, Émile Rohrbach, of France, crashing through the railing that separated the track from the stands. A woman was struck across the eye with his pedal. Rohrbach continued racing while the woman was taken to the hospital for treatment.

On day 1 McNamara was involved in a crash with six other riders that halted the race for an hour. Alphonse Goosens and McNamara were the most seriously hurt. Both were knocked unconscious and had to be taken to the emergency ward down in the Garden's basement. Goosens had a gash on the right side of his head that needed four stitches. McNamara, who rarely grumbled about being hurt, complained about rib pain. Both received bandages and tape and went back into the race.

McNamara crashed twice again on day 2. He remounted immediately both times, but his knees were heavily barked. Despite his accidents, McNamara-Giorgetti held a four-lap lead, and it was looking like they would waltz to the victory.

On day 3 McNamara had another crash that underscored why all his competitors and fans had such profound respect for the grand old man of cycling, not just because he was tough but also because he had a heart of gold. Willie Ratner recounted the story: "Charlie Meyer, one of the veteran trainers around the Newark and New York bike tracks, had just shoved off one of his riders during the sprints and as all trainers do, stood there for a few seconds watching his boy pedal away. The cyclist was down low, near the flat, and Charlie was also on the flat. McNamara was coming along at break-neck pace and when he reached the spot where Meyer was standing he found that he would have to go through low, underneath the man Meyer had pushed away. It was a case of hitting one or the other and Mac ran into the big, good-natured Meyer. He struck Charlie with a terrific crack in the ribs. Meyer and McNamara both went out cold. . . . When Meyer was revived, he started to cry. He was afraid, he said, that McNamara would be out of the race as a result of what he believed was his own carelessness, but that idea was entirely wrong. He was not at fault. The rumors that McNamara had sustained a broken collarbone caused Meyer to go 'out' again, but ten minutes later, when Reggie appeared on the scene, Meyer felt relieved. As soon as McNamara had pulled himself together the first thing he asked was, 'How is Charlie Meyer?'"[4]

Although McNamara never said anything, some had questioned whether Giorgetti pulled his weight when paired with the Iron Man. As a team, this race—March 1927—was perfect, and nobody could claim Giorgetti was a weakness. None of their pickups were "wireless," as they had been in the past, and there was a confidence between them that the crowd could sense. Although they were in the lead from day 1, as a consequence of this confidence and camaraderie, the crowd pulled for them. The old blend of boos and cheers was gone—only cheers.

For six days in a row McNamara was incorporated into the headline of the *New York Times* sports section, page 1. On the final day a throng of twenty-two thousand witnessed McNamara cross the line, once again a winner at Madison Square Garden with his Italian mate, Franco Giorgetti. McNamara rode the final forty-eight hours with broken ribs on his left side and was again greeted at the finish line by his wife, Elizabeth, and their daughter, Eileen.

McNamara's next stop would be in Paris, in the April six-day at the Vélodrome d'Hiver. Howard Freeman, a former professional bike rider turned sportswriter for the *Newark Evening News*, was hopeful but cautious of McNamara's chances in Paris, which he reported "are not as bright as they would be most anywhere else, and it will not be surprising if he fails to win. The Paris race is a tough one. It is held at the Vélodrome d'Hiver, which is almost as big as the Newark Velodrome. Lap stealing is rare on this track, and is not suited to the American style of six-day racing, at which Mac excels. But it would be a magnificent triumph and crowning achievement of the Iron Man's career if he cracked Alf Goullet's six-day record by winning the Paris race."[5]

Altogether, with the prize money, appearance fees, and sprint winnings, McNamara purportedly took home $10,000 for the March 1927 six-day race at the Garden. The richest man in the cycling world just got richer. Waiting to board the RMS *Aquitania* for Cherbourg, local cameramen took a photo of little Regina McNamara seated between her parents and looking up, questioningly, at her father. Eileen remained at home because of school commitments. She must have been disappointed to miss this chance of a lifetime, but she had gone on a European vacation with her mother and sister in the summer of 1925 while her father remained at home.[6]

The French press poked fun at the amount of cycling equipment McNamara brought with him. A sketch was made in *La Presse* of two assistants struggling to carry it all through the Vélodrome d'Hiver's front entrance.

McNamara was teamed with a Belgian, Émile Aerts, who was a European six-day specialist. He was on the winning team in 1922 and 1924 in the Paris six-day; 1922, 1924, and 1925 at the Brussels six-day; and in the Berlin six-day in 1925.

As many as ten thousand people were turned away nightly from the Vélodrome d'Hiver in what was a close battle. Just as Freeman had predicted, it was difficult to gain a lap on a 250-meter track like the Vélodrome d'Hiver. No team had stolen a lap until McNamara and Aerts did on day 4 and suddenly found themselves in first place.

From that point on the pair never relinquished their grasp on the lead and took the overall victory. According to a special cable to the *New York Times*, the end of the race "was the occasion of one of the most uproarious demonstrations ever seen at a Paris sporting event."[7]

Coincidentally, on the very next evening and thousands of miles away at the New York Velodrome, Franco Giorgetti had such a popular motor-paced victory that fans massed out of the bleachers and grandstand and hoisted the little Italian rider to their shoulders and paraded him around the track. Giorgetti beamed as men, women, and children followed along while he was showered with flowers and kisses. Complete strangers thrust money into his hands.[8]

Reggie and family traveled to Italy, where he raced at velodromes in Milan, Pordenone, and Bologna against some of the best Italian riders, such as Costante Girardengo and Alfredo Binda, and then in Rome he met the pope and Benito Mussolini. "Then when we returned to Paris for a few days," wrote McNamara in a letter to Harry Mendel, "my wife and Rennie left me and went to Ireland. I would have gone too, but had to race here."[9]

On the way back across the Atlantic, the McNamaras enjoyed the first-class accommodations of the *Aquitania* again. McNamara was not the only superstar athlete either. The first ever Ryder Cup golf team from Great Britain was also on board. As fate would have it, the United States team, captained by Walter Hagen, had crushed the Brits at Worcester Country Club.

Not only were the McNamaras surrounded by golfing history, there was a possibility of being part of aviation history. Depending on what time the *Aquitania* left the port at Cherbourg, France, on May 21, it was close to the flight path of Charles Lindbergh on his famous nonstop flight from New York to Paris. Lindbergh landed at Le Bourget airport at 10:22 p.m. on May 21. In some Forrest Gump–like happenstance, the *Aquitania* and the *Spirit of St. Louis* may have crossed paths. Perhaps McNamara was outside on deck, smoking a cigar in the night air when Lindbergh flew over.

The *Aquitania* steamed into the New York Harbor on Friday, May 27, 1927, and two days later McNamara was racing at the New York Velodrome in front of twenty-two thousand spectators. Although his hero's welcome was not in the form of a New York City ticker tape parade, like Charles Lindbergh's return, McNamara was given a standing ovation in honor of his thirteenth six-day victory when he came out on to the track. After he beat Alex McBeath in a special match race, showing that he still had a sprint in his legs, the crowd burst into an even greater applause.[10]

With McNamara on top of the cycling world and his incredible streak of eight six-day wins in two and a half years coming to an end, there was only one direction he could go, and that was down. McNamara hoped his fortieth birthday in November 1927 would be celebrated with his fourteenth six-day win. But like old iron left outside exposed to the elements of rain, snow, ice, wind, and sun, at some point it was going to rust and decay.

Flaxen-haired and gap-toothed Charlie Winter was the youngest of his four brothers and three sisters. They were raised in Bronx, New York, inside a five-story apartment complex on Heath Avenue by their Austrian-born parents. In August 1925, at age twenty-one, Winter, riding for the Century Road Club of America, clinched the amateur sprint championship at the Newark Velodrome. A few months later Winter rode in his first professional race—the Chicago six-day, paired with Paul Croley, the rider who took second to Winter in the amateur championship. Although they finished fifth to the winning combination of Freddie Spencer and Bobby Walthour Jr., it was a great experience competing in and finishing the Chicago grind.

Winter's first six-day victory was at Madison Square Garden in December 1927. He was the hometown kid, and amid the confetti thrown from the gallery and the boisterous crowd of more than twenty thousand spectators was an old plumber—Charlie's proud father.

"It certainly was a great thrill," said Winter a few days after his victory. "I felt as if I didn't care about winning another race for the remainder of my career. I wanted to win that one, and I did, and nothing else mattered. But now I feel different. I want to win the next one, as well, and all the other six-day. And don't forget, I have the plumbing business to fall back on."[11]

Winter was the kid Jack Neville had compared with McNamara, saying that "if he wasn't the next McNamara, I don't know my digitalis." Winter and McNamara were built with the same stocky proportions, but Winter was a few inches taller and weighed 180 pounds, whereas McNamara was about 10 pounds less.

In January 1928 John Chapman decided that the next Iron Man, Winter, and McNamara should be paired together in the Chicago six-day. Of the pair Howard Freeman wrote: "With two McNamaras riding as a team there will have to be something radically wrong with one of 'em for the team to finish worse than first. Making up two such powerful jammers is bound to have a beneficial effect on McNamara. Winter is strong and not temperamental and when he's representing the team on the field of battle Reg will know that his interests are perfectly safe. That alone will pump up his morale to the bursting point."[12]

Freeman's words proved prophetic. At the Chicago Coliseum, McNamara, generally considered to be the greatest "shover" in the six-day game, loved having Winter as his partner. "In all my years I have never seen a stronger boy than Winter," grinned McNamara. "The first time Winter relieved me this week he gave me such a shove I thought a truck had hit me. . . . Another fine thing about Winter is you can rely on him to be in the proper spot for a pick-up. It's a relief when you know you don't have to worry about your partner."[13]

On day 3 McNamara said to Winter that he wanted to take the lead—and he did. In the lead by two laps, McNamara was involved in a crash with a number of other riders. When he stood up, a fan close by yelled that McNamara had taken the fall on purpose. Nobody could recall McNamara ever losing his temper with a fan before, but that's just what happened. Before he was able to make his way into the stands, however, a few nearby trainers reacted quickly to restrain him.[14]

As a result of the fall, McNamara continued to ride with a chipped left shoulder bone, and he could hardly lift his arm over his head, much less give big Charlie Winter a good shove. The other riders caught wind of McNamara's injury and took advantage by incorporating continuous jams. McNamara-Winter soon went from being two laps up to three laps down.

The next day, at two in the morning, McNamara locked handlebars with Larry Gaffney and fell on his chipped left shoulder. He slid down the track and ended up at the boards by the track railing, immersed in pain. McNamara had to be carried out and taken to Keystone Hospital. Referee Frank Kramer gave Winter the standard four hours to find a new partner, but he never did find one and was forced out of the race. McNamara arrived back at the Coliseum with his arm in a sling, and he fired the gun for the final hour of racing.

Although it seemed the McNamara-Winter combination was a winning one, they were paired again at Madison Square Garden in March and Paris in April and did not have good results. On April 20 Winter wrote a letter from Paris to Al Everard, the president of his former team, the Century Road Club of America, and provided much insight about the Paris race. "I suppose you all were just thinking how terrible Mac and I rode," he wrote. "We did not go so very bad, but they did not give us the best of everything. And I don't care to have anybody know this bit of news, because I think Mac is OK and I don't want to pan him. But of course he realizes now that he is just about finished as a six-day bike rider and he tells me so very often. He really wanted to quit Wednesday but he said he stayed in for my sake. Because there were many times the old boy was just shook off and I had to bring him back into the field. And there's no such thing as making a wireless pick-up here because they call you a robber and fine you. So two hours before the finish Mac said to the trainers he was going to quit so in one big jam Mac rode off and let me stay on and those dumb frog trainers just let me stay out there jamming but when I did not see Mac, well, I knew he threw in the sponge so that was the finish of that."[15]

Whether Winter was fully truthful in the letter will never be known. But unless McNamara had some physical problem, it is not likely that he would "throw in the sponge" for no reason, as Winter seems to indicate in the letter.

Another rider still fighting to race at the end of a stellar professional career that had started in 1914 was Italian Gaetano

Belloni. To this cycling researcher's knowledge, no other rider, other than Eddy Merckx, had ever won both a Grand Tour and a major six-day race. Belloni had won the Giro d'Italia in 1920, and then in December 1922, with the best partner in the game at the pinnacle of his career, Alf Goullet, he won the six-day race at Madison Square Garden. Belloni also won more than ten stages of the Giro and was second overall in 1919 and 1921.

In the early spring of 1929 Belloni traveled to the United States, where he signed contracts with John Chapman to race in back-to-back six-days—New York in early March and then in Chicago a week later. Paired with American Tony Beckman, he got third overall at the Garden and then got sixth overall in Chicago with fellow Italian Alfonso Zucchetti.

With little time to rest before traveling back to Italy, on May 19, 1929, Belloni won a mountainous stage 1 from Rome to Naples. Alfredo Binda won stage 2 and stage 3, but Belloni still claimed the leader's jersey. But Binda continued his assault, and on May 25 he took stage 4 and the leader's jersey. Binda went on to win five more stages in a row, making it eight straight stages—a Giro record.

On stage 8 Belloni lost fourteen minutes in a crash before he was able to remount and chase the field containing Binda. During his frantic pursuit a young boy darted out in front of him and was killed. The grief-stricken rider climbed off his bike, wept, and abandoned the Giro.[16]

Although nothing could have been worse than what Belloni experienced in the 1929 Giro, McNamara was having bad luck too. Over the course of two years he hadn't come close to winning since he and Émile Aerts turned the trick in Paris in 1927. The press wrote articles that he was jinxed on unlucky six-day victory number 13, but there was that other albatross around his neck—he was getting too old.

Perhaps John Chapman thought it would be humorous to put these two aging stars, both down on their luck, together as a pair at the Chicago six-day in November 1929. With their combined experience, they didn't worry that they had never ridden together as partners. Both needed cycling redemption, especially Belloni, after his accidental killing of a child.

Despite the fact that the race began two weeks after the stock market crash of October 1929, the prelude to the ten-year Great Depression—on McNamara's forty-second birthday—Chicago stadium was absolutely bike crazy. Each night sellout crowds of more than sixteen thousand filled the great venue. According to the *Chicago Tribune*, the bike race had "a big gathering representing most of Chicago's night life in the infield where the customers pay $5.00 to watch the race, sip ginger ale and red pop."[17] In the same issue front-page headlines included a story of police having made four liquor raids. One warehouse stored 170,000 gallons of beer mash. "Machine Gun" Jack McGurn, handsome, bombastic, and one of Al Capone's favorite gangland machine-gun executioners, was often a guest of Capone at the Chicago six-day races.[18] Perhaps Capone and McGurn were there, hiding from police and sipping ginger ale.

On day 5 in Chicago the two grizzled veterans, McNamara and Belloni, struggling to keep up with the leaders for most of the week, started a great jam, and "before any of the record breaking crowd suspected it, the old ironman and his swarthy Italian confrere broke loose and took the lead."[19] The old pair hung on to their one-lap advantage and won the race over the second-place French team of Paul Brocardo and Alfred Letourneur and the third-place combination of Germans Franz Duelberg and Victor Rausch. McNamara finally had his fourteenth victory, and Gaetano Belloni had redemption from his disaster at the Giro d'Italia. Page 1 of the *Chicago Daily Tribune*'s sports section carried a flash photograph of McNamara and a clean-cut Belloni, both smiling with their trainers, with promoter Paddy Harmon, holding up the eighteen-inch trophy cup, between them.[20]

After his November 1929 victory in Chicago, McNamara had back-to-back six-day races, with little time for rest. There was New York in December; Dortmund, Germany, in January; Chicago in February; and New York in March. Although

McNamara's team was in the lead or near the lead in all the races at some point that winter, he had little overall success.

On day 4 in Dortmund, McNamara broke a finger on his right hand by getting it caught in the spokes. On the same finger a deep gash penetrated the bone. Against his wishes the physician, for fear of blood poisoning, ordered him off the track and out of the race. McNamara was nonplussed and vowed never to race at Dortmund again.[21]

For the first time in ten years McNamara made arrangements to go to Australia to visit his parents, Timothy and Honora, who were both in their eighties. He had made several offers to persuade them come out to the United States and live in Newark, but they remained in Australia. McNamara wanted Elizabeth to come along, but she decided to stay behind and look after the girls, now both teenagers.

McNamara had a charmed send-off at Newark's Market Street Station of the Pennsylvania Railroad. Not only did fellow riders and trainers, such as Harvey Black, Pop Brennan, Harry Horan, Harris Horder, and Charlie Ritter, come to see him off, but so, too, did many of his fans. Of course, Elizabeth was there with Eileen and Regina. McNamara accepted packages from Harris Horder to present to his father, George, who lived near the McNamara ranch. The *Newark Evening News*'s Willie Ratner was there to cover the moment. "Mac waved one hand at the crowd and with the other brushed tears away from his eyes," he wrote. "One could hardly believe that this was the same rough fellow of six-day fame, the man six-day crowds thinks has no feelings, no sentiment, no romance. But it was. The 'Iron Man' softened up. This display of loyalty on the part of his friends and his fellow riders, most of them boys in the game who look upon McNamara as one of the wonders of the world."[22]

Perhaps it was on this trip, whether on the train to San Francisco or on the steamer to Sydney or there and back to the United States again, when the alcohol problems began that would plague him in the years ahead. It was very likely that McNamara had a few beers now and again. Even though it was still illegal during Prohibition, drinking was widely accepted and tolerated. But if there was a breakdown in moderate drinking, this trip to Australia may have been the first phase, or at least the root cause of his heavy drinking. By his own admission McNamara said of his 1930 trip to Australia that he was drunk the whole time and was even put in jail briefly.

Similar to his return trip in 1919, Australian newspapers enthusiastically wrote of McNamara's impending arrival. From the ship he radioed to the newspaper *Referee* that he would arrive in Sydney "by the Tahiti about April 12. I will consider racing engagements."[23] Then, at what first seemed to be a promising and lengthy correspondence with the Australian media, the reporting stopped. Perhaps in an attempt to keep his drunkenness a secret the papers chose, instead, to report almost not at all during his month-long stay. Weeks after he left to return to America, a pathetic one-paragraph article entitled "Reg McNamara Ignored" appeared in a newspaper called *The Land*.

He may have not remembered everything for that month in Australia. But McNamara would never forget the shame he brought on his family. He had come to renew acquaintances with his brothers and sisters and meet some of his nieces and nephews for the first time. He knew it may be the last time he would ever see his parents alive. One can merely speculate about what happened there, but it seemed to trigger something that changed his life. Maybe it was just the booze, but maybe it was something more. With inner demons that he could not control, he knew he could always count on keeping motivated by riding his bike.

14

Downward Spiral

If there were a contemporary professional athlete who could compare to McNamara's utter refusal to give into the natural aging process, it would be baseball's Rickey Henderson, who was inducted into the Hall of Fame in 2009. The two had similarly aggressive styles; both were unafraid of serious physical injury and sacrificed their bodies for victory. Reggie was known as the "Iron Man," and Henderson's nickname was "the Man of Steal." Both were professional athletes for nearly three decades.

Approaching his forty-eighth birthday, Henderson said something that McNamara, at the same age, would have agreed with wholeheartedly. "I can't say I will retire," said Henderson. "My heart is still in it . . . I still love the game right now, so I'm going to wait it out and see what happens." In 2005, after spending twenty-four seasons in the major leagues, he finished a season with the San Diego Surf Dawgs in the Golden Baseball League. Henderson helped lead the Surf Dawgs to their league championship. In 2007 Billy Beane, general manager of the Oakland Athletics, considered calling him up for one day, but Henderson didn't want it as a gift. "One day? I don't want one day. I want to play again, man. I don't want nobody's spot. . . . I just want to see if I deserve to be out there. If I don't, just get rid of me, release me. And if I belong, you don't have to pay me but the minimum—and I'll donate every penny of that to some charity. So, how's that hurtin' anybody? . . . Don't say goodbye for me. . . . When I want that one day they want to give me so bad, I'll let you know."[1]

If cycling had a minor league, like baseball, that's where forty-five-year-old McNamara belonged. But like Henderson, he still showed signs of speed and strength—grit was not an issue. Nobody could take his marvelous career away. Promoters knew that a six-day race without Reggie McNamara was no six-day race at all. Whether he was beyond his best years or not, people would pay to see the Iron Man one last time. If he and Norman Hill hadn't won the Cleveland six-day in January 1933, perhaps that would have been his farewell season. But he hung on a few more years.

In the 1930s the number of six-day races increased prohibitively. In 1933 there were at least fifteen in North America. After the Cleveland race in January, there was St. Louis, New York, Chicago, Montreal, Toronto, Boston, Quebec, Detroit, Minneapolis, Montreal (#2), Boston (#2), Chicago (#2), New York (#2), and Cleveland (#2). If Reggie could have been in all of them, he would have. It wasn't uncommon for some professionals to race in more than ten per year. In 1932, for example, Torchy Peden won ten of the fourteen six-day races he competed in. McNamara's youthful wish of competing in a six-day race every month, more or less, came true.

In early March 1933, for a brief time, McNamara and his teammate, Harry Horan, were in the lead at the New York six-day at Madison Square Garden. But before the end of the race, on day 5, he was forced to withdraw by the race physician. His front wheel rubbed the back wheel of another rider, and McNamara went down with a severely bruised shoulder and a concussion. Willie Ratner, WMCA radio commentator and sportswriter for the *Newark Evening News*, reported: "But to those eyes that have looked at many a race and many a rider, there was something missing, and the truth reached home with startling suddenness. Reggie McNamara wasn't out there. Old Mac passed out of this race picture shortly after midnight and in the capacity crowd of 20,000 there was a tear discernable here and there as they carried the gallant old warrior to the basement training quarters."[2]

It was McNamara's thirty-first New York six-day race, and it was the first time he was out before the final gun. From the rub table of the emergency quarters downstairs at the Garden, where McNamara was covered in bandages, he insisted he be allowed to go upstairs to at least watch the race. Over and over he vowed to compete in Chicago's six-day race, which was to start the following week. With his unruly thatch of iron-gray hair, McNamara said, "Put that in your paper." McNamara added that he would be there "or there won't be any Chicago race."[3]

But the Chicago race was more or less a repeat of New York. After a bad crash the doctor ordered him out of the race with another concussion. One newspaper account claimed not to worry about McNamara because only "the first hundred concussions are the hardest."[4]

Undeterred, McNamara started the Boston six-day in late April, just six weeks after his second concussion. The Boston race had a conflicting time schedule with the Montreal six-day. Some of the best cyclists in the business—Jules Audy, Al Crossley, Gérard Debaets, Alfred Letourneur, Torchy Peden, and Tino Reboli—competing in Montreal would not be able to make it to Boston.

But Boston had a number of good riders too. McNamara was there, along with George Dempsey, Franz Duelberg, Freddie Spencer, Bobby Walthour Jr., Jimmy Walthour Jr., Cecil Walker, Charlie Winter, and Ewald Wissel. Promoters thought it wise to team Reggie McNamara with an unproven youngster with the same last name, Hal McNamara.

A few days after Patriots' Day the six-day race began inside the Boston Garden. Early in the morning of day 2 Bobby Walthour and his partner, Wissel, broke away from the field. A furious jam began, and the crowd stood up and came to life. Coming out to relieve his partner, Wissel came out on the track. Walthour, who was just about ready to reach out and give Wissel a good shove, lost his balance. Walthour went to the boards unhurt, but his bike went down in such a way that his pedal took the force of his weight and carved out a chunk of Canadian spruce from Pat Mulvey's track surface.

McNamara was behind, going full speed but in a position to see the danger Walthour was in, lying on the flat of the track. In swinging down suddenly to avoid the fallen rider, McNamara's bike came out from under him, and he slid head first along the track right over the spot where Walthour had dug his pedal into the spruce.

For Walthour's five-year-old son, Bob Walthour III, it may have been one of his earliest memories seeing McNamara that day. A splinter eight inches long and two inches wide penetrated McNamara's body under the left side of his rib cage. "They had to slide him out of it," recalled young Walthour. "I was right there as a little kid, with the crowd around him, and he says, 'Take it easy! Me guts are hangin' out.'"[5]

For Dr. G. Lynde Gately, who had treated cyclists and hockey players for a decade at the Boston Garden and dressed McNamara's wound that day, it was the closest he had seen an athlete come to death without actually being killed. Gately had nearly all he could handle with McNamara insisting on returning to the track to race. Whether it was losing consciousness from the pain or that Gately gave him a sedative, eventually McNamara went to sleep. His condition was so serious that Gately refused to move McNamara immediately to the hospital.

From his bed in Boston, McNamara wrote a letter to Willie Ratner. "I suppose you've heard all the reports of my fall," he began. "It was a simple fall and while sliding along the home stretch I ran into a loose strip extending above the surface. I got quite a jagged cut so Dr. Gately couldn't stitch it up. He laid it back and it's healing nicely. I feel quite OK otherwise. I think I have had more people come to see me than attend the sprints. I've had Boston lawyers, doctors, newspapermen, counts, earls and lords in here to talk to me (but no women). Judging from their interest in my welfare, I am sure the six-day race here will go over. I think it's an even better town than Chicago."[6]

It was not the first time McNamara had track splinters, and

it was not to be his last. In October 1928 he picked up a stubborn one in his right arm in a Detroit six-day. The doctors in Detroit probed but didn't remove it all. The following month he entered the Chicago six-day with Gérard Debaets as his partner. Although McNamara started the Chicago race with a bloodshot eye and was unable to lift his arm over his head, Debaets was the one who was forced to quit because of an ankle injury. At the time Debaets's ankle was wounded, they were closing in on the lead. McNamara finished the race by partnering up with Freddie Spencer. Weeks after the Chicago race McNamara went to New York to have the infected arm treated, and they couldn't get the rest of the splinter out. Finally, in Newark, he had a specialist remove the remaining fragments of wood.[7]

As someone renowned for his durability, he had not finished a six-day race in three attempts—that was a personal record he did not want. He was growing older, and the last three races had put him out for months. But he had no plans to retire. "I suppose folks back home think I am at the end of my career," he said. "I'm going to ride at least 100 six-day races and maybe one or two more. When promoters refuse to use me any longer then I'll retire gracefully."

In the summer of 1933 Canadian promoter Armand Vincent put together a professional road race. The race was to start in Montreal on August 1, with stops in Toronto, Hamilton, Minneapolis, Madison, Milwaukee, Chicago, Detroit, Cleveland, Toledo, Buffalo, and Ottawa and finishing back in Montreal on September 3. The race distance was to be more than forty-three hundred miles—longer than the Tour de France. Vincent offered $25,000 in prize money and selected dozens of professional six-day riders to compete. Among the fifty-four starters were Lew Elder, Reggie Fielding, Harry Horan, Torchy Peden, Tino Reboli, Mike Rodak, Lew Rush, and Freddie Zach—and Reggie McNamara.

They began at Montreal baseball stadium with 150 laps around the field before pushing off to the countryside and into the Laurentian Mountain range. The caravan included a repair truck, an ambulance, and other vehicles for trainers, managers, and the press. On the first day Reggie McNamara crashed on the pavement and was forced to abandon the race with cuts to his face and knees.[8] Surely he was not happy with how things ended—especially so soon—but McNamara must have had a great time racing in the sun and recalling the last time he had been in an outdoor road race nearly thirty years ago in Australia.

Evidence that promoter Vincent had planned poorly and bit off more than he could chew came on full force when the great caravan arrived at the United States border. Customs authorities demanded $1,500 cash. Vincent did not have the money. From that point on Vincent was nowhere to be found, and Willie Spencer, the former cycling great turned promoter, took control of the management of the race. Spencer turned the riders around and headed them back to Montreal, cutting the race well short of the projected forty-three hundred miles.[9]

From late 1933 to early 1934 McNamara signed contracts to compete in as many six-day races as possible. There was Boston in October, Chicago in November, New York in December, Milwaukee and Buffalo in January, New York and Pittsburgh in March, Montreal in April, and Toronto in May. Surely it was a whirlwind adventure, but six-day racing had forever changed. The quantity of races made the competition thin out, and the crowds, with the exception of New York, were thinning too. McNamara's presence at the races was still in demand, and at forty-six years old, just like baseball great Rickey Henderson, he still had the fire in his belly.

In almost every race of this period McNamara and his teammate were either in the lead or somewhere within striking distance of it. In Milwaukee he and Bobby Thomas finished second overall. Then in Buffalo, McNamara and his partner, Tino Reboli, almost pulled out a victory but came in second again. The next stop on his busy schedule was the West Coast. McNamara hadn't raced there since the 1917 six-day race scandal in San Francisco, when he and others suddenly quit the race under protest.

Seventeen years later McNamara didn't have much better luck in San Francisco; he crashed on day 2 while he and his youthful partner, Eddie Testa, were in the lead, and he fractured his left wrist.[10]

But he went out west for more than racing—he was there to help make a film. Joe E. Brown was one of the most famous comedic actors of the day. With his great comic timing and his colossal smile, Brown made a number of sports-related movies. In the late spring of 1934 Brown played Wilfred Simpson in the movie *6 Day Bicycle Rider*, in which he competed with a six-day bike rider for the affection of a girl.

Frank Turano, who resembled Brown, played his double in many of the action scenes on the track, where McNamara and other professionals of the day could occasionally be seen riding in the background. McNamara may not have earned any money for being in the film, but he did earn a credit as a "technical advisor." McNamara was impressed with the leading actor. "Brown is a really good bicycle rider," he said. "Do you know he took the job of becoming a better one seriously? Do you know he had the picture stopped each morning so that he got an hour or two of practice? That is what I call doing a good job."[11]

Sometime between rehabilitating his wrist in May and helping out with the movie in August, McNamara learned about the death of his eighty-six-year-old father, Timothy. The last time he had seen his father was in 1930 in Australia, and he wasn't in a good state of mind then, being drunk for most of the time. In addition, his aging mother and his own little family three thousand miles away in Newark weighed heavily on his mind. Given his sad and lonely condition, there is little doubt that he continued his beer drinking to excess.

Not only did the drinking continue, but so, too, did the six-day racing. In one of his crashes in the November 1934 six-day race in Chicago, a large splinter was lodged in his left arm. Doctors worked to extract it and sewed his arm up with four stitches. Decades later Eddie Raffo, one of the many young riders McNamara raced against, recalled how nonchalant McNamara was during his medical treatment in Chicago. "I once saw McNamara," said Raffo, "the old 'Iron Man,' have an eight-inch splinter taken from one arm while he ate a sandwich with the other."[12]

Although McNamara would not turn fifty years old until November 1937, many of his races, like Chicago in November 1934, perpetuated a myth that he had already passed that milestone. The *Chicago Tribune* described one evening as "Reggie McNamara Night" to celebrate his fiftieth birthday. "The riders and some of Reggie's friends," it was reported, "plan to give him gifts and they will probably cut a birthday cake at the trackside for the veteran of 111 races."[13] Whether McNamara came up with the idea himself or whether promoters used it to sell more tickets remains unknown. For years McNamara insisted he was older than he was, and in 1939 he went so far as to write a letter to a fan to settle an argument. He claimed, falsely, that he had been born on November 7, 1884.[14]

McNamara signed a contract to race in the December 1934 six-day race at Madison Square Garden. But after the Chicago race his condition was not good. In addition to all the little maladies he suffered, he had stomach problems. Whether it was brought on by the splinter he had received six months earlier in Boston or a flare-up from his 1920 operation or his drinking, or a combination of all three, something was nagging at him that he hoped would go away. But it didn't go away. Pressure was mounting, too, because since 1913 he had only missed two New York grinds—in December 1917, while recovering from a broken jaw and fractured skull, and in March 1924, for getting suspended by Frank Kramer in Chicago. At the start of the December 1934 New York six-day, McNamara was a no-show. He had called in sick—a first for certain. Dave Lands was to be McNamara's partner, and at first it looked like he may have had to forfeit his chances. But John Chapman secured a substitute for McNamara, and Charlie Ritter was pressed into service, donning the traditional McNamara team black jersey.[15]

While he continued to search for victories against much younger, stronger, and more agile opponents, even McNamara could look back on his 1934 season and see there was not much success. Although he did have two second-place finishes and he had a little part in making a Hollywood movie, he had been stabbed in the stomach with a splinter, stabbed in the arm with a splinter, broke a wrist, had a number races that he did not finish, called in sick to a race, and his father died.

If he were hoping, at forty-seven years old, that his 1935 season would be any better, he was wrong. But unlike the Oakland A's general manager, Billy Beane, who only wanted Rickey Henderson to come back to Oakland to play one measly game, John Chapman would not deny McNamara the opportunity.

In March 1935 McNamara raced in his final six-day at Madison Square Garden. It was his thirty-fourth six-day race at that venue. He had finished almost all of them and had eight overall triumphs. He was racing against men who were not yet born when he and Eddie Root took third at the Garden in 1913.

He was teamed with Dave Lands, and within five hours they were eleven laps down on the leading team of Franco Giorgetti and Alfred Letourneur. The downward trend continued, and McNamara had a number of crashes, including one in which he "went down, bouncing his head on the wooden track."[16] Sixteen laps in behind, McNamara-Lands began a remarkable comeback, kicking and scratching their way to the leaders. McNamara showed flashes of his old form, and at one time they were tied for the lead. But their day 3 escalation went away, and they tumbled back. By the time the eight o'clock sprints started on day 6, McNamara and Lands had withdrawn.[17] They were given a great ovation by the fifteen thousand fans, who never dreamed it would be the Iron Man's final Garden dismount.

On Wednesday evening, May 8, 1935, McNamara sat waiting at the Newark train station for his next bike adventure out west in San Francisco. He also had tentative plans to travel to Tokyo to introduce six-day riding in Japan. The big noisy train came rolling in and shook the ground where it stopped. As McNamara reached down for his luggage, he noticed a number of Essex County sheriff's deputies closing in.

Mrs. McNamara had learned of her husband's plans to leave for several months, whereupon she went through a great ordeal to obtain a chancery court writ to keep him in the state. McNamara was arrested at the train station and spent the night in the county jail. The next morning he secured bail of $1,000 and was released.

Elizabeth filed a suit for "separate maintenance," which works like alimony but the couple remains legally married. She charged that McNamara had begun to treat her cruelly on about Christmas 1931. On several occasion thereafter, she also alleged that she was forced to seek aid from the domestic relations court. She further purported that on the most recent Thanksgiving Day, McNamara had smashed dishes on their table and was generally and otherwise cruel to her.[18]

This sequence of public events revealed that his family life—or at least life with his wife—was not good. One can only guess what was happening financially. Was all the money gone? Was it being stockpiled in a bank account or under a mattress somewhere? Had they made unwise investments? Was McNamara racing to get money enough just to stay even? Had Reggie and Elizabeth been separated unofficially a long time ago? Although it is impossible to know what was going on financially, what was known was that Reggie continued to drink beer in great quantities and continued six-day racing with limited success.

Not much time was spent in the county court to sort out the couple's domestic problems because on May 20, 1935, McNamara was three thousand miles away, at the starting line of the San Francisco six-day, competing against riders half his age, including American cyclists who had participated in the 1932 Los Angeles Olympics: Jack McCoy, Henry "Cocky" O'Brien, and Eddie Testa. "I feel like a kid," McNamara said, "and I'm not afraid of any of these young bike riders."[19]

A week later McNamara was across the San Francisco Bay, in Oakland, racing inside the Municipal Auditorium. McNamara and his partner, Tony Schaller, were in the lead early on, but they were no match for the eventual winning team of Jules Audy and Reggie Fielding.

Although his results weren't great and he wasn't earning anywhere near his superstar status of 1926, McNamara was still making good money. His appearance fees and the bonuses he received, in the neighborhood of $1,500 per race, were roughly equivalent to $26,000 today. Along with other athletes of the day, his image appeared in newspapers all over the United States in Camel cigarette ads with taglines such as "They don't get your wind" and "So Mild! You can smoke all you want!"[20] With the new "separate maintenance" arranged by the county court, some or most of the money went home to Newark on a mandatory basis.

In November 1935 Reggie McNamara celebrated his forty-eighth birthday, just before the start of what would be his second-to-last six-day race ever. Whether he planned it this way or whether promoters such as John Chapman refused to sign him to another racing contract remains unknown. But one thing is certain: no rider or professional athlete, even Rickey Henderson, could say they were more ready for retirement than Reggie McNamara. In his 121 six-day races and other assorted races he had been beaten up, battered, bruised, and broken. He competed professionally in approximately 150,000 miles of racing, the equivalent of circling Earth six times. Although there were so many published reports of the untold injuries he had suffered over the years, there had to be many injuries that went unreported—perhaps even broken bones—which he kept to himself.

The choice for his partner was a worthy one. Of any of the riders nobody had known McNamara for as long as Bobby Walthour Jr. did. McNamara had raced against his father while the younger Walthour, a pimply preteenager, sat watching from the stands of smoke-filled indoor stadiums such as Madison Square Garden with his mother and sisters. Now, in 1935, Walthour Jr. was a middle-aged man with a wife and three children of his own to support. In bike racing years Walthour was a veteran, and of course McNamara was ancient.

It was Chicago's thirty-fourth international six-day race, and McNamara had been in twenty-six of them. Chicago stadium was jammed with fourteen thousand bike fans as McNamara lined up on the very inside in his black silk jersey at the start. The pop of bright photograph flashes was heard and seen throughout the big building as the football coach of Purdue, Nick Kiser, raised his arm and fired the starting pistol.[21]

The comedian of six-day riders, Belgian Gérard Debaets, who once had a nose-pulling contest with Jimmy Durante and often threw wet sponges at sleeping fans, was in a foul mood. Debaets and his partner, Bobby Thomas, complained to referee Frank Kramer that they were being ganged up on by the German team of Gustave Killian and Heinz Vopel as well as the Canadian team of Jules Audy and Torchy Peden. Kramer told the riders they had been "accused of monkey business" and threatened to suspend them if he caught them red-handed. The warning, however, did little but inspire the teams—especially Audy-Peden and Killian-Vopel—to liven up their performance. According to the *Chicago Daily Tribune*, the German team rode "exactly as the Fuehrer would have them ride. They overpowered the remainder of the field in the afternoon."[22]

By the halfway point the McNamara-Walthour team was in last place. Seeming to lack his normal motivation and inspiration, McNamara merely plugged along and allowed other teams to lap him almost at will. Walthour got tired of their losing battle and stole four laps all on his own, bringing them within seven laps of the leaders. But they were still in last place. On day 5 a photographer snapped a picture of McNamara sleeping in a trackside tent on his right side with his mouth open and shoes on—a figure more pathetic than motivational or inspirational.

In the end Killian and Vopel, as a pair, won their first of many six-day races in the United States. On the opposite end of the scale McNamara and Walthour nearly went the entire distance but were forced to withdraw before the final hour of racing.

In December 1935 McNamara signed his last six-day contract. But it wasn't for the New York grind at Madison Square Garden; it was for the Buffalo six-day. McNamara was the sentimental favorite of the Buffalo crowd, and when he and his teammate, Bob Lipsett, first circled the track during the introductory parade, he was given a genuinely heartwarming reception.

But for McNamara the race went black seconds after he landed on his head on day 2. A woman in the stands sitting directly in front of the crash scene also went blank—she fainted. When McNamara finally regained consciousness, Frank Kramer, perhaps fearing for the racer's life, ordered the grizzled, battle-scarred veteran off the track. Less than a week before Christmas Day 1935, and probably with much reluctance and trepidation, McNamara announced his permanent retirement from bike racing.[23]

15

Grandpa Mac

With his racing career at an end, McNamara looked forward to settling down for a taste of the easy life, like his fellow cycling superstars Alf Goullet and Frank Kramer. Although Kramer worked as a referee for nearly a decade, he did so more for the enjoyment—he didn't need the money. Goullet dabbled in promoting races in his retirement years, but he, like Kramer, did not do it for the money. Goullet retired in Red Bank, New Jersey, along the Navesink River, five miles inland from the Atlantic Ocean. He lived a comfortable retirement with his wife and two children.

If McNamara was hoping for an easy retirement, he was in for a rude awakening. Life was going to get harder for the Iron Man. Of the roughly $500,000 earned during his racing career, McNamara said he could "not account for a cent of it."[1] But financial matters were practically the least of his problems. He had health concerns and marital trouble and had to face the greatest battle of his life—alcoholism.

On September 18, 1936, McNamara sat squinting and sunning himself not on a tropical beach vacation but on the hot roof of the Newark City Hospital.[2] The hospital had been his home for six weeks. While apparently preparing his memoirs at the summer home of a friend at Indian Lake in Denville, New Jersey, McNamara was stricken with internal hemorrhages. As soon as they found out McNamara was sick, his comrades from the Nutley Velodrome lined up to donate blood transfusions.

"Reggie is very dear to us all in the game," said Alf Goullet, "and we are all going to fight to keep him alive."[3]

News of McNamara's sudden illness was reported all over the United States, in Italy, in France, and in Australia. Many, including doctors at the hospital, thought his life was over. But like many of his six-day bike races, he made a remarkable comeback and surprised everyone; he cheated death once again.

McNamara did not slow down either. In the months that followed, he accepted a chairmanship for the Catholic Youth Organization Bicycle Club, he worked at the Gottfried Krueger Brewing Company, and he officiated at six-day bike races.

In March 1937, six months after being released from the Newark City Hospital, McNamara prepared for officiating duties at the Kansas City six-day race. Ted Harper, a rider who idolized McNamara for coaching him and helping him make it to the professional ranks, was also in Kansas City to race. But the night before the race, Harper got word that his mother had died. McNamara told Harper to go home to his family and not worry; the Iron Man would take his place. McNamara rode in Harper's place on borrowed equipment, and nobody knows whether he had worked out since his retirement. Eight months shy of his fiftieth birthday, McNamara did not finish, but he did race for two days and two nights. Considering his age and fitness level, it was an inspired ride and extraordinary physical achievement.[4]

In the 1950s McNamara used to tell his grandson, Kenneth Zink, that he had half a stomach. He may have said it with a wink and a smile, but to some degree it may have been true. He was confined twice more to hospitals for stomach disorders: once in Chicago in March 1938, while he was officiating a race there, and another time in February 1941. Whether it was for the same condition over and over that was never fixed properly or for different conditions, no one may ever know. But since the 1941 operation there were no reported instances of further stomach issues.

During World War II McNamara wasn't able to officiate professional bike races because there weren't any. He left the Gottfried Krueger Brewing Company and acquired a job as a maintenance worker at the Kearny Shipyard on the west bank of the Hackensack River, about three miles from today's Newark Liberty International Airport. The years during World War II were the darkest period of his life. "Once I didn't take my shoes off for eight days," McNamara acknowledged, "I slept in parked cars or in alleyways. Then I would be picked up, sent to jail or the alcoholic ward or a sanitarium. I would promise friends, relatives and priests to quit. But I was too stubborn to admit I couldn't drink as well as the next man."[5]

Time and time again, the former famous bike rider appeared before the judge unwashed, unshaven, and suffering from a hangover. But one judge took pity on McNamara, and instead of sending him to the city prison, he ordered him to the hospital for a medical evaluation. A doctor recommended he join a new organization called Alcoholics Anonymous.

Hearing complete strangers give emotional stories about their alcohol problems encouraged McNamara to share his own story. Providing an excellent example of how well AA worked, McNamara quit drinking forever and credited the organization with having saved his life. He carried a mourning card with the inscription: "Pray for the repose of the soul of Honora McNamara, died Dubbo, NSW, aged 90." Within his "anonymous" union, surely he spoke about the shame he had brought on his family and the regrets he had about visiting Australia in 1930. In February 1947, as a celebration of his sobriety, McNamara gave a cycling exhibition on a set of training rollers on a stage in a Newark auditorium in front of five hundred members of Alcoholics Anonymous and their families.

McNamara was overjoyed when his first grandchild, Rosemary, was born in 1946. Although he and Elizabeth never were truly "together" again, they never officially divorced either. To some degree he did reconcile with his wife and daughters.

With no six-day races in New York since 1939, McNamara

was also happy that cycling promoters in the United States were hoping to make a comeback. In October 1948 a photo appeared in the *Brooklyn Daily Eagle* of several riders working out in Central Park. Most were smiling and relaxing with their hands near the stems of their bikes as the photographer snapped the shot. But along with the group was sixty-year-old McNamara, the only rider in shirtsleeves and a tie. He must have been the first to see the photographer because he put his hands on the drops of his handlebars and went on his own playful jam ahead of the younger riders. Another rider took to the drops and got in behind within McNamara's slipstream. The photo said it all: no matter what his age, McNamara is going to try to win, even for a publicity shot.

The six-day race in 1948 was at the Kingsbridge Armory in the Bronx, and McNamara served as the chief referee. With the armory's big footprint, a seven-lap-to-the-mile track was constructed, and for the opening day 14,500 spectators came out to watch the fun. But with the six-day race not being held at Madison Square Garden, something seemed different. Sportswriter Fred Hawthorne suggested the difference was "the smell of the elephants."[6]

There were some familiar names in the field, most notably McNamara's friend Franco Giorgetti, now forty-six years old. Before the war Giorgetti had left the United States and went home; his savings made him the equivalent of an Italian millionaire. Now he was back in America, where he had achieved most of his professional cycling success, trying to recoup a war-shattered fortune for a mere $100 per day.

Giorgetti paid a dear price for racing in the Bronx six-day: a trip to St. Francis Hospital. He suffered from a fractured skull and broken hip. For so many who idolized Giorgetti, it was sad to see the little Italian being carried out to a waiting ambulance, instead of rekindling his former glory. But for McNamara the sadness went deeper—like déjà vu. More than likely, Giorgetti never raced professionally again.

In the 1950s McNamara, like much of America, had a new

life of relative prosperity. He made a decent living as a kitchen aide in the Essex County Sanatorium. He bought a '55 Plymouth sedan in his favorite color, black.

Both his daughters were married, with children. Regina married Kenneth Zink, a career police officer in New Jersey. Besides Rosemary, born in 1946, they had a son, Ken, in 1949 and another daughter, Theresa, in 1959. In 1936 Eileen married Joseph E. Horter, who worked at the Newark Fire Department. While Joe went off to war, Eileen had to work. When Joe came back, they had son, Joseph K. Horter, born on December 30, 1948. The Horters lived in the Vailsburg neighborhood of Newark, New Jersey.

According to Ken Zink Jr., the first car he ever drove was his grandfather's '55 Plymouth. He remembered that McNamara was not a good driver. More than once he was pulled over by the police for traffic violations with Ken as a youngster in the car. One time he went right through a stoplight and got pulled over. McNamara rolled down the window and smiled. He couldn't make the officer stop writing up a ticket, so he had to tell him who he was—not Reggie McNamara, the famous bike rider, but rather Officer Ken Zink's father-in-law. "Have a nice day," the officer would say as he put his ticket book away and looked at the old man with the hacked-up face and the young kid riding shotgun. "Please don't tell your mother about this," McNamara would say. And Ken never did.

Ken knew about his grandfather's past alcohol abuse, but he never saw him take a single drink. McNamara used to take Ken to his AA meetings. The boy never went into the actual room where the meeting was held, but there was an area with a pool table where Ken played and passed the time with other children. After McNamara and the others filed out of the meeting, he and Ken would go to their favorite Chinese restaurant.

Perhaps not from his grandfather himself, but Ken heard stories about the 1920s and 1930s carousing. After victories McNamara would buy drinks for everyone all night long. McNamara was the life of the party and quite a ladies' man too. He was not faithful to Elizabeth. McNamara would freely admit to Ken that he was an alcoholic and that he had lost considerable money because of the heavy drinking and bad investments. Despite his shenanigans during his bike career, McNamara was a loving, caring, and respectful grandfather.

He taught all his grandchildren the joy of bicycles and always made sure they had a good one to ride. He helped them with minor repairs, but if it became too much of a task, he would take the broken bike to Pop Brennan's shop and have it fixed as good as new. He also made slingshots for the grandchildren, until there was an incident with a neighbor's window.

Ken recalls that despite his age and battle-scarred body, McNamara was a very nimble man. He walked easily without a limp and no unusual movements. But there were scars everywhere on his body: on his hands, his face, his forearms, his calves, and his thighs and a very big one on his lower abdomen. To some, like Walthour's eldest son, Bob, McNamara's physical appearance was frightening and intimidating. But to Ken and McNamara's other grandchildren, he was just grandpa, a man they looked up to and worshipped and loved.

Ken also remembers McNamara's love of the water. He was a terrific swimmer. Once, when McNamara was in his early seventies, they were at the Highlands at Sandy Hook Bay. Ken and McNamara went for a swim, and they swam out farther and farther. They went all the way out to the channel, where one hundred–foot boats started passing them by. Some people on the boats got angry, but McNamara told his grandson not to pay any attention to them. From the shore Ken Zink Sr., the policeman, was keeping tabs on the two and eventually jumped in after them. "Hey Mac, c'mon let's get outta the water," Zink pleaded as he caught up, out of breath.

For Ken Zink, the elder, the incident at Sandy Hook was just one of the many "Reggie stories" about which his eyebrows would go up but at the same time he'd have a twinkle in his eye. He, too, loved his father-in-law's spirit as much as the rest of the family did.

McNamara's grandsons, cousins Ken and Joe, both vividly and independently recall a story that their grandfather told them when they were very young. He told them that at a race in Madison Square Garden, he and his bike went right off the edge of the steepest part of the track. He flew off and landed to the floor some twenty feet below, with twenty thousand people looking on. But with his highly pressurized tires, instead of crashing to the ground, he simply bounced off the floor. Then be bounced again and again and again. He didn't stop bouncing until a quick-thinking policeman shot out his tires. The kids laughed and laughed until they could laugh no more—it was the funniest story they'd ever heard.

In the late 1950s and early 1960s promoters tried to revive six-day racing to its former glory. They knew it was going to be difficult because many of the fans had moved on and lost interest over the years. The younger generation knew next to nothing about the history of the sport. Before then, Brocco, Clark, Giorgetti, Goullet, Grenda, Kramer, McNamara, Spencer, Van Kempen, and Walthour were household names. But the current stock of professional riders were universally unknown.

In January 1959 two images of McNamara appeared in a *New York Times* article, one of him in his prime on a bike and the other of a present-day McNamara—a smiling and respectable old gentleman. "It's a grand sport," the seventy-one-year-old McNamara reminisced at a news conference, "and I'd dearly love to see it come back. Bobby Walthour, whose father was a champion, was my best partner. Frank L. Kramer was the sprint champ—he could beat them all, here and in Europe. I can still hear the fans yelling B-r-r-r-occo. Franco Giorgetti was a great rider I used to team with. Gérard Debaets and Gustav Killian were top-notchers, well known to sports fans in the Twenties and Thirties. We made the most money during Prohibition. Texas Guinan, who had her club in New York, often offered a hundred dollars for a sprint."[7]

But six-day racing in the United States never did come back

to its former glory—not even close. In 1961 John "Drebby" Drebinger, a New York sportswriter as old as McNamara, wrote: "Even the most optimistic old-timer will reluctantly concede the good old days can never be brought back. And yet, they're about to give it another try. In the final week of September they are going to revive the six-day bicycle race in Madison Square Garden. And that should bring out the old boys. Might even intrigue the young. . . . Needless to say, they won't quite be able to match the color and aroma of the event when it was held in the old, old Garden. Particularly the aroma, which had a flavor all of its own."

There hadn't been a six-day race at the Garden since 1939. Like McNamara, Alf Goullet was hopeful that in September 1961 six-day racing would make a successful comeback. "I think the revival is being staged at a most opportune time," he said. "World events just now are drawing all nationalities in this country together and I am certain this event will draw. I know bike riding has almost vanished in this country but it is still tremendously popular in Europe, especially in Italy and France."[8]

But things got fouled up early on. As the starting time quickly approached, with a crowd of eight thousand, and more filtering in, an error in the construction of the track was unraveling. The blueprint drawings were not followed correctly, and some of the surface planks were assembled in such a way that they caused a series of small open spaces on the track. Sixty-two carpenters rushed to the scene to fix the blunder. Hours and hours went by, and the promoting company, Sports International, Inc., was forced to refund money to thousands of would-be fans. The total delay was six hours, and the start did not occur until three o'clock in the morning.[9]

With the inauspicious beginning of the revival at Madison Square Garden, the very shrine of six-day racing in the United States, fans, riders, and promoters were upset but hopeful. "Six-day bike racing has a place in the sports world," said David Paully, president of Sports International. Twelve thousand spectators came out the second night to see riders from the United States, Canada, Portugal, Spain, Italy, Great Britain, France, West Germany, Luxembourg, Argentina, and Switzerland. But the crowd, as big as it was, didn't seem to understand the race. "Where are the crowds that shouted for Goullet and McNamara and Brocco, for Giorgetti and Debaets and Goosens?" wondered a sportswriter from the *New York Times.* "Where are the troubadours that made the galleries ring with their songs and their music?"[10] The whir of the riders' tires along the pine boards was plainly audible, and there was little applause until prompted by the public address announcer, who would say, "This is terrific!" or "Let's give a hand for these riders!"

In the early 1960s cycling historian Peter Nye competed in downtown criteriums in the New York metropolitan area. He was racing as a junior, and many of the former six-day riders used to come out to watch the races. In the sweltering July heat he straddled his bike, waiting at the starting line among the junior field. "Then," he recalled, "some race officials—old guys to me at the time—got excited and called out Reggie's name. 'It's Reggie! Reggie McNamara! The greatest six-day bicycle racer there ever was!'"[11] Nye never saw McNamara that day, but he will never forget the commotion stirred up by the old racer's presence; it was like seeing a scrum of newspaper and television people following Michael Jackson or Princess Diana around.

Several years later, in August 1967, about the time plans for a fourth Madison Square Garden were getting under way, McNamara, just shy of his eightieth birthday, was inducted into the Madison Square Garden Hall of Fame. McNamara's granddaughter Theresa Passione remembers being at the dedication ceremony as an eight-year-old girl. The trophy they presented was bigger than she was. Along with McNamara, eighty-seven other greats were inducted into the Madison Square Garden Hall of Fame, including Gene Autry, P.T. Barnum, Wilt Chamberlain, Buffalo Bill Cody, Bob Cousy, Jack Dempsey, Alf Goullet, Sonja Henie, Gordie Howe, Bobby

Hull, Joe Louis, Jerry Lucas, Joie Ray, Tex Rickard, Oscar Robertson, Roy Rogers, Bill Russell, and Bill Tilden.[12] The present Madison Square Garden Company, however, does not recognize this impressive list of inductees; its Hall of Fame was eliminated around 1988.

Ken Zink recalls a trophy case at the third Madison Square Garden that contained a number of his grandfather's victory pieces. But today, according to Barry Watkins, the executive vice president of communications and administration of the Madison Square Garden Company, the trophies are all gone.

Sometime in the late 1960s McNamara suffered a stroke, and his remaining years were spent at the Essex County Geriatrics Center, a 200,000-square-foot facility that later became the Garden State Cancer Center. On October 10, 1971, McNamara died, one month shy of his eighty-fourth birthday. The indestructible man was gone. Most of the journalists and sportswriters who knew anything about McNamara and six-day racing had passed away too. But one writer, Will Leonard of the *Chicago Tribune*, had a special reason to honor McNamara. Leonard was not a sportswriter by trade. He was a nightlife critic. "Mac was the only athletic hero this columnist ever had," he wrote. He even named his daughter after McNamara. And for that decision Leonard had paid a small price. When Regina was young and she didn't want to go upstairs to bed, she'd say, "Well, you named me after a six-day bike rider, didn't you?" Leonard said that she had a point.[13]

A few years after his death, a Hollywood movie producer approached McNamara's family to make a film about his life, but nothing ever materialized.

Although the Baseball Hall of Fame in Cooperstown, New York, does not require their inductees to have United States citizenship, the U.S. Bicycling Hall of Fame, in Davis, California, does. In other words, a rider such as France Giorgetti— who spent the majority of his brilliant cycling career in America and won many great six-day races, was motor-pacing American champion several times, and was a great fan favorite—is out of luck. In February 2012 I wrote an appeal to the Nomination and Selection Committee at the Bicycling Hall of Fame to reverse this constraint. Although no official documentation responding to my appeal came forward, I did receive an email from the Hall's executive director, Joe Herget, who stated that not only did they not lift the requirement; they had made a move to strengthen it.

In 1988, the very first year of inductions, the U.S. Bicycling Hall of Fame selected two very worthy bicycle riders for its pre-1945 category: Alf Goullet and Frank Kramer. The next year it selected three great ones for the category as well: Major Taylor, Bobby Walthour Sr., and Arthur Zimmerman.

But not until 2004, when McNamara's great-granddaughter, Dr. Lori McGowan, went through a tremendous struggle to make the case, with the assistance of cycling historian Peter Nye, writing to U.S. congressmen and Tom Ridge, the director of Homeland Security, was she was able to prove to the Hall of Fame's satisfaction that McNamara had obtained his U.S. citizenship. McGowan's efforts were rewarded with her great-grandfather's induction into the Hall of Fame. The class of 2004 was a strong one. Enshrined with McNamara were Alexi Grewal, Ron Kiefel, John Tomac, John Vande Velde, and Bill Woodul.

Today anyone curious to know the top ten cyclists of all time can go to Google and search. Most lists will invariably include Tour de France winners such as Eddy Merckx, Fausto Coppi, Gino Bartali, Jacques Anquetil, Bernard Hinault, Greg LeMond, and Miguel Indurain. Those lists will also consistently exclude Reggie McNamara, Alf Goullet, Major Taylor, Frank Kramer, Bobby Walthour, Franco Giorgetti, and Piet Van Kempen. Not even more modern six-day heroes, such as Patrick Sercu and Danny Clark, are mentioned in those lists. Although comparisons between track riders and road riders are difficult to analyze, with time there is hope that the gap between their legendary statuses may close a little tighter.

Perhaps no professional rider other than Reggie McNamara can claim to have raced professionally for three decades. Throughout those thirty years, and his subsequent race officiating, McNamara was the foremost participant from American six-day racing's rise to glory to its inevitable fall from grace. His great passion for the sport he loved should never be forgotten.

Notes

INTRODUCTION

1. Edward A. Harper, *Six Days of Madness* (Stroud, Ontario: Pacesetter Press, 1993).

2. Andrew Homan, "At the Edge of the Garden," *VeloNews*, July 2009, 66–69.

3. Willie Ratner, "Riders Forcing Favorite Team to Keep at Top Pace," *Newark Evening News*, March 9, 1927.

1. RABBITS AND SLINGSHOTS

1. Some documents listed McNamara's birth year as 1888, but by most accounts it was 1887.

2. "Found Drowned," *Australian Town and Country Journal*, March 14, 1885.

3. Irving Crump, "Twenty Years the Crowd's Hero," *Boys' Life*, April 1927.

4. Crump, "Twenty Years."

5. Crump, "Twenty Years."

6. "Honors for M'Namara but He Wins Anyway," *Newark Evening News*, September 16, 1916.

7. "McNamara and His Austral!" *Sydney Morning Herald*, December 7, 1907.

8. "Sporting," *Riverine Grazier*, February 1, 1910.

2. BUSHES TO THE BIG LEAGUES

1. Alfred T. Goullet and Charles J. McGuirk, "The Infernal Grind," *Saturday Evening Post*, May 29, 1926.

2. Andrew Ritchie, *The Flying Yankee: The International Cycling Career of Arthur Augustus Zimmerman* (Cheltenham: John Pinkerton Memorial Publishing Fund, 2009), 109.

3. "The Champion Cyclist," *South Australian Advertiser*, Adelaide, October 2, 1895.

4. "Cycling in Sydney," *Border Watch*, Mount Gambier, SA, November 20, 1895.

5. Andrew Ritchie, *Major Taylor, The Fastest Bicycle Rider in the World* (San Francisco: Cycle Publishing / Van Der Plas Publications, 2010), 136.

6. "Cycling in Sydney," *Adelaide Advertiser*, SA, December 29, 1902.

7. "Sydney Cycling Carnival," *Adelaide Register*, SA, January 22, 1903.

8. "Paced Cycle Racing," *Sydney Morning Herald*, February 9, 1903.

9. Ritchie, *Major Taylor*, 138.

10. "Cycle Racer Attacked Rival," *New York Times*, August 22, 1901.

11. "Race Ends in Free Fight," *Boston Globe*, January 5, 1902, 1.

12. "The Iron Man at 82," *New York Times*, February 28, 1973.

13. Ritchie, *Major Taylor*, 198.

14. *Brisbane Worker*, January 23, 1904.

15. "Cycle Matches in Melbourne," *Sydney Morning Herald*, February 18, 1904.

16. "Cycling Carnival," *Sydney Morning Herald*, March 24, 1904.

17. "The Sydney Thousand," *Sydney Morning Herald*, March 31, 1904.

18. "Lawson and MacFarland," *Sydney Morning Herald*, June 29, 1904.

19. "Floyd MacFarland's Appeal," *Sydney Morning Herald*, July 19, 1904.

20. Newspapers and magazines were split about whether his last name was spelled *Clark* or *Clarke*. For purposes of consistency, this book will use *Clark*.

21. "Cycling," *Newcastle Morning Herald and Minor's Advocate*, April 26, 1906.

22. "Cycling in Sydney," *Sydney Morning Herald*, May 3, 1906.

23. "Pye Makes Good Showing," *Salt Lake City Herald*, May 31, 1906.

24. "Ernest Pye Married at Farmington," *Salt Lake City Herald*, July 25, 1906.

25. "Clarke-Bray," *Salt Lake Herald-Republican*, September 1, 1910.

26. Goullet and McGuirk, *Infernal Grind*.

27. "The Grand Game," *Bicycling World*, May 1990.

3. PROMOTER GOES TO HOLLYWOOD

1. "J. D. Williams, Film Man, Dies," *New York Sun*, August 29, 1934.

2. "Picture Theatre Pioneer," *Melbourne Argus*, August 31, 1934.

3. "Australia's First Six Days' Race," *Sydney Morning Herald*, June 21, 1911.

4. "Kramer-Goullet Both Are Signed," *Newark Evening News*, November 23, 1917.

5. "Declared Kramer the Winner," *New York Sun*, September 4, 1911.

6. "Kramer Wins Championship," *Ogden (Utah) Evening Standard*, September 25, 1911.

7. "Cyclists Start Six Day Grind," *New York Times*, December 11, 1911.

8. H. "Curly" Grivell, *Australian Cycling in the Golden Days* (Adelaide: Courier Press, 1952).

9. "On the Wheel," *Sydney Arrow*, October 7, 1911.

10. "Professional Cycling," *Referee*, October 18, 1911.

11. "Goullet and Grenda," *Sydney Sunday Times*, November 26, 1911.

12. "Amusements," *Sydney Morning Herald*, December 9, 1911.

13. "Six Days' Riding," *Sydney Morning Herald*, January 2, 1912.

14. "Six Days Awheel," *Sydney Morning Herald*, January 6, 1912.

15. "The Huge Crowd," *Sydney Sunday Times*, January 7, 1912.

16. "Promoter Gratified," *Sydney Sunday Times*, January 7, 1912.

17. "Six Days' Cycle Race," *Sydney Sunday Times*, January 7, 1912.

18. "Australia Wins," *Sydney Morning Herald*, January 8, 1912.

19. "A. J. Clarke's Return," *Queenslander (Brisbane)*, February 3, 1912.

20. "Six Days' Cycle Race," *Adelaide Advertiser*, February 26, 1912.

21. "Another Bombshell," *Sydney Morning Herald*, February 1, 1913.

22. "Statement by Mr. Williams," *Sydney Morning Herald*, February 1, 1913.

23. "Mr. Williams Reinstated," *Sydney Morning Herald*, February 6, 1913.

4. ACCIDENTAL ROMANCE

1. "R.M.S. Marama," *Sydney Morning Herald*, April 9, 1912.

2. "Cycling," *Adelaide Daily Herald*, June 25, 1912.

3. "Eight-Hour Night Carnival," *Sydney Referee*, November 6, 1912.

4. "Finish of the Six Days' Cycling," *Barrier Miner (NSW)*, January 8, 1913.

5. "Six Days' Cycling," *Sydney Morning Herald*, January 6, 1913.

6. "The Winners Interviewed," *Sydney Sunday Times*, January 5, 1913.

7. "McNamara Would Ride One a Month," *Bathurst Times*, January 2, 1913.

8. "Six Days' Cycling Race," *Adelaide Advertiser*, February 27, 1913.

9. "New From Spears," *Sydney Referee*, June 11, 1913.

10. Andrew Homan, interview with Theresa Passione, November 16, 2012.

11. Reggie McNamara Collection, *Newark Evening News*, December, 1916.

12. "McNamara Will Do," *Newark Evening News*, July 13, 1913.

13. "Bob Spears Attacked by Eddie Root and Wife after Finish," *New York Sun*, July 7, 1913.

14. "Cyclist Leaves for Australia to Collect Inheritance," *Newark Evening News*, September 18, 1913.

15. "Boston Six-Day Race Fiasco," *New York Sun*, November 10, 1913.

16. "Six-Day Cyclists Conclude Training," *Newark Evening News*, December 5, 1913.

17. "Three Cycle Riders Spilled at Garden," *New York Times*, December 9, 1913.

18. "Rough Crowds Rush to Six-Day Race," *New York Times*, December 11, 1913.

19. Arthur Daley, "The Race to Nowhere," *New York Times*, September 20, 1961.

20. "Gunmen's Battle Fought at Garden," *New York Times*, December 13, 1913.

5. SAFE IN AMERICA

1. "Bike Riders Strong after Long Grind," *New York Times*, December 15, 1913.

2. "Money Paid Over to Six-Day Riders," *Newark Evening News*, December 15, 1913.

3. "Cyclists Grumble over Race Affairs," *Newark Evening News*, December 18, 1913.

4. "Yankees Win Abroad," *New York Tribune*, March 22, 1909.

5. "Moran Badly Injured in Fall Compelled to Quit Cycle Grind," *Newark Evening News*, December 9, 1913.

6. "Americans Third in Brussels Grind," *Bicycling World and Motorcycle Review*, February 10, 1914.

7. "De Zesdagenkoers van Brussel," *De Volksstem*, February 10, 1914.

8. "Don Kirkham's Experiences," *Sydney Morning Herald*, October 14, 1914.

9. "McNamara Wins Four Successive Long-Distance Race," *Sydney Referee*, August 12, 1914.

10. Max Hastings, *Catastrophe 1914: Europe Goes to War* (New York: Knopf, 2013), 181.

11. "Cyclisme," *Le Matin*, August 1, 1914.

12. "French Bicyclists Hard Hit," *Bicycling World and Motorcycle Review*, November 3, 1914.

13. Hastings, *Catastrophe 1914*, 84.

14. "Don Kirkham's Impressions," *South Bourke and Mornington Journal*, October 22, 1914.

15. "British Ship Sunk to Koenigin Luise as She Placed Mine," *New York Evening World*, August 5, 1914.

16. "2064 More Here on Refugee Ships," *New York Times*, August 21, 1914.

17. "French Liner Chicago Brings Shipload of Americans Home," *New York Evening World*, August 24, 1914.

18. "2064 More."

19. "Moral—Don't Wear Ear Trumpets while in Paris," *Washington Herald*, August 24, 1914.

20. "Goullet Captures Ten-Mile Contest," *Newark Evening News*, August 27, 1914.

21. "Old Hard Luck Picks Out McNamara," *New York Sun*, September 4, 1914.

22. New York City Department of Records and Information Services, Municipal Archives.

6. POLITICS OF RACING

1. Michael C. Gabriele, *The Golden Age of Bicycle Racing in New Jersey.* (Charleston SC: History Press, 2011).

2. "Cycling at New Track," *New York Sun*, April 17, 1911.

3. "Ban on Motor Cycle Racing," *New York Times*, September 15, 1912.

4. "Grand Jury Recommends Law to Stop Bike Racing," *Elmira New York Star Gazette*, October 28, 1912.

5. Andrew M. Homan, *Life in the Slipstream: The Legend of Bobby Walthour Sr.* (Washington DC: Potomac Books, 2011), 89.

6. "Racing Cyclists Talk Grievances," *Newark Evening News*, May 17, 1913.

7. "Sport Lore and Comments," *Newark Evening News*, May 19, 1913.

8. "Velodrome Will Increase Purses," *Newark Evening News*, May 21, 1913.

9. "Seven European Cyclists Coming," *Newark Evening News*, May 27, 1913.

10. "Pat Powers Again in Charge of 6 Day Race," *New York Sun*, June 29, 1913.

11. "Sport Lore and Comments," *Newark Evening News*, June 17, 1913.

12. "Powers Describes Cycling Situation," *Newark Evening News*, July 3, 1913.

13. "Cycle Promoters Sign Peace Pact," *Newark Evening News*, August 1, 1913.

14. "Cyclers' Outlaw Movement Ended," *Salt Lake City Tribune*, August 2, 1913.

15. "Bike Race Promoters Pool Their Interests," *New York Sun*, August 2, 1913.

16. "Wordy War Brings Peace to Cyclists," *Newark Evening News*, August 7, 1913.

7. THE WAR YEARS

1. "Rutt to Defend Cycling Title," *New York Times*, April 12, 1914.

2. "Grenda's Cycle First," *New York Times*, August 30, 1914.

3. "Sport Lore and Comment," *Newark Evening News*, October 17, 1914.

4. "Cyclist Hall Writes of Things Abroad," *Newark Evening News*, October 28, 1914.

5. "Wizard of the Cycle Racing Game," *Boston Daily Globe*, November 8, 1914.

6. "New Six-Day Race Features Promised," *New York Times*, November 8, 1914.

7. "Features of This Year's Race," *Bicycling World and Motorcycle Review*, November 10, 1914.

8. "Australian after American Title," *Ogden Standard*, January 23, 1915.

9. "Goullet Prepares for Title Battle," *Newark Evening News*, February 26, 1915.

10. "Brighton Construction to Begin," *Newark Evening News*, April 14, 1915.

11. "Floyd MacFarland Stabbed to Death," *New York Times*, April 18, 1915.

12. "Cycling, McNamara in U.S.A.," *Sydney Referee*, June 9, 1915.

13. "MacFarland to Be Buried in Buffalo," *Syracuse Daily Journal*, April 21, 1915.

14. "Tragedy Robs Sport of Cycle Racing of Its Forceful Dominating Leader," *Newark Evening News*, April 19, 1915.

15. "Lantinberg, Slayer of MacFarland, Acquitted," *Buffalo Evening News*, June 25, 1915.

16. "Woman Will Feed Convention," *New York Sun*, June 12, 1924.

17. "Grenda and Hill Win Six-Day Bicycle Race," *New York Tribune*, December 12, 1915.

18. "Packey Boxes before 12,000 at Bike Show," *Chicago Daily Tribune*, February 3, 1916.

19. "Kid Team Wins Favor of Fans at Cycle Race," *Chicago Daily Tribune*, February 7, 1916.

20. "Six-Day Race to 'Kangaroos' in Final Hour," *Chicago Daily Tribune*, February 9, 1916.

21. "Regulars Stage a Battle with the Outlaw Brigade," *Newark Evening News*, April 11, 1916.

22. "McNamara Outrides Goullet in Sprints," *New York World*, December 20, 1916.

23. "Three Teams Lose Lap in Cycle Race," *New York Times*, December 19, 1916.

24. William Hennigan, "Egg and Dupuy Win Six-Day Bicycle Race," *New York World*, December 24, 1916.

25. "Six-Day Race Won by Egg and Dupuy," *New York Times*, December 24, 1916.

26. Willie Ratner, "Bobby Walthour Sr., Colorful Cyclist, Dies in Boston at 71," *Newark Evening News*, September 3, 1949.

27. "McNamara's Jaw Only Lacerated," *Newark Evening News*, November 5, 1917.

28. "Spears Fricassees Magin after Race," *Newark Evening News*, November 12, 1917.

29. "Famous Bike Rider Wants to Be an Aviator," *Washington Herald*, January 9, 1918.

30. Graham Healy, *The Shattered Peloton: The Devastating Impact of World War I on the Tour de France* (Halcottsville NY: Breakaway Books, 2014).

8. THE PRODIGAL SON RETURNS

1. Bede Carroll, "Cycling," *Sydney Referee*, September 10, 1919.

2. "Bike Riders Will Be Covered against Accidents," *New York Tribune*, November 23, 1918.

3. "Dupuy Worries Six-Day Riders by Jams," *New York World*, December 6, 1918.

4. Reggie McNamara Collection, "What Jake Says," *Newark Evening News*, December 6, 1918.

5. "Veteran Cyclists Take Six-Day Race," *New York Times*, December 8, 1918.

6. "Kramer, Despite Manifold Bruises and Cuts, Intends to Ride in Grand Prize Final Match," *Newark Evening News*, May 31, 1919.

7. "Kramer had Broken Rib," *New York Times*, August 7, 1919.

8. "Four Teams Lapped amid Wild Scenes," *New York Times*, December 5, 1919.

9. "Spencer and Osteritter Win Six Days' Race, *Sydney Referee*, January 7, 1920.

10. Bob Spears, "Spears Became World Champion on His 27th Birthday," *Adelaide News*, September 9, 1937.

11. "James Reginald McNamara: The 'Iron Man of Cycling,'" *Sydney Referee*, March 22, 1933.

12. "The Scrapped Iron Man," *Newark Evening News*, October 12, 1920.

13. Bebe Carroll, "E. J. Ohrt's Impressions," *Sydney Referee*, April 21, 1920.

14. Bebe Carroll, "Rejoinder to E. J. Ohrt," *Sydney Referee*, April 28, 1920.

15. "McNamara Victor in Ten-Mile Chase," *Newark Evening News*, September 15, 1921.

9. TRAINING OLD SCHOOL

1. "Tom Eck Talks on Changed Methods of Training," *Auburn Citizen*, February 8, 1908.

2. Reggie McNamara Collection, *Newark Evening News*, n.d.

3. Willie Ratner, "Punching the Bag," *Newark Evening News*, March 3, 1931.

4. "Art Spencer Spills Championship Dope," *Newark Evening News*, July 28, 1921.

5. "Clark Is Out for Honors This Year," *Newark Evening News*, February 17, 1915.

6. "Training in a Show Window Brings Its Own Rewards," *New York World*, December 7, 1922.

7. "Wellman Again to Meet Kramer," *Newark Evening News*, November 21, 1917.

8. Alexander Sandow, Richard Lockridge, and Harold Ross, "Iron Man," *New Yorker*, February 25, 1933.

9. "McNamara Begins Stage Work in Newark Monday," *Newark Evening News*, December 14, 1926.

10. Harold C. Burr, "Harris Horder Adds His Words in Praise of Reggie McNamara," *Brooklyn Daily Eagle*, December 5, 1931.

11. "Drugs a Factor in Six Day Contest," *New York Herald*, December 15, 1900.

12. "Walthour Wins Six Day Race in Desperate Chase," *New York Herald*, December 15, 1901.

13. Christy Mathewson, "Polo Grounds May Have Cycle Track," *New York Times*, November 2, 1919.

14. Goullet and McGuirk, "Infernal Grind."

15. "Alf Goullet, Best of the Bike Hopes," *Newark Evening News*, March 24, 1915.

16. "Attempt to Stop Grind Doesn't Worry Chapman," *Newark Evening News*, February 17, 1921.

17. "Three Bike Sprinters in Velodrome Feature," *Newark Evening News*, September 10, 1920.

18. "Arthur Spencer to Ride in 100-Kilometer Race," *Newark Evening News*, September 15, 1920.

19. "Bike Cinderella Who Fits the Silver Zipper," *Newark Evening News*, December 16, 1927.

20. Frank Deford, Peter Nye, Jeff Groman, and Mark Tyson, *The Six-Day Bicycle Races: America's Jazz-Age Sport*, (DVD, Jazz Sport, 2006).

21. René de Latour, *Sporting Cyclist*, November 1967, 28.

22. "Six-Day Bike Rider Earned a Fortune and Title of 'Iron Man,'" *Daily Mirror*, June 6, 1988.

10. LET THE ROARING TWENTIES BEGIN

1. "Cyclists Divide $40,000," *New York Times*, March 16, 1920.

2. "Kramer Is Winner in Newark Opening," *New York Times*, March 29, 1920.

3. "The Scrapped Iron Man," *Newark Evening News*, October 12, 1920.

4. "Team Steals Lap Twice at Garden," *New York Times*, December 7, 1920.

5. Bob Spears, "Bob Spears' Exciting Experience in New York Contest," *Adelaide News*, September 16, 1937.

6. "Ringling and Uppercu Buy Big Velodrome," *New York Evening World*, February 24, 1922.

7. "Rickard Get 10-Year Lease on Madison Square Garden," *New York Tribune*, July 13, 1920.

8. "Our Amateur Scribe Laughs at Hearing Bike Riders Get Paid," *Newark Evening News*, March 9, 1926.

9. "Six-Day Bike Race Starts in Garden," *New York Times*, March 6, 1922.

10. Patterson McNutt, "Egg-Eaton Team Still Holds Lead in Six-Day Race," *New York World*, March 8, 1922.

11. "Two Teams Steal Lip in 6-Day Grind," *New York Times*, March 8, 1922.

12. Robert Boyd, "How Grenda Rates Chances of Rival Six-Day Riders," *New York Evening World*, March 10, 1922.

13. "Les Six Jours de Paris," *L'Ouest-Éclair*, April 10, 1922.

14. "Comment on Current Events in Sports," *New York Times*, May 31, 1922.

15. "Kramer Fails to Break His Record," *New York World*, July 26, 1922.

16. "20,000 Fans Watch Kramer's Last Ride," *New York Times*, July 27, 1922.

17. "Four Teams are Lapped during Series of Furious Sprints," *New York Tribune*, December 5, 1922.

18. "Goullet's Entry Completes List for 6 Day Race," *Chicago Tribune*, February 4, 1923.

19. "Bike Racers Set for Final Dash Tonight," *Chicago Tribune*, February 17, 1923.

20. "Kockler-Lawrence Gain Lap on Field," *New York Times*, December 7, 1923.

21. "Goullet Says Heat Slowed Bike Race," *New York Times*, December 10, 1923.

11. THE ITALIANS ARE COMING!

1. In the United States, Giorgetti's name was spelled incorrectly as *Georgetti*. In this book I use the correct spelling throughout.

2. Reggie McNamara, "The Race Is to the Swift—Sometimes," collection of Lori McGowan.

3. "M'Namara Improves, Rally Amazes Doctors," *Philadelphia Inquirer*, August 12, 1936.

12. MAC STRIKES GOLD

1. "Four Riders Thrown Out of Bike Race; Egg-Grenda Lead," *Chicago Daily Tribune*, January 11, 1924.

2. "M'Namara Winner with Van Kempen," *New York Times*, December 7, 1924.

3. "Goullet Resting after Operation," *New York Times*, December 14, 1924.

4. "Bicycling," *New York Times*, December 8, 1924.

5. Walter Eckersall, "Belgian Teams Get Early Lead in Six Day Grind," *Chicago Daily Tribune*, February 9, 1925.

6. Walter Eckersall, "McNamara and Walthour Lead Bike Race by a Lap," *Chicago Daily Tribune*, February 13, 1925.

7. "Three Teams Tied for Bike Race Lead," *New York Times*, March 6, 1925.

8. "Two Teams Retain 2-Lap Six-Day Lead," *New York Times*, December 4, 1925.

9. "Debaets-Goosens Win Six-Day Race," *New York Times*, December 6, 1925.

10. "Debaets and McNamara Figure in Severe Accident in Berlin Race," *Newark Evening News*, January 20, 1926.

11. "McNamara and Horan Sensational in Last Hour of Wild Sprinting," *Newark Evening News*, January 21, 1926.

12. "Germans Proclaim McNamara as Greatest Six-Day Rider," *New York Times*, January 22, 1926.

13. "Harry Horan's Tales of Hofbrau Keep Six-Day Riders Interested," *Newark Evening News*, February 11, 1926.

14. "Harry Horan's Tales."

15. "Walthour Jr., Bike King, Takes Bride in Florida," *Buffalo New York Courier*, January 4, 1926.

16. "Chicago Grind Stopped for Two Hours by Accident to Leading Contender," *Newark Evening News*, February 19, 1926.

17. Goullet and McGuirk, "Infernal Grind."

18. "McNamara Is the Genuine 'Iron-Man,'" *Newark Evening News*, February 23, 1926.

19. "Pal's Kiss Greets McNamara after Winning the Six-Day Bicycle Race," *Newark Evening News*, March 15, 1926.

20. "Horan reprend la course," *La Presse*, April 7, 1926.

21. Howard B. Freeman, "Evening Muse," *Newark Evening News*, December 13, 1926.

22. Willie Ratner, "Rabid Bike Fans Boo McNamara; Cheer Goullet," *Newark Evening News*, December 8, 1926.

23. "M'Namara-Linari Win Six-Day Race," *New York Times*, December 12, 1926.

24. Howard B. Freeman, "Evening Muse," *Newark Evening News*, December 13, 1926.

13. RUSTY IRON

1. "Ruth's Salary Ranks Him Second Only to Gene Tunney," *Newark Evening News*, March 3, 1927.

2. Willie Ratner, "Goosens Pummels Dinale and Chases Harris Horder," *Newark Evening News*, March 3, 1927.

3. "Six-Day Rider Crashes into Box on First Night of Grind," *Newark Evening News*, March 7, 1927.

4. Willie Ratner, "Meyer Took a Hard Crack When McNamara Rode Low," *Newark Evening News*, March 10, 1927.

5. Howard B. Freeman, "Evening Muse," *Newark Evening News*, March 14, 1927.

6. Ellisisland.org, Elizabeth, Eileen and Regina McNamara aboard RMS *America*, July 9–17, 1925.

7. "M'Namara Takes Paris 6-Day Race," *New York Times*, April 11, 1927.

8. "Bike Fans Parade as Georgetti Wins," *New York Times*, April 11, 1927.

9. "Reg McNamara Raced a Lot on Continent," *Newark Evening News*, May 24, 1927.

10. "22,000 Cheer McNamara's Victory at Velodrome Here," *New York Times*, May 30, 1927.

11. "Bike Cinderella Who Fits the Silver Zipper," *Newark Evening News*, December 16, 1927.

12. Howard B. Freeman, "Evening Muse," *Newark Evening News*, January 5, 1928.

13. Willie Ratner, "Night of Worst Jamming Seen in Chicago Grind," *Newark Evening News*, January 12, 1928.

14. Walter Eckersall, "Six-Day Malady Half Over; All Are Doing Well," *Chicago Daily Tribune*, January 12, 1928.

15. Charlie Winter, letter to Al Erverard," Jeff Groman Collection, April 20, 1928.

16. Bill and Carol McGann, *The Story of the Giro d'Italia* (Cherokee Village AR: McGann Publishing, 2011).

17. French Lane, "American and Belgian Team Lead on Points," *Chicago Sunday Tribune*, November 10, 1929.

18. John H. Lyle, "The Story behind the St. Valentine's Day Massacre," *Chicago Tribune*, February 21, 1954.

19. Edward Burns, "McNamara and Belloni Lead Six-Day Bike Race," *Chicago Daily Tribune*, November 13, 1929.

20. "M'Namara-Belloni Win 6 Day Bike Race," *Chicago Daily Tribune*, November 14, 1929.

21. "McNamara Signs Up for Six-Day Grind," *Yonkers Statesman*, February 6, 1930.

22. Willie Ratner, "As the 'Iron Man' Pulled Out for 'Frisco and Australia," *Newark Evening News*, March 14, 1930.

23. "Reggie McNamara Back Next Week: Will Race in Australia," *Sydney Referee*, April 9, 1930.

1. "Rickey Not Ready for a Token Farewell," *Times Herald Record*, Associated Press, January 1, 2008.

2. Willie Ratner, "Physician Orders Reggie to Quit Grind in Garden," *Newark Evening News*, March 4, 1933.

3. Willie Ratner, "Punching the Bag," *Newark Evening News*, March 14, 1933.

4. "Concussion," *Lowell Sun*, March 27, 1933.

5. Frank Deford, Peter Nye, Jeff Groman, and Mark Tyson, *The Six-Day Bicycle Races: America's Jazz-Age Sport*, (DVD, Jazz Sport, 2006).

6. Willie Ratner, "Punching the Bag," *Newark Evening News*, May 1, 1933.

7. "Van Nek Teams with M'Namara," *Standard Union*, February 20, 1929.

8. "Reggie McNamara Cut in Face during Bike Road Race," *Buffalo Courier Express*, August 2, 1933.

9. "Disappointed Pedal Pushers," *Long Island Daily Press*, August 25, 1933.

10. "Reggie McNamara Badly Hurt in S.F. Bike Crash," *Fresno Bee Republican*, May 14, 1934.

11. Raymond Hull, "Reggie McNamara—The Iron Knight of the Bike World," *Arena and Strength*, December 1934.

12. Don Rodda, "Flushing's Eddie Raffo, Marathon Pedal Pusher," *Long Island Star-Journal*," January 20, 1959.

13. "Honor Reggie McNamara on 50th Birthday," *Chicago Tribune*, November 11, 1934.

14. Reggie McNamara letter addressed to Ernest Branson, Jeff Groman Collection, November 28, 1939.

15. Joseph C. Nichols, "16,000 See Start of Six-Day Race," *New York Times*, December 3, 1934.

16. "Testa, with Illness Over, Makes Bike Race Comeback," *New York Post*, March 8, 1935.

17. Joseph C. Nichols, "Letourneur's Team Takes 6-Day Race by 3-Lap Margin," *New York Times*, March 10, 1935.

18. "Wife on Iron Man M'Namara Had Him Jugged," *Buffalo Courier-Express*, May 10, 1935.

19. "Reg M'Namara, though 50, Is Still Racing," *Oswego Palladium-Times*, May 22, 1935.

20. Camel advertisement, *Brooklyn Daily Eagle*, June 5, 1935, 12.

21. Edward Burns, "First Spill of Race Puts Out Letourneur," *Chicago Daily Tribune*, November 11, 1935.

22. Edward Burns, "Referee Says Get Going and They Do!" *Chicago Daily Tribune*, November 13, 1935.

23. "American Mile Aces Prep for Olympic Spots," *Post-Star, Glen Falls*, December 20, 1935.

1. "McNamara Fit after AA Cure," *Nassau Daily Review Star*, February 10, 1947.

2. "Reggie M'Namara Recovering from Serious Illness," *Niagara Falls Gazette*, September 18, 1936.

3. "Associates Rush to the Aid of Stricken Reg McNamara," *Buffalo Courier-Express*, August 12, 1936.

4. Harper, *Six Days of Madness.*

5. "A Six-Day Rider Went on the Wagon," *Cairns Post*, March 8, 1947.

6. Tommy Holmes, "Six-Day Madness Hits the Bronx," *Brooklyn Daily Eagle*, October 20, 1948.

7. William R. Conklin, "McNamara Pushing Pedals Again," *New York Times*, January 29, 1959.

8. John Drebinger, "A Past Age Comes Back," *New York Times*, August 9, 1961.

9. "Bike Race Starts Six Hours Late," *New York Times*, September 23, 1961.

10. Frank M. Blunk, "Capacity Crowd Is Due at Finale," *New York Times*, September 28, 1961.

11. Andrew Homan, Peter Nye interview, March 5, 2015.

12. "Garden Hall of Fame," *Sunday Star Ledger*, August 27, 1967.

13. Will Leonard, *Chicago Tribune*, October 16, 1971.

Index

ica, 40–42; birth of, 1, 177; breakup with trainer, 79, 108; called in sick, 177; and cartoon with Jack Neville and Charlie Winter, 114; childhood homes of, 1, 3; and close calls with death, 101, 139, 173, 183–84; as "Country Champion" (Australia), 6; and cycling exhibition, 96, 185; and cycling war, 69–70, 74, 84–86; death of, 192; diet of, 105–6; domestic abuse allegations against, 179; and driving, 187; drug use of, 114; early career of, 5–6; essay by, 132–39; fame and popularity of, 148–49, 152–53, 189, 191, 193; and father's death, 1, 176; fiftieth birthday of, 177; financial losses and trouble of, 94, 179, 183, 188; financial winnings and wealth of, xi, 6, 51, 54, 75, 84, 86, 87, 88, 96, 99, 120, 157, 161, 180, 183; first bicycle of, 4; first professional race of, 5; and Rickey Henderson, 170–71, 175; honored, 152–53; inducted into Madison Square Garden Hall of Fame, 191–92; inducted into U.S. Bicycling Hall of Fame, 193; injuries of, 32, 41–43, 55, 61, 86, 89–90, 109, 117–18, 127–28, 151, 155, 159, 160, 164, 168, 171–72, 173, 174, 175, 176–77, 178, 180, 182; as "Iron Man," xi–xii, 90, 137, 139, 140, 151, 156, 160, 167, 168, 170, 171, 177; as "king of the dirt tracks," 24; as ladies' man, 187–88; and loss of fingertip, 2–3; and Floyd MacFarland's death, 81; marriage of, 61–62; medical issues of, 101, 119, 139, 177, 183–84, 192; memoirs of, 139, 183; as mentor to younger riders, 111; and mother's death, 185; as movie extra, 176; and Benito Mussolini, 138, 162; and NCA reinstatement of, 84, 141–42; and officiating, 184; and Pope Pius, 138,

162; post-retirement employment of, 185, 187; post-retirement racing of, 184; as pursuit racer, 45; and racing in Europe, 51–59, 162; as referee, 186, 230; and "Reggie stories," 188–89; retirement of, 182, 183; as road racer, 24, 174–75; and separation from wife, 179, 180; and six-day-race winning streak, 140–56; as six-day racer, xii, 19, 24–26, 29, 31–32, 35, 36–38, 39–47, 49–50, 51, 52, 53–54, 77, 79, 82–83, 84, 86–88, 90, 93–96, 98–99, 109, 118–20, 122–24, 127–29, 132–39, 140–56, 158–63, 164–65, 166–68, 171–74, 175–78, 180–82, 193–94; and smoking, 114–15, 180; sobriety of, 185; as spectator, 126; as sprinter, 25, 35, 80, 100–101, 162; stroke of, 192; suspension by NCA of, 141–42; and team race, 58; track testing of, 122; training of, 25, 43, 52–53, 79–80, 89, 101, 108–9, 110, 154, 158–59; U.S. citizenship of, 103, 193; as "Western Champion" (Australia), 6; and world record, 118, 158; and World War I, 91, 93; as "world's greatest rider," 148–49

McNamara, Sybil (sister of RM), 4

McNamara, Timothy (father of RM), 1, 2, 168, 176

McNutt, Patterson, 123

Meithe, Werner, 149

Melba Theatre (Melbourne), 21

Melbourne Exhibition Ground (Australia), 12, 31

Merckx, Eddy, 11, 166, 193

Meyer, Charlie, 159–60

Meyer, Otto, 57

Michael, Jimmy, 105

Mihlon, Frank, 51, 52, 64, 70–73, 81

Milan–San Remo race, 56, 88, 154

Milan Velodrome, 161

Miner's Empire Theatre (Newark), 80

Schaller, Tony, 180
Scheps, F. H., 13, 14, 15
Scott, Bert, 36
Sercu, Patrick, 193
Sérès, Georges, 78, 124–25
Simpson, Wilfred, 176
"the Sioux," 78. *See also* Linart, Victor
6 Day Bicycle Rider, 176
six-day races: Amsterdam, 109; Berlin, 35, 53, 54, 77, 109, 147–49, 151, 156, 161, 225; Boston, 10, 35, 43–44, 77–78, 82, 89, 109, 171, 172, 173, 175; Breslau, 109; Brussels, 52, 53–54, 109, 161, 182; Buffalo (New York), 175; Chicago, 82, 83–84, 109, 114, 128–29, 136–37, 140–41, 142, 143–44, 149–51, 152, 153, 156, 163, 164–65, 166–67, 171, 172, 173, 175, 177, 181; Cleveland, 109, 171; Detroit, 109, 171, 174; Dortmund (Germany), 167–68; Kansas City (Missouri), 109, 184; London, 109; Los Angeles, 109; Marseille, 109; Melbourne, 21, 30–32, 35, 37–39, 93; Milwaukee, 109, 175; Minneapolis, 109, 171; Montreal, 109, 171, 172, 175; New York (Kingsbridge Armory, Bronx), 186; New York (Madison Square Garden), 16, 19, 21, 23–24, 26, 35, 44–50, 51, 53, 70–71, 73, 75, 77–79, 82–83, 86–88, 90, 91, 94–96, 98–99, 108–9, 110, 111–12, 113, 116–17, 118–24, 127–28, 129–30, 132, 133–36, 137, 141–43, 144–47, 151–52, 153–56, 158–60, 161, 163, 165, 166, 167, 171–72, 175, 177, 178, 186, 187, 189, 190–91; New York (Twenty-Second Regiment Armory), 118; Paris, 35, 52, 53, 109, 114, 124–25, 128, 152–53, 160–61, 165, 166; Philadelphia, 109; Pittsburgh, 109, 175; Quebec City, 171; San Francisco, 109, 175–76, 179; St. Louis, 171; Stuttgart, 109; Sydney, 21, 23, 24–30, 35–37, 93–94, 98,

100, 102; Tokyo, 178; Toronto, 109, 171, 175
six-day racing, xi, xiii–xiv, 19, 21, 23, 35, 91, 98, 109, 116; Berlin scoring system of, 77, 79, 82, 84; counterfeiting tickets at, 129–30; drugs and, 111–14; gun fight at, 119–20; Italian influence at, 131–39, 146; at Madison Square Garden, 116–17; "outlaw," 118; revival of, 185–86, 189–91
slipstream, 186
smoking, 79, 86, 104, 114–15, 142
Snell, Charles, 56
South Mountain Reservation (New Jersey), 158
Speaker, Tris, 157
Spears, Robert "Bob," 43; and arrival in America, 40–41; and championships, 103; and cycling war, 70, 84–85; fight of, 89–90; financial winnings of, 84, 86, 88; NCA reinstatement of, 84; and racing in Europe, 101, 118; and rollers, 39; as six-day racer, 19, 36, 37, 38, 39, 57, 82–83, 84, 86–88, 89–90, 93–94, 98, 99–100, 102, 119–120; as sprinter, 22, 43, 97, 100–101, 103; training of, 80, 85
Speedwell Mile Road Race (Australia), 6
Spencer, Arthur "Art," 97, 117, 126, 135
Spencer, Freddie, 136–37, 145–46, 147, 149, 153, 154, 163, 172, 174
Spencer, William "Willie," 89, 93, 97, 100, 108, 113–14, 175, 189
Sportpalast (Berlin), 147–48, 149
Sports International, Inc., 190
sprint championships, 13, 21–22, 23, 30, 57, 101, 163
Stein, Charley, 106, 107
Stevens, Orlando, 65
Stockelynch, Harry, 145–46, 149–50, 153, 155
Stockholm, Carl, 128, 140, 155
stock market crash (1929), 167